JOURNAL FOR THE STUDY OF THE OLD TESTAMENT
SUPPLEMENT SERIES

394

Women, Ideology, and Violence

Critical Theory and the Construction of Gender in the Book of the Covenant and the Deuteronomic Law

Cheryl B. Anderson

T & T CLARK INTERNATIONAL
A Continuum imprint
LONDON • NEW YORK

A Continuum imprint

Published by T&T Clark International
The Tower Building, 11 York Road, London SE1 7NX
15 East 26th Street, Suite 1703, New York, NY 10010

www.tandtclark.com

British Library Cataloguing-in-Publication Data
A catalogue record for this book is available from the British Library

Library of Congress Cataloging-in-Publication Data
A catalogue record for this book is available from the Library of Congress

Typeset by CA Typesetting, Sheffield
Printed on acid-free paper in Great Britain by CPI Bath

ISBN 0-8264-6767-9 (hardback)

Contents

ACKNOWLEDGMENTS

I have benefited from the support of others, in various forms, during the process of researching and writing this monograph. Because this work is based on the doctoral dissertation I submitted to Vanderbilt University in May 2000, I benefited greatly from the guidance and contributions of my dissertation committee. My committee consisted of Douglas Knight (dissertation director), Peter Haas (second reader), Renita Weems, Victor Anderson, Idit Dobbs-Weinstein and D. Don Welch. Their individual academic backgrounds encompassed the Hebrew Bible and its laws, contemporary legal theory, critical theory, and ethics. The contributions from their various backgrounds greatly enriched my work. Gratitude must also be expressed to David J.A. Clines and Philip A. Davies for agreeing to publish my work in the Journal for the Study of the Old Testament Supplement series. I am particularly grateful to Professor Clines and the anonymous reader whose insightful and detailed comments were instrumental in transforming my dissertation into a book. Prompted by these comments, I have incorporated my more recent reflections on matters covered in the dissertation as well as newer scholarly developments pertinent to that earlier research. At Continuum, Rebecca Mulhearn, Katherine Savage and Sylvia Marson offered excellent guidance during the publication process and I thank them for their work.

While writing the revisions, it has been my honor to be among faculty colleagues at Garrett-Evangelical Theological Seminary such as Phyllis Bird, Rosemary Radford Ruether and James Poling whose scholarly work has helped to shape my own. During the re-writing process, important words of encouragement, advice, and direction have come also from Cristina Traina of Northwestern University, Tikva Frymer-Kensky and Martha Roth of the University of Chicago, and Carolyn Pressler of United Seminary of the Twin Cities. Along with the help from these academic colleagues, I was fortunate enough to receive help from my student research assistants: Katy Valentine, Kimberly Bechtel, and Christina Itson. Furthermore, Cindy Kaynor did a fine job typing the final manuscript and Brooke Lester was kind enough to enter the needed electronic versions of the Hebrew and transliteration fonts.

A very special word of gratitude must be expressed to Robert A. Johnson, Jr, and Diane Capitani for their roles as discussion partners during the writing and then the re-writing of my dissertation, respectively. Their willingness to give of their time enabled me to sharpen my thinking, write more efficiently, and, ultimately, to meet my deadlines.

Financial support for this project has come in two forms. First, as a Garrett-Evangelical faculty member, I received research funds from the seminary president, Ted

Campbell, and the academic dean, Jack Seymour. Second, I was awarded a summer research grant from the Wabash Center for Teaching and Learning in Theology and Religion that allowed me to finish the majority of the re-writing during the summer of 2003. I could not have completed these revisions without these two sources of funding.

Finally, this work is dedicated to my parents:

> To my mother, for being a strong woman, and
> To my father, for loving one.

Cheryl B. Anderson
Evanston, Illinois

LIST OF ABBREVIATIONS

AfOB	Archiv für Orientforschung: Beiheft
BA	*Biblical Archeologist*
BibInt	*Biblical Interpretation: A Journal of Contemporary Approaches*
BJS	Brown Judaic Studies
BN	*Biblische Notizen*
BZAW	Beihefte zur *ZAW*
CBQ	*Catholic Biblical Quarterly*
FCB	Feminist Companion to the Bible
HdO	Handbuck der Orientalistik
HTR	*Harvard Theological Review*
JAAR	*Journal of the American Academy of Religion*
JBL	*Journal of Biblical Literature*
JESHO	*Journal of the Economic and Social History of the Orient*
JJS	*Journal of Jewish Studies*
JNES	*Journal of Near Eastern Studies*
JPS	Jewish Publication Society
JSOT	*Journal for the Study of the Old Testament*
JSOTSup	*Journal for the Study of the Old Testament*, Supplement Series
JSS	*Journal of Semitic Studies*
NIB	*New Interpreter's Bible*
OBO	Orbis biblicus et orientalis
OBT	Overtures to Biblical Theology
OTL	Old Testament Library
RB	*Revue biblique*
SBL	Society of Biblical Literature
SBLDS	SBL Dissertation Series
SBLMS	SBL Literature Monograph Series
SBLSP	SBL Seminar Papers
SBLSS	SBL Semeia Studies
SBLWAW	Society of Biblical Literature: Writings from the Ancient World
TS	*Theological Studies*
VT	*Vetus Testamentum*
VTSup	*Vetus Testamentum*, Supplements
WMANT	Wissenschaftliche Monographien zum Alten und Neuen Testament
ZA	*Zeitschrift für Assyriologie*
ZAW	*Zeitschrift für die alttestamentliche Wissenschaft*

List Of Abbreviations: Laws

Biblical Laws

BC	Book of the Covenant (Exod. 20.23–23.14)
DL	Deuteronomic Law (Deut. 12–26)
HC	Holiness Code (Lev. 17–26)

*Ancient Near Eastern Laws**

HL	Hittite Laws
LE	Laws of Eshnunna
LH	Laws of Hammurabi
LL	Laws of Lipit-Ishtar
LNB	Neo-Babylonian Laws
LU	Laws of Ur-Namma
MAL	Middle Assyrian Laws
SLEx	Sumerian Laws Exercise Tablet

* These abbreviations are taken from Martha Roth, *Law Collections from Mesopotamia and Asia Minor* (SBLWAW, 6; Atlanta: Scholars Press, 2nd edn, 1997), p. xiv.

Chapter 1

WOMEN, IDEOLOGY, AND VIOLENCE: CRITICAL THEORY AND THE CONSTRUCTION OF GENDER IN THE BOOK OF THE COVENANT AND THE DEUTERONOMIC LAW

1. *Introduction*

The treatment of women in the Book of the Covenant (BC) and the Deuteronomic Law (DL) is the subject of this study.[1] Generally, the BC (Exod. 20.23–23.19) is traced conventionally to the premonarchic period (1200–1000 BCE) because it contains no references to a king.[2] The DL, however, has been associated with the law found in the Jerusalem temple (2 Kgs 22–23) during the reign of King Josiah (640–609 BCE). The DL has been described as 'a rather direct descendant of the Book of the Covenant' because many of its provisions are 'restatements' of those found in the BC.[3] Indeed, seven of the laws on women in the BC are also found in the DL (Deut. 12–26), although with modifications.[4]

1. Laws concerning women also exist in the priestly laws, especially in the Holiness Code found in Lev. 17–26, but those laws are not part of this analysis. Because of the degree of overlapping provisions in the BC and DL, they are a logical unit to cover; whereas the post-exilic priestly material has 'its own distinctive rhetorical features, theological leanings, and political emphases'. See J. David Pleins, *The Social Visions of the Hebrew Bible: A Theological Introduction* (Louisville, KY: Westminster/John Knox Press, 2001), pp. 54–62.

2. Later dates for the BC have been proposed. See, for example, Douglas A. Knight, 'Village Law and the Book of the Covenant', in Saul M. Olyan and Robert C. Culley (eds.), *A Wise and Discerning Mind: Essays in Honor of Burke O. Long* (BJS, 325; Providence, RI: Brown Judaic Studies, 2000), pp. 163–79 (monarchic period); and John Van Seters, *A Law Book for the Diaspora: Revision in the Study of the Covenant Code* (New York: Oxford University Press, 2003) (exilic period).

3. Dale Patrick, *Old Testament Law* (Atlanta: John Knox Press, 1985), p. 97. In other words, it is assumed that the similarities between the Book of the Covenant and the Deuteronomic Law are due to the reworking of the chronologically earlier provisions of the Book of the Covenant in the later law. However, an alternate explanation for these similarities has been proposed – that there was a deuteronomistic revision of the Book of the Covenant's provisions after the premonarchic period. Lohfink and Levinson have rejected that explanation. See Norbert Lohfink, 'Poverty in the Laws of the Ancient Near East and of the Bible', *TS* 52 (1991), pp. 34–50 (39); and Bernard M. Levinson, *Deuteronomy and the Hermeneutics of Legal Innovation* (New York: Oxford University Press, 1997), pp. 11–13.

4. The following laws involving women appear in both the Book of the Covenant and the Deuteronomic Law: apostasy (Exod. 22.19 [22.20] and Deut. 13.7-19 [13.6-18]); sorcery (Exod. 22.17 [22.18] and Deut. 18.9-14); widows (Exod. 22.21-23 [22.22-24] and Deut. 24.17-22); release of debt slaves (Exod. 21.2-11 and Deut 15.12-18); participation of women in cultic practices

This study presumes that biblical laws construct identity and therefore builds on earlier work that identifies such a function in the Deuteronomistic History,[5] the Pentateuch,[6] and, particularly, the book of Genesis.[7] Although the basic argument is the same, that biblical texts can shape identity, two differences exist. First, these earlier studies relate the identity structured to a particular historical time period – usually the post-exilic period – and its political and cultic dynamics; but this analysis is done without reference to a historical period. Second, earlier analyses focused on only the national identity of the ancient Israelites, but this study examines how the BC and DL construct national identity as well as other identities.

In the next chapter, the laws concerning women in the BC and DL are differentiated based on gender – the oppositional attributes ascribed to men and women. On that basis, we will see that some laws treat women and men similarly (inclusive laws) and that some treat women and men differently (exclusive laws).[8] Because the biblical laws on women are both inclusive and exclusive, it follows that women have both symmetrical and asymmetrical gender roles. Specifically, a woman's treatment under these laws can be the same as that of a man, hence symmetrical with respect to their children, if he is the patriarch and she is the matriarch. Nevertheless, that hypothetical woman's treatment in other areas of her life would be asymmetrical compared to her husband's treatment or that of any other Israelite male. For example, as will be argued later, the wife's sexuality is to be controlled by her husband, but she neither controls his sexuality nor can she participate in cultic activities in the same manner as an Israelite male.

In Chapter 3, the specific identities created by the inclusive and exclusive laws of the BC and DL will be explored. The discussion there will show (1) that the inclusive laws create national, generational and class identities that apply to both men and women; and (2) that the exclusive laws, which treat women differently, present subordination to men as the gender role for women.

Because gender refers to the oppositional attributes given to each sex, to discuss the construction of the feminine identity necessarily implies the construction of the masculine identity. Using feminist legal theory, the construction of masculinity as male dominance in these same laws will be documented in Chapter 4. In that same

(Exod. 23.17 and Deut. 16.16); respect for parents (Exod. 21.15, 17 and Deut. 21.18-21); and intercourse with an unbetrothed virgin (Exod. 22.15-16 [22.16-17] and Deut. 22.28-29).

5. E. Theodore Mullen, Jr, *Narrative History and Ethnic Boundaries: The Deuteronomistic Historian and the Creation of Israelite National Identity* (SBLSS; Atlanta: Scholars Press, 1993).

6. Mullen, *Ethnic Myths and Pentateuchal Foundations: A New Approach to the Formation of the Pentateuch* (Atlanta: Scholars Press, 1997). See also Regina M. Schwartz, *The Curse of Cain: The Violent Legacy of Monotheism* (Chicago: University of Chicago Press, 1997).

7. Mark G. Brett, *Genesis: Procreation and the politics of identity* (Old Testament Readings; New York: Routledge, 2000), and R. Christopher Heard, *Dynamics of Diselection: Ambiguity in Genesis 12–36 and Ethnic Boundaries in Post-Exilic Judah* (SBLSS, 39; Atlanta: Society of Biblical Literature, 2001). Somewhat in contradiction to one another, Brett thinks that Genesis is a counter-narrative to the 'holy seed' construction of national identity found in Ezra and Nehemiah; whereas Heard argues that Gen. 12–36 seeks to establish the claims to the land made by those who had returned from exile and so implements a policy of exclusion.

8. The texts of the biblical laws covered in this study are provided in Appendix A.

chapter, the construction of gender as male dominance/female subordination is found to constitute the repression of the feminine which, drawing from the work of such theorists as Theodor Adorno and Max Horkheimer, is construed to be an act of violence. Then, the connection is made between the inherent violence of that paradigm and actual violence against women today in Chapter 5.[9] Chapter 5 also discusses the ethical issue of interpreting violent texts, including these biblical laws, in today's culture of male violence against women.

Four basic concepts are necessary for the analysis of the laws being undertaken: the concept of law as a form of ideology; the law's ability to shape various identities based on its status as 'speech acts;' gender, the differences between men and women, as a type of socially-constructed identity; and the theoretical understanding of law as a form of violence. Because these concepts are of crucial importance to the arguments presented here, each of them will be discussed more fully in the following sections.

A. *Law as Ideology*

Laws are normally considered solely in relationship to a society's civil and criminal procedures. However, in contemporary legal theory, laws can be thought of as 'discourses' which are defined as 'linguistic framings or stylized appeals to parts of ideologies'.[10] Consequently, an analysis of a law can reveal its underlying ideologies;[11] where the term, 'ideology' refers to the 'socially produced assumptions'[12] that operate in an intellectual system. Stated differently, 'ideology' refers to the values and interests that are embedded in a text. A critique of biblical laws in this manner can reveal these laws' underlying values, as will be shown in the following chapters.

Ideological criticism can include a two-part analysis – an extrinsic analysis and an intrinsic analysis. As discussed by Gale Yee, an extrinsic analysis 'investigates the social and historical worlds in which these texts were produced', and an intrinsic analysis 'focuses on what the text actually says (content) and how it says it (rhetoric)'.[13] Yet one of the consequences of a written law (as opposed to an oral

9. In his work on the status of women in biblical times, Meir Malul finds that the male dominance/female subordination paradigm is prevalent but he issues a warning 'that we must be careful not to apply our modern notions, and particularly not to use our system of values in judging our subject matter'. Malul, *Knowledge, Control, and Sex: Studies in Biblical Thought, Culture, and Worldview* (Tel Aviv-Jaffa: Archaeological Center Publications, 2002), p. 367. At the same time, though, he contends that 'the ancients' perception of the matter', even if contrary to feminist concerns, 'has nothing to do with practical issues pertaining to the fate and status of women in modern society'. Malul, *Knowledge, Control, and Sex*, p. 328. To the contrary, this study will argue that, given the pervasive cultural influence exerted by the Bible, those ancient attitudes do affect women (and men) today. As a result, a feminist critique of the dominance/subordinate paradigm is neither anachronistic nor ethnocentric but imperative.

10. Martha Albertson Fineman, *The Neutered Mother, the Sexual Family, and Other Twentieth Century Tragedies* (New York: Routledge, 1995), p. 21.

11. Fineman, *The Neutered Mother*, p. 21.

12. A.K.M. Adam, *What is Postmodern Biblical Criticism?* (Guides to Biblical Scholarship; Minneapolis: Fortress Press, 1995), p. 48.

13. Gale Yee, 'Ideological Criticism: Judges 17–21 and the Dismembered Body', in Gale Yee

law) is that it becomes 'decontextualized'.[14] As a result, completing an extrinsic analysis is rendered more speculative.[15] Moreover, an 'intrinsic analysis', which examines just the text, is adequate under current legal theory.

The goal of studying biblical laws, then, does not have to be learning more about ancient Israelite judicial administration or about a sociohistorical context purportedly giving rise to these laws. Instead, these laws can be studied for their ideological content. That content is important because, by expressing appropriate behavior, it constructs identities.[16] With such an analysis, the laws themselves are the concrete material on which a non-historical, text-immanent reading is based, and, as language, these laws constitute a 'reality' that can be analyzed in and of itself.

B. *Law as Speech Acts*

The law's ability to construct identity is reinforced by its status as a 'speech act'. Notably, in his work on the semiotics of biblical law, Bernard S. Jackson used speech act theory, the notion that 'certain uses of language did not merely make statements, but performed actions', as part of his analysis.[17] His initial example of a

(ed.), *Judges & Method: New Approaches in Biblical Studies* (Minneapolis, MN: Fortress Press, 1995), pp. 146–70 (147).

14. Anne Fitzpatrick-McKinley, *The Transformation of Torah from Scribal Advice to Law* (JSOTSup, 287; Sheffield: Sheffield Academic Press, 1999), p. 74. This observation by Fitzpatrick-McKinley is based on the work of Jack Goody in his book, *The Logic of Writing and the Organization of Society* (Cambridge: Cambridge University Press, 1986).

15. Completing an extrinsic analysis is complicated further by varying opinions on the reconstruction of ancient Israelite history. Analysis is still possible, however, given the consensus of cultural continuity in ancient Israel from the Late Bronze Age (1550–1200 BCE) through the Iron Age (1200–587 BCE). Jon L. Berquist, *Controlling Corporeality: The Body and the Household in Ancient Israel* (New Brunswick, NJ: Rutgers University Press, 2002), pp. 13–14.

16. Laws function to shape identity by establishing notions of 'who it is possible or appropriate or valuable to be'. Craig Calhoun, *Critical Social Theory: Culture, History, and the Challenge of Difference* (Oxford: Basil Blackwell, 1995), p. 213. Similarly, as phrased by the legal scholar Robert Cover, legal traditions 'establish the paradigms for behavior'. Robert Cover, 'Nomos and Narrative', in Martha Minow, Michael Ryan and Austin Sarat (eds.), *Narrative, Violence, and the Law: The Essays of Robert Cover* (Ann Arbor: The University of Michigan Press, 1992), pp. 95–172 (101).

17. Bernard S. Jackson, *Studies in the Semiotics of Biblical Law* (JSOTSup, 314; Sheffield: Sheffield Academic Press, 2000), p. 43. Jackson's discussion here is based on J.L. Austin's, *How to Do Things with Words* (Cambridge, MA: Harvard University Press, 2nd edn, 1975). According to Austin, certain conditions have to be met before a speech act could occur: a conventional procedure had to be established that included specific words said by particular persons in given circumstances, and that procedure must be invoked by the appropriate persons and completed correctly and completely. Austin, *How to Do Things with Words*, Chapter 3, cited in Jackson, *Studies in Semiotics*, pp. 43–44. Jackson notes, however, that more recent theoretical work has determined that valid speech acts can occur even when some of the classical conditions as articulated by Austin have not been met. Jackson, *Studies in Semiotics*, p. 44. See also Judith Butler, *Excitable Speech: A Politics of the Performative* (New York: Routledge, 1997), pp. 2–4; Dennis Kurzon, *It is Hereby Performed: Explorations in Legal Speech Acts* (Pragmatics & Beyond VII, 6; Amsterdam/Philadelphia: John Benjamins, 1986), p. 9; and Marina Sbisà and Paolo Fabbri, 'Models(?) for a Pragmatic Analysis', *Journal of Pragmatics* 4 (1980), pp. 301–19.

speech act is the naming of a ship: 'I name this ship the Exodus'. As described by Jackson, this statement functions as a speech act for the following reason:

> [it] does not describe the naming of the ship or claim that the ship has that name: rather, it performs the act of naming. Before the utterance, the ship did not have that name; after the utterance, the ship does have that name. The utterance has an effect in the world (albeit the world of social knowledge and consciousness).[18]

Jackson then relates this concept of naming in speech acts to the process of classification in biblical laws, using Num. 35.16–18 as an example.[19]

> Numbers 35.16–18 contains a sequence of homicide provisions, expressed in the following form: 'But if he struck him down with an instrument of iron, so that he died, he is a murderer – *rotseach hu* (רצח הוא) – the murderer shall be put to death'.[20]

Although some scholars have argued that the declaration, 'he is a murderer' (*rotseach hu*) is 'logically superfluous', Jackson finds that it is a necessary speech act.[21] Such a statement is required, Jackson contends, to classify the perpetrator as a murderer 'without the evidence of ambush or prior hatred that the biblical sources normally require for the offense of murder'.[22]

> God instructs Moses to tell the children of Israel that he, God, says that the accused in these circumstances is a murderer. The institutional speech act of naming is here incorporated into the narrative structure, and indeed into the very structure of the legal norm itself. The audience will not doubt that this offender now really is a murderer, given that it is God who has applied that name to him.[23]

Jackson's application of speech act theory to a law in Numbers applies to the laws under discussion in the BC and DL. For example, the law against adultery (Deut. 22.22) functions to classify a man who has intercourse with the wife of another (Israelite) man and the woman involved as adulterers. Furthermore, as Jackson rightly surmised, the narrative context of the laws in the Pentateuch means that God has named them in that way.

Indeed, biblical laws can be thought of as a category of 'the speech acts of God', as E.A. Levenston does in his article with that title.[24] As Levenston writes, 'the commonest speech act performed by God is legislating' and '[i]n the Bible, God legislates by speaking; it is by virtue of his having said to Moses 'thou shalt not seethe a kid in its mother's milk', that the law has been enacted'.[25] Levenston then describes how 'biblical divine legislation' can be identified by the presence of 'an

18. Jackson, *Studies in Semiotics*, p. 43.
19. Jackson, *Studies in Semiotics*, p. 49.
20. Jackson, *Studies in Semiotics*, p. 49
21. Jackson, *Studies in Semiotics*, pp. 49–50.
22. Jackson, *Studies in Semiotics*, p. 50.
23. Jackson, *Studies in Semiotics*, p. 51.
24. E.A. Levenston, 'The Speech Acts of God', *Hebrew University Studies in Literature and the Arts* 12 (1984), pp. 129–45.
25. Levenston, 'Speech Acts of God', pp. 139–40.

enacting formula, a form of words which functions performatively and establishes the legislative force'.[26] Such an enacting formula, 'These are the laws which you shall set before them', may precede the legislation, as is done in the BC (Exod. 21.1) and, correspondingly, the DL (Deut. 12.1).[27]

The significance of speech act theory applied to biblical laws is that it offers another way of understanding the ability of these laws to shape identity. John Searle, who developed further the work of Austin, offers a significant insight on the matter. Earlier, in *How To Do Things with Words*, Austin had identified three aspects of speech acts: locutionary (the behavior of speaking), illocutionary (utterances that have performative force) and perlocutionary (the effects of speaking such as persuasion). As defined by Searle, directives are types of utterances that have performative force (illocutionary) and the verbs used in directives include 'ask', 'order', 'command', and 'pray'.[28] Consequently, biblical laws, because they command, order, and prohibit, are forms of directives.

Searle then distinguishes between types of illocutionary force: words-to-world and world-to-words. Assertives, another category of illocutionary acts, assert 'the truth of the expressed proposition' and their force is the language of words-to-world since the words conform to the world.[29] In contrast, directives have the illocutionary force of world-to-words because they represent attempts 'by the speaker to get the hearer to do something' (or, not to do something) and, if successful, the world conforms to the words.[30] Biblical laws, therefore, are directive statements that have illocutionary force in the direction of world-to-words. It is that illocutionary force which prompts the hearer to conform his or her actions to the words. In turn, that force, that ability to affect behavior, helps to explain the ability of biblical laws to shape identity. In one sense, biblical laws can classify those who behave in a certain manner, as Jackson contends. Continuing to use adultery as our example, Deut. 22.22 defines adultery and labels a man who has intercourse with the wife of an Israelite man and the woman involved as adulterers. Yet, that law's influence

26. Levenston, 'Speech Acts of God', p. 140.

27. Levenston, 'Speech Acts of God', pp. 140–41. Levenston mentions two other ways that the enacting formula can be found: following the legislation (as in Exod. 27.21, 28.43 and 29.9) and introducing a set of regulations as in the book of Leviticus.

28. John R. Searle, *Expression and Meaning: Studies in the Theory of Speech Acts* (Cambridge: Cambridge University Press, 1979), pp. 13–14.

29. Searle, *Expression and Meaning*, p. 12, 18.

30. Searle, *Expression and Meaning*, p. 13, 18. Searle explains the differences between world-to-word and word-to-world with the following example, originally provided by Elizabeth Anscombe. 'Suppose a man goes to the supermarket with a shopping list given him by his wife on which are written the words "beans, butter, bacon, and bread". Suppose as he goes around with his shopping cart selecting these items, he is followed by a detective who writes down everything he takes. As they emerge from the store, both shopper and detective will have identical lists. But the function of the two lists will be quite different. In the case of the shopper's list, the purpose of the list is, so to speak, to get the world to match the words; the man is supposed to make his actions fit the list. In the case of the detective, the purpose of the list is to make the words match the world; the man is supposed to make the list fit the actions of the shopper'. Searle, *Expression and Meaning*, p. 3. See also Searle, *Intentionality: an essay in the philosophy of mind* (Cambridge: Cambridge University Press, 1983).

does not end there. Not only does the same law shape identity through classification but it also functions to define appropriate behavior for Israelite men and women in general – Israelites are not to commit adultery – and its illocutionary force influences individuals to behave accordingly.[31]

Although his work does not address the BC and DL specifically, Searle's analysis demonstrates that biblical laws, whether spoken by God or promulgated by religious institutions, may constitute valid speech acts.[32] Using speech act theory, then, demonstrates that biblical laws, given their illocutionary force, have the ability to shape identities. Moreover, their divine origin serves to legitimate the laws themselves as well as the national and gender identities constructed by the laws.[33]

C. *The Construction of Gender*

Gender theory challenges the traditional notion that familiar gender attributes are natural. In conventional terms, a person's sex – whether male or female – is thought to be natural, biologically determined, and the constructed characteristics associated with that sex are seen as inherent. According to gender theory, however, the attitudes and behavior associated with one's sex are the product of nurture, provided by one's cultural context, rather than nature. In other words, the terms 'male' and 'female' are biological descriptions but the terms 'man' and 'woman', which connote the appropriate behavior attributed to each sex, are sociologically defined terms. Indeed, the notion that gender – the spectrum of attributes associated with the male or female sex respectively – is a social construction and not a biological fact is a basic concept of gender theory.

Most importantly, 'gender' is defined as the 'mutually exclusive scripts for being male and female'.[34] Consequently, gender refers only to the polarized attributes assigned to men and women respectively. An example of a polarized attribute, a 'gender construction', is the traditional notion that women are to work inside the home and men are to work outside the home. Thus a discussion of gender does not include necessarily any and all laws that mention women because different treatment for men and women is not described in each and every law. As a corollary, then, not all laws concerning women construct gender.

Such a definition of the term, 'gender', though, has not been a stable one. As Joan Wallach Scott writes in the revised edition of her book, *Gender and the*

31. It is worth noting that narratives may influence behavior, too, but they do so indirectly whereas laws directly prescribe and proscribe behavior.

32. Searle finds that institutions such as 'the church', 'the state' and 'the law', among others, are valid contexts in which speech acts can occur. Furthermore, 'supernatural declarations' such as God saying 'Let there be light', are exceptions to the need for an institutional setting. Searle, *Expression and Meaning*, p. 18. See also Levenston, 'The Speech Acts of God', pp. 132–35, and Anthony C. Thiselton, *New Horizons in Hermaneutics: The Theory and Practice of Transforming Biblical Reading* (Grand Rapids: Zondervan, 1992), pp. 291–98.

33. For additional discussions of speech act theory and biblical interpretation, see Hugh C. White (ed.), 'Speech Act Theory and Biblical Criticism', *Semeia* 41 (1988).

34. Sandra Lipsitz Bem, *The Lenses of Gender: Transforming the Debate on Sexual Inequality* (New Haven: Yale University Press, 1993), pp. 80–81.

Politics of History, 'gender' and 'sex' are often used synonymously in both popular and academic conversations, and the distinction between 'nature' and 'nurture' is blurred by a greater awareness that even our concept of biological sex is socially constructed.[35] In response, Scott offers two proposals for clarifying the concepts involved – both of which are followed here. First, Scott thinks that our point of departure must be the ways in which laws and other discourses establish these differences.[36]

> If sex, gender, and sexual difference are *effects* – discoursively and historically produced – then we cannot take them as points of origin for our analysis. Instead we must ask the following questions: How do laws, rules, and institutional arrangements refer to and implement differences between the sexes? In what terms? How have different societies organized gender relationships? In what terms has sexual difference been articulated?[37]

Consequently, in Chapter 3, the BC and DL will be shown to construct the female body as a body that (1) submits to male authority, (2) is meant for sex with men, and (3) is meant for maternity. The significance of this discussion is that it does not cover traditional qualities attributed to women, such as nurturance, but actually demonstrates how laws, as discourses, construct bodies.

Second, to counter allegations of 'essentialism', where the treatment of women is assumed to be universal, Scott suggests that links be made between sexual difference and other kinds of difference such as race, class, and ethnicity.[38] Therefore, this study recognizes that gender constructions are multidimensional and vary in content when race and class considerations are included, a process that has been called 'intersectionality'.[39] For example, in today's 'culture wars' where white middle class mothers are encouraged to stay at home with their children, welfare mothers (presumed to be black and brown) are required to go to work. Obviously, then, even in the same culture, the concept of 'mother' varies according to race and class. Consequently, this analysis of the treatment of women in the BC and DL will acknowledge differences, based on whether the women are slave/free or Israelite/

35. Joan Wallach Scott, *Gender and the Politics of History* (New York: Columbia University Press, rev edn, 1999), p. 200. See also Thomas Laqueur, *Making Sex: Body and Gender from the Greeks to Freud* (Cambridge: Harvard University Press, 1990). As a result, 'sex' must be defined as 'the application of socially agreed upon biological criteria for classifying human beings as females or males'. Candace West and Sarah Fenstermaker, 'Ethnomethodology and "Idealist Determinism": A Reply to John Wilson', in Paula England (ed.), *Theory on Gender/Feminism on Theory* (New York: Aldine De Gruyter, 1993), p. 358.

36. Scott, *Gender and Politics of History*, p. 200.

37. Scott, *Gender and Politics of History*, pp. 201–202 (italics in the original).

38. Scott, *Gender and Politics of History*, p. 202. See also Myra Jehlen, 'Gender', in Frank Lentricchia and Thomas McLaughlin (eds.), *Critical Terms for Literary Study* (Chicago: University of Chicago Press, 2nd edn, 1995), pp. 263–73 (272).

39. Kimberlé Crenshaw, 'Demarginalizing the Intersection of Race and Sex: A Black Feminist Critique of Antidiscrimination Doctrine, Feminist Theory and Antiracist Politics', *University of Chicago Legal Forum* 129 (1989), pp. 139–67, reprinted in D. Kelly Weisberg (ed.), *Feminist Legal Theory: Foundations* (Philadelphia: Temple University Press, 1993), pp. 383–95.

non-Israelite, and include those same factors as they pertain to the construction of the female body in Chapter 3.

D. *Law as Violence*

To date, scholars have highlighted narrative and metaphorical descriptions of violence against women in the Pentateuch and Deuteronomistic History,[40] as well as the prophetic literature.[41] In the legal corpus, violence against women has been seen to result either from a law's act of omission or commission. The act of omission is found in Carolyn Pressler's article on sexual violence and the deuteronomic laws. There, Pressler notes the laws' failure to recognize rape as an assault against the female.[42] Similarly, as an act of commission, Harold Washington finds that the metaphors in the deuteronomic laws of warfare equate masculinity with being victorious whereas femininity is equated with being vanquished and submitting to violence.[43] By addressing violence against women in the Hebrew Bible, this study situates itself within these earlier discussions. However, a different conceptualization of violence is now offered. Rather than trying to identify rhetorical violence in literary descriptions or metaphors, the present attempt is to reveal the inherent violence of biblical laws, based on a philosophical understanding of the power of language. Although that concept of inherent violence will be developed more fully in Chapter 4, an initial explanation is warranted here.

According to Michel Foucault, knowledge and power are related phenomena that serve to reinforce each other.[44]

> We should rather admit that power produces knowledge...that power and knowledge directly imply one another; that there is no power relation without the correlative constitution of a field of knowledge, nor any knowledge that does not presuppose and constitute at the same time power relations.[45]

Because laws constitute a form of knowledge, they therefore have power. Traditionally, power has been equated with that exercised by a centralized state. How-

40. Phyllis Trible, *Texts of Terror: Literary-Feminist Readings of Biblical Narratives* (OBT; Philadelphia: Fortress Press, 1984), and Mieke Bal, *Death & Dissymmetry: The Politics of Coherence in the Book of Judges* (Chicago: University of Chicago Press, 1988).

41. Renita J. Weems, *Battered Love: Marriage, Sex, and Violence in the Hebrew Prophets* (OBT; Philadelphia: Fortress Press, 1995).

42. Carolyn Pressler, 'Sexual Violence and the Deuteronomic Law', in Athalya Brenner (ed.), *A Feminist Companion to Exodus to Deuteronomy* (FCB, 6; Sheffield: Sheffield Academic Press, 1994), pp. 102–12.

43. Harold C. Washington, '"Lest He Die in the Battle and Another Man Take Her": Violence and the Construction of Gender in the Laws of Deuteronomy 20–22', in Bernard M. Levinson, Victor H. Matthews and Tikva Frymer-Kensky (eds.), *Gender and Law in the Hebrew Bible and the Ancient Near East* (JSOTSup, 262; Sheffield: Sheffield Academic Press, 1998), pp. 185–213.

44. Michel Foucault is not considered to be a critical theorist. However, his work shares with critical theory the recognition that knowledge is ideological and serves the purposes of power. See Peter Dews, *Logics of Disintegration: Post-Structuralist Thought and the Claims of Critical Theory* (London: Verso, 1987), p. 150.

45. Foucault, *Discipline and Punish: The Birth of the Prison* (trans. Alan Sheridan; New York: Random House, 1977), p. 27.

ever, Foucault rejects any dualist concept of power that only extends 'from the top down'.[46] Instead, he perceives power to be omnipresent and omnidirectional.[47] The significance of Foucault's approach is that laws can have power even if they were not enforced by a centralized authority.

Furthermore, his approach relates power to violence. In his exploration of sexuality, he wonders how discourses are 'used to support power relations' and suggests that 'rather than referring all the infinitesimal violences that are exerted on sex, all the anxious gazes that are directed at it', any analysis of such discourses should be done 'in the field of multiple and mobile power relations'.[48] In this way, Foucault hints at a conflation of power and violence that is part of an ongoing debate in philosophical circles.[49] At this juncture, our ability to connect laws with violence (because laws, as forms of knowledge have power and power is equated with violence) means that we need to have a different definition of 'violence'. As Beatrice Hanssen noted,

> Stretched beyond its former clearly demarcated boundaries, meaning 'the use of physical force' (a characterization still to be found in standard dictionary definitions), violence now includes such phenomenologically elusive categories as psychological, symbolic, structural, epistemic, hermeneutical, and aesthetic violence.[50]

For our purposes, therefore, laws can constitute forms of symbolic violence and they will be discussed as such in Chapter 4. The significance of an expanded definition of violence is that biblical laws can become forms of violence if they exclude female perspectives and outlooks, for example, as well as when they describe or condone physical violence against women.

2. *Previous Research on the Role of Biblical Law*

Prior research on biblical laws has often grappled with two questions – whether the laws were used in the judicial systems of ancient Israel and whether ancient Israelite society can be reconstructed from these laws. Within the context of the laws under discussion, the laws on women in the BC and DL, the following answers are offered: (1) these laws have primarily a non-juridical function and that function is to construct identity; and (2) ancient Israelite society cannot be reconstructed from these laws. Although these answers might appear to be novel, in fact, they are quite consistent with some of the current thinking on these matters.

The nature and function of ancient Israel's biblical law have been lively areas of scholarly inquiry. Specifically, scholars have long noted that ancient Near Eastern

46. Foucault, *The History of Sexuality: An Introduction*, I (trans. Robert Hurley; New York: Vantage Books, 1990), p. 94.

47. Foucault, *The History of Sexuality (Vol. 1)*, p. 93.

48. Foucault, *The History of Sexuality (Vol. 1)*, pp. 97–98.

49. For a detailed analysis of the philosophical constructions of violence, see Beatrice Hanssen, *Critique of Violence: Between Poststructuralism and Critical Theory* (Warwick Studies in European Philosophy; New York: Routledge, 2000).

50. Hanssen, *Critique of Violence*, p. 9.

laws,[51] including those of the Hebrew Bible, fail to cover adequately a range of topics and decision-making procedures. As one scholar observed, these ancient laws 'provide only minimal information on marriage and divorce, inheritance and property, and the usual methods of conducting trials'.[52] In addition, there is no indication that biblical laws, or the other ancient Near Eastern laws for that matter, were ever implemented as part of a system of judicial administration. Indeed, even the use of the widely disseminated Code of Hammurabi in settling disputes is doubted because no contemporaneous verdicts, decisions or agreements appear to refer to its provisions as authority.[53] Likewise, scholars have questioned the relationship between biblical laws and their ancient sociocultural settings. Stated in another way, some scholars doubt that using biblical laws to reconstruct ancient Israelite society yields reliable information. Answers to each of these questions have been debated since Albrecht Alt's groundbreaking work on biblical laws and the trends in those debates are summarized below.

A. *Did the Laws Serve a Legal Purpose?*

In his work on the laws in the Hebrew Bible, Albrecht Alt recognized that the limited guidance provided in biblical laws undermined the ability of some of these laws to function as judicial vehicles.[54] Consequently, he distinguished between the conditional (casuistic) laws that were judicial instruments and the unconditional (apodictic) laws that were not. With respect to casuistic laws, Alt observed that each of them could 'be used as it stands in the work of the ordinary courts' and that these laws were 'presumably composed, then, to fulfill the needs of these courts'.[55] In contrast, he found that the apodictic laws fail to treat matters in a manner 'adequate to the practical needs of secular jurisdiction'.[56] For example, Alt notes that homicide is prohibited in an apodictic form in Exod. 21.12 but there is a failure to distinguish between murder and manslaughter as is done in the laws that immediately follow it (Exod. 21.13-14). Consequently, Alt concludes that apodictic laws are sacred rather than secular in function because they deal with 'the sacral realm of man's relations with the divine' and with 'sacred areas within the community'.[57]

51. The ancient Near Eastern laws referred to generally in this study include specific law collections from a variety of cultures. The laws of Ur-Namma (LU) and Lipit-Ishtar (LL) are written in Sumerian. The laws written in Akkadian are those of Eshnunna (LE), Hammurabi (LH), and Neo-Babylonia (LNB). The Middle Assyrian (MAL) and Hittite (HL) law codes are also included under the rubric of ancient Near Eastern laws. The abbreviations provided here in parentheses for each law code are used in this study. These abbreviations are taken from Martha T. Roth, *Law Collections from Mesopotamia and Asia Minor* (SBLWAW, 6; Atlanta: Scholars Press, 2nd edn, 1997), p. xiv.

52. Hans Jochen Boecker, *Law and the Administration of Justice in the Old Testament & Ancient East* (trans. Jeremy Moiser; Minneapolis: Augsburg Publishing House, 1980), p. 55.

53. Jean Bottéro, *Mesopotamia: Writing, Reasoning, and the Gods* (trans. Zainab Bahrani and Marc van de Mieroop; Chicago: University of Chicago Press, 1992), pp. 163–64.

54. Albrecht Alt, 'The Origins of Israelite Law', in *Essays on Old Testament History and Religion* (trans. Robert A. Wilson; Garden City, NY: Doubleday, 1967), pp. 101–71.

55. Alt, 'Origins of Israelite Law', p. 116.

56. Alt, 'Origins of Israelite Law', p. 160.

57. Alt, 'Origins of Israelite Law', p. 146.

Since Alt's work, various explanations have been offered for the law's incomplete coverage of subjects and procedures. Niels Peter Lemche argues that most laws were not written down in the Western Asia of antiquity because no such laws were needed.[58] The explanation Lemche provides is that in the ancient Near Eastern setting most disputes were handled within lineage systems rather than by state officials.[59] Similarly, Jay Marshall adopted anthropological models in his discussion of biblical law to demonstrate that in preindustrial societies such as ancient Israel, valid law can exist without the law being written and in the absence of a centralized state to enforce the law.[60] Furthermore, Raymond Westbrook has argued that biblical and cuneiform law collections were meant to function as academic treatises rather than binding rules and regulations.[61] In this respect, the law codes served to provide general guidelines for legal administrators rather than statutory authority.[62] The common element in each of these explanations for the apparent deficiencies in ancient Near Eastern laws is the insistence that these laws, to some extent or another, did in fact serve a judicial purpose.

To the contrary, there are other scholars who suggest that instead of a juridical function, these laws have primarily a non-juridical one. Bernard Jackson, in his examination of biblical criminal law, reached such a conclusion. Jackson, citing the first and second person formulations of the biblical laws, the frequent absence of sanctions and the presence of many of the types of motive clauses, found that these 'characteristic features of Biblical drafting' indicated that they were not legal documents.[63] As a result, Jackson asserts that to compare the biblical law and the Code of Hammurabi is to compare two 'religious literary texts' and not 'two legal systems'.[64] In the same way, Waldemar Janzen concluded that even if the biblical law codes had served a judicial purpose 'at one time', that purpose was later transcended as these laws 'were communicated in exhorting form to elicit assent, shape character, and renew commitment to the God who had saved his people'.[65] The

58. Niels Peter Lemche, 'Justice in Western Asia in Antiquity, Or: Why No Laws Were Needed!', *Chicago-Kent Law Review* 70 (1995), pp. 1695–1716.

59. Lemche, 'Justice in Western Asia', pp. 1705–706. More generally, Lemche suggests that a patronage system was operative in which the smaller number of those in wealthier lineage systems extended protection to the more numerous poor members of the community. See Lemche, 'Justice in Western Asia', pp. 1709–710.

60. Jay W. Marshall, *Israel and the Book of the Covenant: An Anthropological Approach to Biblical Law* (SBLDS, 140; Atlanta: Scholars Press, 1993), pp. 27–32.

61. Raymond Westbrook, 'Cuneiform Law Codes and the Origins of Legislation', *ZA* 79 (1989), pp. 201–22 (222). Similarly, Bottéro states that the Code of Hammurabi is not an authentic law code but a 'treatise on jurisprudence'. Bottéro, *Mesopotamia*, p. 183.

62. Westbrook, 'Cuneiform Law Codes', p. 222.

63. Bernard S. Jackson, 'Reflections on Biblical Criminal Law', in *Essays in Jewish and Comparative Legal History* (Studies in Judaism in Late Antiquity, 10; Leiden: E.J. Brill, 1975), pp. 25–63 (29).

64. Jackson, 'Reflections', pp. 53–54.

65. Waldemar Janzen, *Old Testament Ethics: A Paradigmatic Approach* (Louisville, KY: Westminster/John Knox Press, 1994), p. 62.

approach here, then, is entirely consistent with these recent considerations of biblical law as non-juridical material.[66]

Current research has also identified the construction of identity as the purpose of these laws' ideologies. For example, Harold Washington, recognizing that biblical law may or may not actually have been applied in antiquity, proposes that by the time the Deuteronomic Law reached its present form, the 'sermonizing appropriation of the legal tradition is directed more toward the inculcation of values and the creation of identity than the juristic imposition of rules'.[67] Although Washington's statement refers only to the Deuteronomic Law, the ability of a law to construct identity applies more widely. By punishing some types of conduct and rewarding others, laws shape and define the behavior deemed appropriate for an adherent of that value system.[68] In the context of biblical laws, their ability to define appropriate behavior for an Israelite, whether male or female, a married free woman, a slave man, and so forth is the way that these various identities are developed.[69] Some approaches would seek to justify the apparent deficiencies in biblical laws as

66. The approach to biblical laws as non-juridical documents followed here differs from Calum Carmichael's position that these laws are non-juridical and solely literary in nature. In one of his earliest books, *Women, Law, and the Genesis Tradition* (Edinburgh: Edinburgh University Press, 1979), Carmichael argues that the deuteronomic laws do not arise from responses to the everyday life of the Israelites. Instead, he suggests that they are a response to Israel's literary traditions found in Genesis. For example, according to Carmichael, the guidelines in Deut. 21.15-17, concerning the inheritance rights of the first-born son of a disliked wife versus those of the son whose mother is loved, reflect the story of Jacob and his two wives, Rachel (loved) and Leah (the first wife but less favored) and their sons, Joseph (Rachel's son who inherits) and Reuben (Leah's son). Carmichael finds that the law reflects 'the Deuteronomist's sensitivity to the humiliation of women'. Carmichael, *Women, Law and the Genesis Tradition*, p. 32. In a more recent book, *The Origins of Biblical Law: The Decalogue and the Book of the Covenant* (Ithaca, NY: Cornell University Press, 1992), Carmichael presents his argument that the Book of the Covenant responds to situations presented in the patriarchal narratives on Jacob and Joseph. Consequently, for Carmichael, the social setting of these law codes is less important than the events reported in Israel's literary traditions. Although the biblical laws are considered to be non-juridical documents, the notion that their content was never used in administrative settings goes beyond any foundational premises needed in this inquiry. For a more detailed critique of Carmichael's approach, see Bernard M. Levinson, 'Calum M. Carmichael's Approach to the Laws of Deuteronomy', *HTR* 83 (1990), pp. 227–57. But in *The Transformation of Torah*, Anne Fitzpatrick-McKinley thinks 'Carmichael's view that the setting for the production of Israel's codes is the scribal school rather than the practical life of Israel, is an appropriate starting point'. Fitzpatrick-McKinley, *The Transformation of Torah*, p. 108.

67. Washington, 'Violence and the Construction of Gender in the Hebrew Bible: A New Historicist Approach', *BibInt* 5 (1997), pp. 324–63 (344).

68. Calhoun, *Critical Social Theory*, p. 213.

69. That laws considered to be unenforceable or impractical influence attitudes and behavior and so construct identity has been recognized already. See Joseph R. Gusfield, *Symbolic Crusade: Status Politics and the American Temperance Movement* (Urbana: University of Illinois Press, 2nd edn, 1986); and David A. Leiter, 'The Unattainable Ideal: Impractical and/or Unenforceable Rules in the Ancient Israelite Legal Collections' (unpublished doctoral dissertation, Drew University, 1994). Addressing the ideological content of the BC and DL, therefore, means that even those laws normally discounted as unenforceable or impractical must be considered.

judicial instruments in various ways; but the assumption here is that these same factors indicate that the laws may have served a different purpose in ancient Israel. In brief, the laws influenced behavior even as non-juridical expressions and so functioned to construct identities.[70]

B. *Can Ancient Israelite Society Be Reconstructed from the Biblical Laws?*
In addition to addressing the previous issue of the function of biblical laws, Alt broached this subject when he distinguished between apodictic laws, casuistic laws, and their respective origins. In Alt's formulation, the apodictic (unconditional) laws were cultic in origin and unique to ancient Israel, but the casuistic (conditional) laws were secular and common among other ancient Near Eastern peoples. Alt's typologies and their designated settings within Israelite society established a relationship between biblical laws and particular sociocultural practices in ancient Israel, but they have been challenged. Boecker and Patrick have proposed alternative linguistic distinctions between the apodictic and casuistic laws.[71] Most importantly, though, scholars have sought to determine more accurately the laws' sociohistorical settings. Noth traced the apodictic laws to the earliest gatherings of the Israelite tribes.[72] However, Mendenhall noted parallels between apodictic law forms and corresponding forms in Hittite treaties.[73] Gerstenberger agreed with Mendenhall that the apodictic laws were not unique to ancient Israel and then traced those laws to the clan setting rather than a cultic one.[74] Beneath these scholars' interest in a legal form's original setting appears to be an interest in using the laws to elucidate aspects of social organization in ancient Israel.

70. A precept that helped to define modernity was the Cartesian assertion: 'I think, therefore, I am'. According to this statement's logic, knowledge is dependent on the individual, and one's self-concept is independent of societal influence. See Calhoun, *Critical Social Theory*, p. 194. Postmodern thought has thoroughly rejected that logic, based on the understanding that the individual is shaped by society. Specifically, the argument is made that identity, whether collective or individual, is socially constructed. As a result, the construction of 'identity' is intimately related to that of the 'reality' or culture constituted by the laws themselves. See Alberto Melucci, 'The Process of Collective Identity', in Hank Johnston and Bert Klandermans (eds.), *Social Movements and Culture* (Social Movements, Protest, and Contention, 4; Minneapolis: University of Minnesota Press, 1995), pp. 41–63; and Hank Johnston, Enrique Laraña and Joseph R. Gusfield, 'Identities, Grievances, and New Social Movements', in Hank Johnston, Enrique Laraña and Joseph R. Gusfield (eds.), *New Social Movements: From Ideology to Identity* (Philadelphia: Temple University Press, 1994), pp. 3–35.

71. Boecker, *Law and the Administration of Justice*, pp. 201–205; Patrick, *Old Testament Law*, pp. 23–24.

72. Martin Noth, 'The Laws in the Pentateuch: Their Assumptions and Meaning', in *The Laws in the Pentateuch and Other Studies* (trans. D.R. Ap-Thomas; Edinburgh: Oliver & Boyd, 1966), pp. 1–107 (7).

73. George E. Mendenhall, 'Ancient Oriental and Biblical Law', *BA* 17 (1954), pp. 29–30.

74. Erhard S. Gerstenberger, 'Covenant and Commandment', *JBL* 84 (1965): pp. 38–51. See esp. Gerstenberger's book, *Wesen und Herkunft des 'Apodiktishen Rechts'*, WMANT 20 (Neukirchen–Vluyn: Neukirchener Verlag, 1965). Gemser and Sonsino identify wisdom rather than cultic circles as the origin of apodictic law. See B. Gemser, 'The Importance of the Motive Clause in Old Testament Law', VTSup 1 (1953), pp. 50–66, and Rifat Sonsino, *Motive Clauses: Biblical Forms and Near Eastern Parallels* (SBLDS, 45; Chico, CA: Scholars Press, 1980).

Similarly, Rhonda Burnette-Bletsch sought in her work to use the biblical laws as the basis for reconstructing agrarian family life in ancient Israel. Burnette-Bletsch's project was to reconstruct agrarian family life in ancient Israel using the biblical text, so she had to face squarely the issue of the biblical text's relationship to an external reality. Recognizing that the biblical text was 'the best primary source for this purpose', she nevertheless acknowledges that 'the societal practices described in normative documents like the Hebrew Bible are inevitably removed to some degree from social reality'.[75] She develops specific guidelines to help determine the accuracy of information on the Israelite agrarian family provided in the biblical text.[76] Two such guidelines are that traditions which serve the compilers' interests, such as the requirements for offerings of crops and animals to the priesthood, are to be discounted, but traditions that run counter to the compilers' interests, such as the notion of inalienable land tenure, are more likely to depict actual social practices.[77]

Clearly, attempting to glean information about ancient Israelite society from biblical law is at best a delicate balancing act. Successfully making the connection between law and ancient Israelite society, though, has become more complicated. Apparently, reconstructing ancient Israelite society from the laws rests on two assumptions. One assumption, now undermined, is that Israelite laws, the ones that were operative in ancient Israel, are the same as biblical laws.

> Israelite laws belong to the actual legal systems operating in the Israelite society, either at the level of the centralized state or within the more immediate communities of the people. They are the laws that actually existed in order to affect behavior in that society according to enforceable controls and to help the judicial system decide a case involving crimes and conflicts between parties. Biblical laws, in contrast, are literature. They probably include some of the Israelite laws – that is, the 'living laws' – but any number of laws (quite plausibly the vast majority) existing in that society during some part of its long history or within the diverse regions and villages of the country were not incorporated in the Hebrew Bible.[78]

The second assumption is that legal development is directly related to social development. If that is the case, then, changes in laws reflect social changes and vice versa. As Anne Fitzpatrick-McKinley effectively argues in her work on biblical laws, however, that notion of 'a correlative relationship between law and soci-

75. Rhonda J. Burnette-Bletsch, 'My Bone and My Flesh: The Agrarian Family in Biblical Law' (unpublished doctoral dissertation, Duke University, 1998), pp. 42–43.

76. Burnette-Bletsch, 'The Agrarian Family', pp. 40–50.

77. Burnette-Bletsch, 'The Agrarian Family', pp. 43–45. Two other such guidelines privilege older traditions over newer ones and information provided incidentally within a text rather than that claimed explicitly. For an example of the latter guideline, she cites the motif of barren women as unreliable proof that fertility was a problem in ancient Israel because it appears so explicitly throughout the Hebrew Bible. Burnette-Bletsch, 'The Agrarian Family', pp. 45–46.

78. Douglas A. Knight, 'Whose Agony? Whose Ecstasy?: The Politics of Deuteronomic Law', in David Penchansky and Paul L. Redditt (eds.), *Shall Not The Judge Of All the Earth Do What Is Right: Studies on the Nature of God in Tribute to James L. Crenshaw* (Winona Lake, IN: Eisenbrauns, 2000), pp. 97–112 (104).

ety' is questionable because laws, once written, function more or less autonomously.[79] Specifically, Fitzpatrick-McKinley asserts that neither socio-economic conditions nor presumed underlying societal values are as determinative of legal growth as are, among other factors, the borrowing of legal texts from other legal traditions and the interests of the elite individual or groups who draft the laws.[80]

Setting aside questions about the relationship between biblical law and ancient society, as done in the present study, offers two advantages. First, as mentioned earlier, because the law, as language, constitutes its own 'reality', it can be analyzed on its own terms. Yet, not only can the laws be analyzed as constituting a 'reality' or 'culture'[81] in and of themselves, but there is the realization that this reality may or may not reflect a historical reality. It is Jacques Derrida who asserts that there is no 'objective' external referent outside of the text: '*il n'y a pas de hors texte*'.[82] For him, writing marks 'the disappearance of natural presence'.[83] As a result, an approach to these biblical laws can focus on the biblical text as a writing whose meaning can be determined in the absence of any 'natural' setting.[84] Instead of having to establish guidelines for translating legal content into social reality, it can be admitted that the relationship between the 'reality' constructed on the basis of these laws and an actual historical social setting may be tenuous. Indeed, it is more likely that the only 'reality' reflected in the text conveys the political, economic, and theological interests of the elite groups who produced and conserved the biblical text.[85] It bears repeating that these values are significant, nevertheless, because they shape behavior.[86]

Second, a historical approach eliminates the need to search elsewhere in the Hebrew Bible for law-related materials that are thought to complete the picture of societal practices in ancient Israel. For example, Deut. 22.22 prescribes the death penalty for a married woman and a man other than her husband who are caught in the act of adultery. Yet Prov. 6.32-35 seems to imply that the husband could accept

79. Fitzpatrick-McKinley, *The Transformation of Torah*, pp. 11–19.

80. Fitzpatrick-McKinley, *The Transformation of Torah*, pp. 54–80.

81. In this context, a 'culture' refers to 'symbolic forms' such as language or ritual practices 'through which people experience and express meaning'. Ann Swidler, 'Culture in Action: Symbols and Strategies', *American Sociology Review* 51 (1986), pp. 273–86 (273).

82. Jacques Derrida, *Of Grammatology* (trans. Gayatri Chakravorty Spivak; Baltimore: The Johns Hopkins University Press, 1976), p. 158 (italics in original).

83. Derrida, *Of Grammatology*, p. 159.

84. In this sense, the Derridean approach adopted here directly contradicts the nineteenth-century German approach which presumed the existence of a reality external to the text that could be known objectively by historians through that text. See Robert A. Oden, Jr, 'Hermeneutics and Historiography: Germany and America' (*SBLSP*, 19; Chico, CA: Scholars Press, 1980), pp. 135–57; and *The Bible Without Theology: The Biblical Tradition and Alternatives to It* (San Francisco: Harper & Row, 1987).

85. Knight, 'Whose Agony? Whose Ecstasy?', pp. 99–100.

86. A law's influence extends beyond the preferences of a given segment of society because it is 'part of a reward and punishment system that aims to coerce, when necessary, behavior that conforms to a view of the kind of society we should have'. D. Don Welch, 'Introduction: The Moral Dimension of Law', in D. Don Welch (ed.), *Law and Morality* (Philadelphia: Fortress Press, 1987), pp. 1–27 (1).

financial compensation for the offense instead.[87] Those who would use the laws to reconstruct an actual social reality have to address the issue of which genre reflects actual practices – the law, the wisdom literature, or both. Moreover, Derrida's work forces the recognition that incorporating material from other biblical materials will not provide more accurate access to a historical reality.[88] Bracketing the search for an 'objective' historical reality means that biblical law can be analyzed independently, because it constitutes its own reality, without reference to other parts of the canon.

3. *Methodological Considerations*

From the preceding discussions, it should be evident that this study employs a variety of methodological approaches and that these approaches are borrowed from the fields of hermeneutics, critical theory, and poststructuralism. The range of theorists referred to so far include Foucault (poststructuralism), Derrida (deconstruction), and, in Chapter 4, the work of Mary Jo Frug will be used (postmodern legal theory). Some of the additional theorists whose works have shaped the approach used here include Judith Butler and Judith Lorber (gender theory) and Patricia Hill Collins, Susan Bordo, Martha Albertson Fineman, and, especially, Julia Kristeva (feminist theory). In the same way, several disciplines will be represented and included among them are anthropology (Peggy Sanday), theology (Rosemary Radford Ruether), and pastoral care (James Poling). Considered collectively, the insights of these scholars and disciplines significantly advance this discussion of laws in the Hebrew Bible.

Without a doubt, an eclectic analytical approach is used here and having the term 'critical theory' in the title implies an expanded definition of 'critical theory'. In its narrower sense, critical theory refers to the method developed by a group of scholars that includes Theodor Adorno, Max Horkheimer, and Walter Benjamin who first came together in Germany during the 1930s. Known collectively as the Frankfurt School, this group of neo-Marxist scholars identified a critical theory of society that emphasized an interdependent relationship between theorists and their social worlds.

In its broader sense, though, critical theory refers to the notion of the 'social construction of knowledge,'[89] where laws, as knowledge, are produced in an environment, and then these laws act upon the environment that produced them.[90] A

87. Laws that confer upon the husband the right to determine the wife's punishment rather than a judge or the king can be found in the Middle Assyrian laws. See MAL(A) 14–16.

88. Derrida's work would suggest that any external referent, whether another literary genre or the presumed author, are 'texts' so that, as a result, there are no 'points of reference which transcend the text and provide privileged points of access into it'. Yvonne Sherwood, *The Prostitute and the Prophet: Hosea's Marriage in Literary-Theoretical Perspective* (JSOTSup, 212; Sheffield: Sheffield Academic Press, 1996), pp. 169–70.

89. Peter L. Berger and Thomas Luckmann, *The Social Construction of Reality: A Treatise in the Sociology of Knowledge* (New York: Anchor Books/Doubleday, 1966).

90. As such, an immanent critique results because the ostensibly external as well as internal

valid question does arise here, however. What is the common thread that weaves these different methodological and hermeneutical perspectives together? To a great extent, the approaches used fall within the category, 'socio-critical hermeneutics' because they recognize that 'texts can be used for social manipulation or control, or to authorize, or to appear to authorize, values which serve the interests of some individual or corporate entity'.[91] Correspondingly, their task is to 'unmask these social interests through an emancipatory critique'.[92]

In addition, there are basically two common features that apply to most of the approaches borrowed from other disciplines in this work. One feature is the awareness that 'the meanings within a literary work are never fixed and reliable, but always shifting, multi-faceted and ambiguous'.[93] With such an understanding, biblical texts can be read in new and creative ways. Specifically, the gaps in the biblical laws are considered to be instructive. For example, there is no law in the Book of the Covenant or the Deuteronomic Law that permits a wife to initiate a divorce, whereas there is a law that refers to the husband's ability to divorce his wife (Deut. 24.1-4). Admittedly, the lack of such a law does not mean necessarily that women did not have this right in ancient Israelite society. To the contrary, a woman may indeed have had that right in ancient Israel.[94] In the context of this study, though, the absence of such a law is instructive because it communicates information concerning the appropriate behavior for a wife, namely, that she was not to initiate a divorce.

Significantly, some gaps in biblical laws become more apparent if the latter are compared to the ancient Near Eastern laws which are their temporal and geographical counterparts. A relevant illustration can be seen in the absence of laws on a woman's dowry and/or bridewealth in the Hebrew Bible when such laws exist in those law collections.[95] The absence of dowry and bridewealth laws is striking because of the numerous parallels between ancient Near Eastern and biblical laws. In fact, the similarities between the bodies of law have led some scholars, such as Westbrook, to suggest that there was a common legal heritage.[96]

forces that impinge on the process of developing intellectual constructs are acknowledged. Adam, *Postmodern Biblical Criticism*, pp. 15–16.

91. Thiselton, *New Horizons in Hermeneutics,* p. 6.

92. Thiselton, *New Horizons in Hermeneutics,* p. 12. The other hermeneutics according to Thistleton's schema that are most relevant for this project are metacritical (trans-contextual) and socio-pragmatic (reader-response) hermeneutics.

93. Peter Barry, *Beginning Theory: An Introduction to Literary and Cultural Theory* (Manchester: Manchester University Press, 1995), p. 35.

94. It may be that women were treated more harshly in the legal codes than in custom. Ze'ev Falk, *Hebrew Law in Biblical Times* (Provo, UT: Brigham Young University Press, 2001), p. 109.

95. LU 15; LL 29; LE 25; LH 142, 159–161, 162–164; MAL(A) 38; and HL 27–30, 34, 36. According to social anthropology, the difference between bridewealth and dowry is that the former is an exchange between families (from the groom's family to the bride's family) and the latter is an exchange within a family (from the father of the bride to the bride). See Katarzyna Grosz, 'Bridewealth and Dowry in Nuzi', in Averil Cameron and Amélie Kuhrt (eds.), *Images of Women in Antiquity* (Detroit: Wayne State University Press, rev. edn, 1993), pp. 193–206.

96. Raymond Westbrook, *Studies in Biblical and Cuneiform Law* (Cahiers de la *RB* 26; Paris: J. Gibalda, 1988), pp. 1–8.

With so many commonalties, one wonders why the gap in these particular laws exists in the Hebrew Bible. Specifically, the questions can be directed towards the ideological underpinnings beneath the failure to include such laws. Where a conventional approach would focus on whether that gap relates to a social reality, under this approach, the investigation focuses on the ideological motivation for the gap and the gap's effect on the construction of identities. For example, the absence of laws on dowry and brideprice in the biblical laws arguably maintains a woman's economic dependence on men and reinforces male control of females.

Another theme common to most of the theorists and approaches referenced is the concept that 'politics is pervasive'.[97] The phrase 'politics is pervasive' means that any knowledge is influenced by the pertinent social context and the privileged interests within that context.[98] Recognizing such political influence in this study means that, since the individuals who redacted and preserved these laws were privileged males, the laws assume that perspective – whether or not those individuals intended the laws to do so. Specifically, Carol Meyers has written that 'the Bible as a whole is androcentric, or male-centered, in its subject matter, its authorship, and its perspectives'.[99] Consequently, the analysis in this study will reveal that the laws distinguish between 'us' and 'them', from the perspective of elite Israelite males, and indicate appropriate behavior for themselves and for those who from that vantage point are 'Other'. Given the status of the redactors, it stands to reason that these laws would not only privilege males over females but also the free person over the slave and the Israelite over the foreigner. However, of the groups that fall within the category of 'Other', gender, defined as the different behaviors set out for males and females, is the identity developed most completely in the laws.[100]

Critical hermeneutics, therefore, facilitates the recognition of political influences on texts in antiquity and the present. But the influence of politics in the shaping of these texts extends further. I have to admit that my own interest in such an analysis is politically motivated. Because gender is a social construction, it is legitimated by mechanisms that label its requirements as given, natural and inevitable, and then those requirements are reinforced by punishing those who do not comply.[101] According to Seyla Benhabib, then, a 'defetishizing critique' is 'a procedure of analysis whereby the given is shown to be not a natural fact but a socially and historically constituted, and thus changeable, reality'.[102] As a Christian (Protestant) and feminist/womanist African-American female who lives in a culture of violence

97. Barry, *Beginning Theory*, p. 36.

98. Such a premise is also found in Critical Legal Studies (CLS). For an analysis of biblical laws based on CLS, see Harold V. Bennett, *Injustice Made Legal: Deuteronomic Law and the Plight of Widows, Strangers, and Orphans in Ancient Israel* (Grand Rapids: Eerdmans, 2002).

99. Carol Meyers, 'Everyday Life: Women in the Period of the Hebrew Bible', in Carol A. Newsom and Sharon H. Ringe (eds.), *Women's Bible Commentary* (Louisville, KY: Westminster/ John Knox Press, revised and expanded, 1998), pp. 251–59 (251).

100. See Appendix B.

101. Judith Butler, *Gender Trouble: Feminism and the Subversion of Identity* (New York: Routledge, 1990), p. 140.

102. Seyla Benhabib, *Critique, Norm, and Utopia: A Study of the Foundations of Critical Theory* (New York: Columbia University Press, 1986), p. 47.

against women, I have an interest in 'defetishizing' these laws, to use Benhabib's term, as well as the male dominance/female subordination gender paradigm that they encode.

To reveal the privileging of the interests of elite male redactors is to challenge the notions of class, gender, and so forth that are presented in the laws as natural categories of human interaction. Rather than considering such categories to be natural, critical liberationist approaches such as this one seek to unmask their inherent biases and so undermine their claims to absolute and transhistorical truth. By demonstrating that the male dominance/female subordination gender paradigm, found in both ancient and contemporary laws, is not natural and harmful to men and women alike, the hope is that change will occur. Ultimately, as expressed by Drucilla Cornell and Seyla Benhabib, the feminist goal for both men and women is a 'social life characterized by nurturant, caring, expressive, and nonrepressive relations between self and other, self and nature.[103]

103. Benhabib and Drucilla Cornell, 'Introduction: Beyond the Politics of Gender', in Seyla Benhabib and Drucilla Cornell (eds.), *Feminism as Critique: On the Politics of Gender* (Minneapolis: University of Minnesota Press, 1987), pp. 1–15 (4). See also Rosemary Radford Ruether, *Gaia and God: An Ecofeminist Theology of Earth Healing* (San Francisco: HarperSanFrancisco, 1992).

Chapter 2

A SURVEY OF THE LAWS ON WOMEN IN THE BOOK OF THE COVENANT AND THE DEUTERONOMIC LAW

1. *Introduction*

In the previous chapter, we learned that 'gender' refers to traits assigned to males and females that are socially constructed, and that these traits for males and females are defined in opposition to one another. An illustration of a polarized gender trait is found in descriptions of men who are valued as 'aggressive' but women who are valued as 'passive'. In this chapter, we will see that, since only polarized traits construct gender, not all laws concerning women construct gender. To the contrary, some of the laws treat men and women in the same way. Therefore, the laws of the BC and DL can be divided between those that treat men and women similarly ('inclusive laws') and those that treat men and women differently ('exclusive laws').

Consequently, exclusive laws, the laws that construct gender, are those that prescribe or proscribe behavior and attributes for women only. Exclusive laws consist of laws that (1) specifically apply only to women, (2) laws that specifically exclude women, and (3) those that determine a woman's treatment based on her relationship to a male. In contrast, inclusive laws are those that prescribe or proscribe attributes and behavior for both males and females. Inclusive laws can be subdivided then according to those that call for such treatment explicitly or implicitly.

An issue on women's gender roles in biblical laws has emerged from recent investigations by Naomi Steinberg,[1] Carolyn Pressler,[2] and Rhonda Burnette-Bletsch.[3] The issue is whether the roles for men and women are symmetrical and interdependent or if the roles for women, in relation to men, are asymmetrical and subordinate. Distinguishing between inclusive and exclusive laws as done in this study offers an explanation as to why the different opinions were reached. Because these opinions will be explored more fully at the end of this chapter, it is sufficient to say here that Steinberg and Burnette-Bletsch focus more on the inclusive laws and so find interdependence and symmetry in male/female roles. Pressler, by comparison, bases her conclusions on the deuteronomic family laws. Since these laws

1. Naomi Steinberg, 'Adam's and Eve's Daughters Are Many: Gender Roles in Ancient Israelite Society' (unpublished doctoral dissertation, Columbia University, 1984).

2. Carolyn Pressler, *The View of Women Found in Deuteronomic Family Laws* (BZAW, 216; Berlin: W. de Gruyter, 1993).

3. Burnette-Bletsch, 'The Agrarian Family'.

in the DL are exclusive laws, she finds male/female roles to be asymmetrical. The perspectives of Steinberg, Pressler, and Burnette-Bletsch are emphasized in this chapter because the current discussion builds upon their work.[4]

The following analysis, though, differs from the work of Steinberg, Pressler and Burnette-Bletsch in two respects. First, they attempt to reconstruct actual historical contexts based on the laws and pertinent narratives. For example, in her discussion of the laws on the betrothed girl in Exod. 22.15-16 [22.16-17] and Deut. 22.28-29, Pressler suggests that the prohibition of divorce in the later law may result from an increased frequency of divorce in the deuteronomic period.[5] In this case, as a non-historical and text-immanent analysis, the sociohistorical context of the laws is not sought. Second, rather than focus on why a law exists or how a law relates to an ancient context, the motivating question here is whether or not a law constructs gender. In other words, the interest here is in the laws' content and whether that content treats men and women alike or differently. The following survey, therefore, examines the laws' underlying values and attitudes, that is, their ideologies.

2. *Inclusive Laws*

Inclusive laws prescribe or proscribe treatment that applies to both males and females either explicitly or implicitly. Explicit laws include those on slaves, the family, and the cult. Implicit laws are those that refer to only males or only females specifically but nonetheless appear to apply to both men and women. Laws that are inclusive by implication are those on sorcery and apostasy.

A. *Inclusive Laws that Explicitly Refer to Men and Women*

1. *Inclusive laws: the treatment of male and female slaves.* When biblical laws concerning women are discussed, the laws concerning slaves are usually not considered. However, these laws are relevant because females are specifically covered in each of their provisions. These laws on slaves include those on injuries to slaves caused by their owners or by a goring ox, and the release of debt slaves.

a. *Striking a male or female slave (Exod. 21.20-21 and 26-27).* A slave owner can be punished if a male or female slave dies immediately after the owner has struck him or her with a rod – but not if the slave survives for a day or two (Exod. 21.20-21). Although the requisite punishment for the immediate death of a slave from the striking is not specified in the law, Hans Jochen Boecker has proposed that blood-revenge is referred to, which means that the life of the slave is equated with that of a free Israelite.[6]

Exodus 21.26-27 provides further that if the slaveowner, by striking, destroys an eye or knocks out the tooth of a male or female slave, the owner must free the

4. The scope of this investigation which covers the treatment of women in the BC and DL, however, is different from that of Steinberg, Pressler, and Burnette-Bletsch. Steinberg and Pressler cover just the DL family laws. Only Burnette-Bletsch discusses both the BC and the DL, but her analysis focuses only on those laws that provide information about kinship patterns.

5. Pressler, *Family Laws*, pp. 40–41.

6. Boecker, *Law and the Administration of Justice*, p. 162.

slave. Correspondingly, Boecker finds that this provision creates a slave's 'right to bodily integrity'.[7] Unlike Boecker, Shalom Paul does not think that talion applies when the slave dies immediately because 'a slave is not considered the peer of a freeman'.[8] Nevertheless, he does agree with Boecker's conclusion that Exodus 21.26-27 offers some protections to the slave who is considered 'a person in his own right and must be treated with proper restraint'.[9]

Both Boecker and Paul view these laws favorably, noting that there is no cuneiform law that addresses the issue of death or injury caused by the owner to his or her own slave.[10] Referring to Exod. 21.20-21, Paul maintains that this law offers a unique evaluation of a slave's worth in the ancient Near Eastern context.[11]

Dale Patrick and Jay Marshall, however, offer a very different interpretation of these laws. Patrick deems Exod. 21.20-21 more favorable to the slaveowners than to the slaves because it confers upon owners the right to use force on slaves to compel them to work.[12] Furthermore, if the slave dies from physical punishment, according to Patrick, the law presumes that 'it is in the nature of an accident' and the slave owner 'suffers economic loss'.[13] Similarly, concerning the permanent injury caused by striking covered in Exod. 21.26-27, Marshall argues that the talionic formula is not required here because the loss of the eye or tooth of a free person in return for the lost eye or tooth of a slave would exact too great a penalty from the free person.[14] Instead, the slave is freed to become part of the economically underprivileged, an intermediate status between free and slave.[15]

These laws provide equivalent treatment for male and female slaves; therefore, gender construction is not involved. Yet, following the analysis of Patrick and Marshall, these laws do offer stark contrasts between the treatment of those who are slaves and those who are free. Because a distinction is made between slave and free, these laws contribute to the construction of class identity and will be discussed as such in Chapter 3.

b. *Male or female slave gored by an ox (Exod. 21.28-32).* The laws here provide that if an ox gores a man or woman to death, the ox must be killed (and its flesh must not be eaten) but the owner of the ox is not liable. Yet, if the ox has gored before, the owner has been warned but failed to restrain the animal, and the ox then kills a man or a woman, both the ox and the owner shall be put to death. A ransom may be imposed upon the owner, though, which allows him to redeem his life and pay compensation instead. The same rules apply if the ox gores a boy or a girl but, if a slave is involved, the penalty is different. If a male or female slave is gored, the owner must pay 30 shekels of silver to the slaveowner and the ox is to be stoned.

7. Boecker, *Law and the Administration of Justice*, pp. 162–63.
8. Shalom M. Paul, *Studies in the Book of the Covenant in the Light of Cuneiform and Biblical Law*, (VTSup, 18; Leiden: E.J. Brill, 1970), p. 78.
9. Paul, *Studies*, p. 78.
10. Paul, *Studies*, p. 69; Boecker, *Law and the Administration of Justice*, p. 162.
11. Paul, *Studies*, p. 69.
12. Patrick, *Old Testament Law*, p. 76.
13. Patrick, *Old Testament Law,* p. 76.
14. Marshall, *Israel and the Book of the Covenant*, p. 121.
15. Marshall, *Israel and the Book of the Covenant*, p. 121.

Ancient Near Eastern parallels to the BC's goring ox laws can be found in both the Laws of Eshnunna (Sections 54–55) and the Code of Hammurabi (Sections 250–252).[16] Boecker points out in his discussion of these sets of laws that they agree on only two details: (1) whether the dangerous nature of the animal was previously known to the owner determines the owner's liability, and (2) that a slave-owner is due compensation for the loss of a slave.[17] Boecker observes that, in all other respects, these laws differ.[18] According to him, the most essential differences between the biblical law and its ancient Near Eastern counterparts concern the stoning of the animal and the punishment of the negligent ox-owner.[19] Each of these elements of Exod. 21.28-32 will now be addressed separately.

Unlike the comparable cuneiform laws, the BC requires that the ox be killed if a person has been killed.[20] The rationale for the biblical requirement offered by Moshe Greenberg is that, because humans are made in the image of God, 'a beast that kills a man destroys the image of God and must give a reckoning for it'.[21] Consequently, Greenberg sees the requirement to stone the guilty ox as an affirmation of the value of human beings, and the 'Babylonian law on the subject reflects no such theory as to the guilt the peculiar value of human life imposes on all who take it'.[22]

According to Boecker, the second significant difference between the biblical law and the Babylonian versions is the punishment of the animal owner who has been negligent.[23] Exodus 21.29 provides that the owner of the ox can be subject to the death penalty if the owner knew of the animal's goring nature but failed to restrain the ox. Jackson suggests that the owner's liability stems from the failure to protect the community.[24] Specifically, his rationale for the law is that the owner knew the ox had a propensity for goring but failed to slaughter the animal and so, if the ox kills a person, the owner is liable for the death that could have been prevented.[25] Although the death penalty is called for in Exod. 21.29, the subsequent legal

16. Laws on a goring ox are not unique to the ancient Near East and have been found in the legal traditions of other cultures. See Sophie Lafont, *Femmes, Droit et Justice dans l'Antiquité orientale: Contribution à l'étude du droit pénal au Proche-Orient ancien* (OBO, 165; Göttingen: Editions Universitaires Fribourg Suisse/Vandenhoeck & Ruprecht, 1999), pp. 2–3. See also J.J. Finkelstein, *The Ox That Gored* (Philadelphia: The American Philosophical Society, 1981).

17. Boecker, *Law and the Administration of Justice*, p. 164.

18. Boecker, *Law and the Administration of Justice*, p. 164.

19. Boecker, *Law and the Administration of Justice*, pp. 164–65.

20. Patrick, *Old Testament Law*, p. 77; and Paul, *Studies*, p. 79.

21. Moshe Greenberg, 'Some Postulates of Biblical Criminal Law', in M. Haran (ed.), *Y. Kaufmann Jubilee Volume* (Jerusalem: Detus Goldberg, 1960), pp. 5–28 (15–16). Greenberg's approach to the law of the goring ox has been vigorously challenged by Bernard Jackson. Jackson argues that the function of stoning the ox was utilitarian initially – to protect the community from future goring – and any rationales, religious or otherwise, are later interpretations. Jackson, 'The Goring Ox', in Jackson, *Essays in Jewish and Comparative Legal History* (Studies in Judaism and Late Antiquity, 10; Leiden: E.J. Brill, 1975), pp. 108–52 (115–16).

22. Greenberg, 'Postulates', pp. 15–16.

23. Boecker, *Law and the Administration of Justice*, p. 165.

24. Jackson, 'The Goring Ox', p. 127.

25. Jackson, 'The Goring Ox', p. 127.

provision allows the life of the owner to be redeemed. Patrick finds that the owner's life could be redeemed under these circumstances because negligence and not intentional homicide was involved.[26]

However, one difference between the laws on the goring ox in the BC and the Babylonian ones that is generally not emphasized is that the biblical version specifically mentions the female in each provision – as a (free) woman, a female child or a female slave.[27] As in the laws on injuries to slaves discussed previously, the equivalent treatment of males and females means that gender is not at stake here. Yet, just as in the slave laws, class issues are raised because Exodus 21.32 specifies that if a male or female slave is gored the ox must be killed, but the owner is only required to pay 30 shekels of silver. Along with the previous law on striking a slave, this law will be discussed in Chapter 3 as laws contributing to the construction of class identities.

c. *Male or female debt slave (Exod. 21.2-11 and Deut. 15.12-18).* According to Exod. 21.2-6, a Hebrew male debt slave[28] who is purchased must be released in the seventh year as a free person without debt. If the slave was married when he began his period of servitude, his wife may go out with him. However, a woman whom the master gave in marriage to a male slave during that time and any children they have had remain the property of their master. Instead of becoming free, the male slave may renounce his freedom, by declaring that he loves his master, wife, and children, and having his ear pierced. He will then remain a slave for life.

A different process is called for when a female is to be sold into debt servitude and the onus is on the master who purchases a Hebrew female slave. Exod. 21.7-11 provides that if the master designates her for himself but she does not please him, then he must allow her to be redeemed and must not sell her to a foreign people. If the master takes her as a wife and then marries another woman, he must not diminish her food, clothing, or marital rights. If he does not do these three things for her, then she shall go out without debt and without payment of money. If he designates the female slave for his son, he shall deal with her as with a daughter.

In the deuteronomic version of the law on debt slaves, the female is to be treated in the same way as the male. Deut. 15.12-18 specifies that an Israelite who pur-

26. Patrick, *Old Testament Law*, p. 78.

27. Scholars have noted also an implicit difference between the relevant ancient Near Eastern laws and the biblical one that concerns the punishment resulting from the death of a child. In the BC, the punishment for a child's death is identical to that of an adult (Exod. 21.31). Citing LH 116, 210 and 230, scholars have determined that specifying this punishment and only this punishment was necessary in a sociocultural context where what is referred to as 'vicarious talion', the execution of the perpetrator's child, might be required. See Paul, *Studies*, p. 83; Patrick, *Old Testament Law*, p. 78; and Anthony Phillips, *Ancient Israel's Criminal Law: A New Approach to the Decalogue* (New York: Schocken Books, 1970), p. 91.

28. Because the slave is to be released after a few years of service, 'debt slave' or 'indentured servant' are the preferable translations here of the Hebrew term עבד. See Marshall, *Israel and the Book of the Covenant*, p. 116; and Burnette-Bletsch, 'The Agrarian Family', p. 185 n. 27. It is worth noting, however, that the law only applies to Hebrews for whom 'the situation of slavery has been occasioned through debt'. Ronald E. Clements, 'Deuteronomy', *NIB* II (Nashville: Abingdon Press, 1998), p. 405.

chased and had a Hebrew man or woman work for him six years should free the person in the seventh year. That freed person should not go out empty-handed but should be liberally provided for by the owner. The law goes on to state that the owner should not consider losing the slave a hardship because the master had that person's services for six years. If the debt slave decides to remain with the owner, the slave's earlobe is to be pierced and that person will remain the master's slave forever.

Patrick notes the following five differences between the BC and DL versions of this law: (1) a female slave comes under the same provisions as a male, which Patrick takes to mean that a female's purchase to become a wife or concubine has been discontinued; (2) there is no reference to the master's giving the slave a wife and her remaining with the master if the slave is freed; (3) without the master's ownership of a slave's wife and children, a primary motive for entering lifelong servitude has been removed; (4) the ceremony to remain a lifelong servant has been removed from the sacred sphere and now there is a symbolic attachment to the household; and (5) servitude has been reduced to the ownership of a person's labor, not of the person.[29]

Generally, the reformulation of the laws concerning women and indentured servitude in Deuteronomy has been viewed favorably. For example, Paul Hanson cites the elimination of the discriminatory practice between men and women in the law of release as indicative of 'a new level of equity and humaneness within the biblical legal tradition'.[30] Similarly, Philips, who determined that women were not covered in the release law in Exodus, found that under the deuteronomic laws, 'male and female slaves now enjoyed the same rights and privileges'.[31] Yet Pressler questions whether the usual assumptions concerning the treatment of female slaves in the BC are valid. She refutes the assumptions that all female slaves had been excluded from the release in the first part of the law (Exod. 21.2-6) and that all female slaves were covered in the second part of the law (Exod. 21.7-11). For example, Pressler thinks that the first part of the law of release would apply to some females such as widows and abandoned wives who were particularly vulnerable economically and might have sold themselves 'as general household slaves'.[32]

To further her argument, Pressler suggests that this second part of the law of release does not apply to all freeborn bondswomen. Instead, she asserts that the second provision covers only any unbetrothed girls sold into bondage, and the

29. Patrick, *Old Testament Law*, p. 113. Similar differences were noted by Anthony Phillips in his analysis of these laws. See Phillips, 'The Laws of Slavery: Exodus 21.2-11', *JSOT* 30 (1984), pp. 55–56. In addition, the deuteronomic version 'imposes on the owner the obligation of a liberal gift to give the slave a new start in honor and dignity'. Richard D. Nelson, *Deuteronomy: A Commentary* (OTL; Louisville, KY: Westminster/John Knox Press, 2002), p. 197.

30. Paul Hanson, 'The Theological Significance of Contradiction Within the Book of the Covenant', in George W. Coats and Burke O. Long (eds.), *Canon and Authority: Essays in Old Testament Religion and Theology* (Philadelphia: Fortress Press, 1977), pp. 110–31 (127).

31. Phillips, 'The Laws of Slavery', p. 56.

32. Pressler, 'Wives and Daughters, Bond and Free: Views of Women in the Slave Laws of Exodus 21.2-11', in Matthews, Levinson and Frymer-Kensky (eds.), *Gender and Law*, pp. 141–72 (167).

subcases mentioned in the law cover circumstances that will occur only if an unbetrothed girl is to be in the master's household.[33] Pressler found that it was 'overly narrow' to assume that a master would purchase an unbetrothed girl only for himself or his son, given that the girl could be purchased 'for sexual use and to get heirs or to increase one's possession of slaves'.[34] As a result, Pressler contradicts the conclusion that the elimination of the male/female distinction in Deuteronomy was evidence that women were not included in the Exodus version of the law. To the contrary, Pressler finds that Deut. 15.12-18 was simply making explicit that women who were not under male protection when enslaved should be released too.[35]

Burnette-Bletsch found, on the same grounds as did Pressler, that the Exodus version of the law of release would have applied to some categories of women.[36] But not only does Burnette-Bletsch think that some females would have been covered under the Exodus law of release; she also thinks that, for those sold into concubinage, becoming a concubine would have been a somewhat positive option. In her opinion, concubinage extended to impoverished women a means of support that 'provided a woman with some of the rights and privileges associated with full wives'.[37] Accordingly, Burnette-Bletsch argues that these laws on indentured servants are benign methods for poor members of the community to support themselves while providing more affluent members with additional labor.[38]

Even though Pressler and Burnette-Bletsch interpreted the law of release similarly, they evaluated the law in different ways. To Pressler, it is a law that points to the wife's status being determined by that of her husband.[39] Yet Burnette-Bletsch finds that, even though the laws have an androcentric bias, they do not necessarily 'provide evidence for the lived experience of ancient Israelite women'.[40] To her, these laws are evidence of the importance of being within a household for survival in ancient Israel.[41]

Traditionally, the law on debt slaves in Exodus has been viewed as discriminatory towards women, but this may not be the case. As Pressler and Burnette-Bletsch have found, some women would have been released under the general provisions, and not all women were concubines in the master's household. Consequently, there may be less difference between the treatment of males and females under this law than previously thought. Nevertheless, the preceding laws on debt slaves, as well as

33. Pressler, 'Wives and Daughters', pp. 155, 158.

34. Pressler, 'Wives and Daughters', p. 158.

35. Pressler, 'Wives and Daughters', pp. 171–72.

36. Burnette-Bletsch, 'The Agrarian Family', pp. 191–92.

37. Burnette-Bletsch, 'The Agrarian Family', pp. 192–93.

38. Burnette-Bletsch, 'The Agrarian Family', p. 194.

39. Pressler, 'Wives and Daughers', p. 161. Specifically, she writes: 'The law of the Hebrew slave assumes that the wife of a free man has no independent legal status. Verse 3 rules that if a man is married when he is enslaved, his wife is released when he is released. The rule does not explicitly indicate that the wife has been enslaved with him; it assumes that if her freeborn husband is forced into bondage, she is enslaved with him'.

40. Burnette-Bletsch, 'The Agrarian Family', p. 192 n. 43.

41. Burnette-Bletsch, 'The Agrarian Family', p. 194.

this one, recognize debt slaves as a distinct group from free members of the Israelite community. Therefore, these laws do not construct gender but they do demarcate class differences between privileged and non-privileged Israelites.

2. *Inclusive laws: the treatment of men and women in family matters*. The second type of inclusive laws on women in the BC and the DL involves family and kinship matters. These laws address concerns of the parent-child relationship and the treatment of widows. Interestingly, both of these topics are found in both the BC and DL.

a. *Respect for mothers and fathers (Exod. 21.15, 17 and Deut. 21.18-21)*. In the Book of the Covenant, striking or cursing one's parents is punishable by death (Exod. 21.15, 17). In Deut. 21.18-21, a procedure is set forth that allows the mother and father of a disrespectful son to lodge a complaint against him before the elders and can result in the son being stoned to death by all of the town's men. Steinberg thought that this law 'establishes the authority of both the mother and father over their offspring while limiting the potential of unjust use of patriarchal power'.[42] Similarly, Nelson found that 'emphasizing the role of the mother seems to be a further way of limiting the father's exclusive authority' and 'the influence of the elders can modify an unrestrained paternal authority'.[43] Patrick has surmised that, if the precedent in Exodus permitted a summary execution of the son by the parents, then the corresponding law in Deuteronomy 'is instituting safeguards against the unlimited authority of parents over their children'.[44]

Both Pressler and Burnette-Bletsch reject the notion that the inclusion of a legal procedure in Deuteronomy means that a father had such extreme authority.[45] Furthermore, Burnette-Bletsch submits that the law's purpose is to protect the family unit and intergenerational stability, which were important matters for inheritance purposes and the support of elderly parents.[46] Most importantly, given the concerns of this study, she noted that these generational duties were entrusted to sons and not daughters.[47] Burnette-Bletsch suggests that daughters are not covered under these provisions since they 'would leave the family unit during early puberty and their obedience would, in effect, become someone else's concern'.[48]

As for the role of the mother in these laws, Burnette-Bletsch envisions her as an equal partner with the father and that 'the authority of both parents is at stake in every law demanding filial obedience'.[49] Steinberg, Pressler, and Burnette-Bletsch have agreed that both mother and father have authority in these laws on parental respect.[50] Acknowledging that these laws do not contribute to gender distinctions,

42. Steinberg, 'Adam's and Eve's Daughters', p. 250.
43. Nelson, *Deuteronomy*, p. 261.
44. Patrick, *Old Testament Law*, p. 129.
45. Burnette-Bletsch, 'The Agrarian Family', pp. 232–34; and Pressler, *Family Laws*, pp. 17–19.
46. Burnette-Bletsch, 'The Agrarian Family', pp. 235–36.
47. Burnette-Bletsch, 'The Agrarian Family', p. 236.
48. Burnette-Bletsch, 'The Agrarian Family', p. 236.
49. Burnette-Bletsch, 'The Agrarian Family', pp. 233–34.
50. Burnette-Bletsch, 'The Agrarian Family', pp. 233–34; Pressler, *Family Laws*, p. 20; and Steinberg, 'Adam's and Eve's Daughters', p. 250.

they will be discussed in Chapter 3 as laws involved in the construction of a generational identity.

b. *Widows (Exod. 22.21-23 [22.22-24] and Deut. 24.17-22)*. Exodus 22.21-23 [22.22-24] prohibits the abuse of any widow or orphan. Because a female is mentioned, this text does involve the treatment of women.[51] The initial question for the purposes of this study is whether it constructs gender: Does it treat women differently from men? Any findings of discrimination based on sex seem unlikely because similar language applies to the resident alien[52] and protection for the poor.[53] In other words, the protections extended to the widow are the same as those extended to orphans, the poor, and resident aliens in the BC even though the specific formula of 'the stranger, the orphan, the widow', referred to collectively as the *personae miserae*, does not appear before Deuteronomy.[54]

Continuing the protections offered in Exodus, Deuteronomy prohibits depriving the resident alien or orphan of justice and taking the widow's garment in pledge (Deut. 24.17-18). Similarly, gleanings of the field are to be left for the alien, widow, and orphan (Deut. 24.19-22). Another reference to these groups is found in Deut. 26.12-15: the third year of tithes is to go to the Levites, the aliens, the orphans, and the widows.

The element that unites each of these groups is that they have no means of support through kinship patterns and/or the possession of landed property.[55] To understand that common element, a redefinition of the term 'widow' is needed. In the Bible, a 'widow' is not just a woman whose husband has died; she is a woman who has no male relatives such as sons or a father-in-law to support her financially.[56] Similarly, the stranger (*gēr*) is a person whose ties with family had been severed. It is thought that the *gēr* refers to the northerners who migrated to the southern kingdom after the fall of Samaria but that cannot be known with any certainty.[57] Regardless of the particular circumstances that led to the displacement, the *gēr* is one who lives outside of his or her own geographical area and so is without relatives or land. Therefore, the widow and the *gēr* share a common plight because they are without kinship ties in a society where such ties provided identity.

51. Women are mentioned twice in Exod. 22.21-23 [22.22-24] which provides that, if the proscribed abuse of widows and orphans occurs, the wives and children of the abusers will become widows and orphans. Only the reference to females in 22.21 [22.22] will be considered in this discussion. But the reference in 22.23 [22.24] is worth noting. Dana Nolan Fewell and David M. Gunn see this law as one requiring the wives and children to pay for the sins of their husbands and fathers. Fewell and Gunn, *Gender, Power, & Promise: The Subject of the Bible's First Story* (Nashville: Abingdon Press, 1993), p. 102. Their interpretation contrasts sharply with that of Phillips who, on the subject of vicarious talion, has written: 'there is no occasion in Israelite criminal law where someone was punished instead of another'. Phillips, *Ancient Israel's Criminal Law,* p. 91.

52. Exod. 22.20 [22.21] and 23.9.

53. Exod. 22.24-26 [22.25-27] (against abusing the poor when money is lent) and 23.6-8 (against perverting justice to the poor).

54. Lohfink, 'Poverty', p. 40.

55. Lohfink, 'Poverty', p. 44.

56. Paula S. Hiebert, '"Whence Shall Help Come to Me?": The Biblical Widow', in Peggy L. Day (ed.), *Gender and Difference in Ancient Israel* (Minneapolis: Fortress Press, 1989), p. 137.

57. Lohfink, 'Poverty', p. 41.

> The Hebrew *'almānâ* then, like the *gēr*, existed on the fringes of society. In a society where kinship ties gave one identity, meaning and protection, both the *'almānâ* and the *gēr* had no such ties. Unlike the *gēr*, however, the *'almānâ* lives in this liminal zone as a woman.[58]

To a large extent, the stranger, widow, and orphan are treated similarly and so these laws do not construct gender. Nevertheless, gender differences are identifiable. In her article on biblical widows, Hiebert states that the widow suffers more 'on the fringes of society' than the *gēr* because 'not only was she bereft of kin, but she was also without a male who ordinarily provided a woman with access to the public sphere'.[59] Similarly, Phyllis Bird argues that the concern expressed for the poor in biblical legislation and the prophetic literature is for 'their brothers' – males who are disadvantaged – and, with the exception of the widow, not females.[60]

Most significantly, the Israelite widow is disadvantaged primarily because, as a female, she cannot inherit her husband's estate. As pointed out by Léon Epsztein, the Israelite widow had fewer resources with which to survive on her own than a comparable Mesopotamian widow.

> According to the Code of Hammurabi and the Assyrian laws, the formal situation of the widow would seem to have been better than in Israel. In Babylon she had a right to some of her husband's estate. The widow or the repudiated wife could even in some cases enjoy part of the estate equivalent to that received by a child and regain full control over her dowry. The Assyrian laws seem to contain analogous dispositions. By contrast, the Israelite widow did not enjoy any right of succession and the estate fell entirely into the hands of the sons of the dead man, and if he had none, those of his daughters. If he did not have any children, the estate went to his brothers, his father's brothers or the nearest relative.[61]

Consequently, the laws taken together construct gender indirectly because the widow cannot inherit her husband's property, a fact that contributes to her eco-

58. Hiebert, 'The Biblical Widow', p. 130.

59. Hiebert, 'The Biblical Widow', p. 130.

60. Phyllis A. Bird, 'Poor Man or Poor Woman: Gendering the Poor in Prophetic Texts', in *Missing Persons and Mistaken Identities: Women and Gender in Ancient Israel* (OBT; Minneapolis: Fortress Press, 1997), pp. 67–80 (78).

61. Léon Epsztein, *Social Justice in the Ancient Near East and the People of the Bible* (trans. John Bowden; London: SCM Press, 1986), pp. 113–14 (interlineal citations omitted). The specific laws to which Epsztein refers from LH are sections 137, 172–173, and 180–182. As for the Assyrian references, Epsztein cites the work of Roland de Vaux in *Ancient Israel: Its Life and Institutions*, (trans. John McHugh; New York: McGraw-Hill, 1961). On this matter, de Vaux states that although under Assyrian law [MAL(A) 37] a husband could divorce his wife without providing any compensation at all, marriage contracts can provide otherwise. According to de Vaux, Assyrian marriage contracts reveal 'still more onerous conditions for the husband' and that such special clauses were probably negotiated by the wife's parents to protect her interests. De Vaux, *Ancient Israel*, p. 36. Furthermore, even if contractual arrangements had not been made, the Assyrian law may have presumed that the husband who divorced his wife 'had to restore her dowry and personal possessions'. Sophie Lafont, 'Mesopotamia: Middle Assyrian Period', in Raymond Westbrook (ed.), *A History of Ancient Near Eastern Law* (HdO, 72/1; Leiden: E.J. Brill, 2003), pp. 521–63 (542).

nomic marginalization. Considered by themselves, though, these specific biblical laws do not treat the widow differently than males in these marginalized groups. As argued by Norbert Lohfink, the deuteronomic laws envisioned a situation where these groups who were not in a position to live off their own land would be supported.[62] According to him, these laws were intended 'to create a world in which one can be a stranger, an orphan, or a widow without being poor'.[63]

Because the categories, then, of widow, orphan, and stranger necessarily include both males and females, these laws concerning the widow do not create differences between her treatment and that of a similarly situated male. As a result, these laws do not construct gender expressly. These and other legal provisions for marginalized members of the Israelite community, however, presume an economically privileged audience and require that they care for the less privileged. As observed by Nelson, 'these laws reflect the fundamental social division between the landowners and the landless classes: aliens, the fatherless, and widows, along with daily wage earners'.[64] Such provisions, therefore, assume the perspective of privileged Israelite males and will be evaluated accordingly in Chapter 3.

3. *Inclusive laws: the treatment of men and women in the cult.* Along with the laws pertaining to slaves and the family, two laws that have been associated with cultic practices, but are now thought to have non-cultic purposes, expressly apply to both males and females. These laws address the issues of cross-dressing and prostitution and they are inclusive laws because, whatever the prohibited activities might be, the prohibitions apply to both males and females.

a. *Male and female cross-dressing (Deut. 22.5).* As provided in Deut. 22.5, a man is not permitted to wear a woman's clothes and vice versa. Phillips offers the more traditional interpretation of this law by associating its prohibition with anti-Canaanite measures.[65] Apparently, the practice of cross-dressing was understood to reflect sexual practices in the foreign cult, and cross-dressing was banned for fear that it 'might contaminate the purity of the Israelite faith'.[66]

Moving away from that stance, Patrick noted that, although designating the practice an 'abomination to Yahweh'[67] does indicate an anti-foreign cult purpose, 'the law is quite understandable as a rejection of actions exhibiting confusion of sexual identity'.[68] Most recently, Nelson relates the prohibition against cross-dressing to the prohibition against 'violating or blurring natural or social boundaries' as seen in Lev 19.19 so that 'failing to differentiate gender boundaries is forbidden'.[69] Developing this concept of sexual identity further, in Chapter 4,

62. Lohfink, 'Poverty', p. 44.
63. Lohfink, 'Poverty', p. 44.
64. Nelson, *Deuteronomy*, p. 293.
65. Phillips, *Deuteronomy* (Cambridge: Cambridge University Press, 1973), p. 145.
66. Phillips, *Deuteronomy*, p. 145.
67. The Hebrew word תוֹעֵבָה translated by Patrick as 'abomination' is translated as 'abhorrent' in the NRSV.
68. Patrick, *Old Testament Law*, p. 130.
69. Nelson, *Deuteronomy*, pp. 267–68.

Deut. 22.5 will be cited as a law with a secular purpose, the maintenance of gender identity, rather than a cultic one.

b. *Male and female prostitution (Deut. 23.18-19 [23.17-18])*. This provision is usually thought to enjoin the sons and daughters of Israel from participating in what was believed to be temple prostitution, and monies earned from prostitution by men or women were not to be brought into the Temple. Generally, this law has been associated with the anti-Canaanite legislation of the deuteronomic reforms, based on the assumption that the Canaanites participated in fertility cults, and the Israelites had adopted their practices.[70] However, some scholars now question earlier statements about 'sacred prostitution' in the ancient Near East and doubt that such practices existed.[71]

Specifically, in her analysis of these laws, Bird found that the coupling of verses 18 and 19 'brings *qdšh* into parallelism with *zwnh*', and '*zwnh* is paired with a masculine term, *klb* "dog", which has commonly been understood to designate a male prostitute'.[72] As a result, the two verses are usually read as parallel prohibitions against both cultic and secular prostitution. However, Bird points out that the verses are not parallel in structure or in content. For example, she notes that 'the first law proscribes the existence of a "professional" class within the Israelite population;' and the second law 'prohibits an action: dedication of income from sexual commerce (male and female)'.[73] The apparent parallelism of the laws, she argues, is 'a parallelism created by editorial activity, based on an identification of *qdšh* and *zwnh*'.[74]

Assessing the use of the term, *qdšh* (literally, 'a consecrated woman') in Genesis and Hosea, among other things, Bird concludes that it 'describes a class of cult-related women associated with outlying sanctuaries in pre-Josianic times' whose cultic service was once accepted but later rejected.[75] The intentional parallelism of *qdšh* and *zwnh,* she then states, is 'a polemical identification' through which the reader 'is meant to understand that the "consecrated woman" is "simply" a kind of prostitute'.[76] As a result, Bird rejects the term 'sacred prostitute' as a translation of *qdšh* because 'it incorporates into the name of the class an identification with prostitution that is lacking in the Hebrew term'.[77] Furthermore, Bird finds no evidence of a male (homosexual) cult prostitute, as *qdš* is usually translated, and she sug-

70. Philips, *Deuteronomy*, pp. 156–57; and Patrick, *Old Testament Law*, pp. 133–34; and Clements, 'Deuteronomy', *NIB* II, p. 468.

71. See, for example, Jeffrey H. Tigay, 'Excursus 22: The Alleged Practice of Cultic Prostitution in the Ancient Near East', in Jeffrey Tigay (ed.), *JPS Torah Commentary: Deuteronomy* (Philadelphia: Jewish Publication Society, 1996), pp. 480–81; and Oden, *The Bible Without Theology*, pp. 131–53.

72. Bird, 'The End of the Male Cult Prostitute: A Literary-Historical and Sociological Analysis of Hebrew *Qādēš-Qĕdēsîm*', in J.A. Emerton (ed.), *VTSup 1995 Congress Volume* (Leiden: E.J. Brill, 1997), pp. 37–80 (47).

73. Bird, 'Male Cult Prostitute', p. 47.

74. Bird, 'Male Cult Prostitute', p. 48.

75. Bird, 'Male Cult Prostitute', p. 46.

76. Bird, 'Male Cult Prostitute', p. 40 n. 13.

77. Bird, 'Male Cult Prostitute', p. 43.

gests that the term *qdš* may be just 'a literary creation, introduced for comprehensiveness and balance'.[78] In the same way, Nelson notes that the phrase in v. 18, 'the earnings of a dog', is 'traditionally interpreted as the fee of a (presumably) homosexual male prostitute'.[79] He, too, finds that this translation is 'largely based on the poetic parallelism of this verse' and no ANE texts suggest that the term 'dog' refers to a male prostitute.[80]

As seen here, these laws do not refer to cultic prostitution as once thought. Furthermore, they apply to men and women, which means that they do not expressly construct gender differences. Nevertheless, these prohibitions define an aspect of national identity – Israelites (as opposed to other groups) are not to engage in such practices – whatever the exact practices might be. These cultic prohibitions and their role in the construction of an Israelite identity will be discussed further in Chapter 3.

B. *Inclusive Laws that Implicitly Refer to Men and Women*

On the whole, inclusive laws are those that treat women and men similarly and, in addition to the laws previously discussed that are expressly inclusive, there are laws that are inclusive by implication. These are laws that, in terms of their linguistic forms, refer to either males or females but have been interpreted to cover both sexes. Such gender-specific laws that have been given a general application are those on apostasy and sorcery.

1. *Female reference: sorcery (Exod. 22.17 [22.18]).* This prohibition that is literally against a female sorcerer (מכשׁפה) usually has been translated inclusively so that it covers both men and women. In her early work, *The Israelite Woman,* Athalya Brenner favored the more inclusive interpretation of the law because, in her words, 'why should female witches receive a treatment different from that of their male counterparts?'[81] In that book, Athalya Brenner defined sorcery and magic as related concepts: sorcery is 'malevolent magic' that 'caus[es] harm to communities or individuals by manipulating destinies, casting spells, and so on'.[82] In general, she found that magic and various occult activities were condemned in the prophetic literature because they were associated either with foreign pagan

78. Bird, 'Male Cult Prostitute', p. 50. See also Nelson, *Deuteronomy*, p. 281 ('the questionable translation 'male cult prostitute' is based solely on the parallel with *qĕdēsâ*'.)

79. Nelson, *Deuteronomy*, p. 281.

80. Nelson, *Deuteronomy*, p. 281. Nelson also mentions that the term could refer to a 'devoted follower' of a pagan god or that it might even refer to a real dog. In particular, Nelson argues that, since a dog is a 'pariah animal', it is possible that funds made from the sale of a dog could not be used to fulfill a vow.

81. Athalya Brenner, *The Israelite Woman: Social Role and Literary Type in Biblical Narrative* (Sheffield: JSOT Press, 1985), p. 76.

82. Brenner, *The Israelite Woman*, p. 69. Brenner seems to distinguish between 'magic' whether positive or negative and 'religion' according to supposed substantive differences. It is now thought that the difference between socially acceptable practices (religion) and socially unacceptable practices (magic) is political rather than phenomenological. See Nancy Bowen, 'The Daughters of Your People: Female Prophets in Ezekiel 13.17-23', *JBL* 118 (1999), pp. 417–33.

belief systems or with false prophecy within Israel.[83] Brenner also concluded that, although women may have practiced some branches of magic and witchcraft more than men, they did not have a monopoly and 'members of both sexes are included in the negative attitude displayed by the religious establishment to magic of all sorts'.[84]

More recently, the importance of the feminine participle used has been reclaimed. Brenner, after having supported the inclusive translation earlier, now finds that the gender-specific language of the prohibition holds a key to the law's meaning. Relating sorcery to the theme of sexuality that is found in the verses surrounding it, Brenner proposes that the activity proscribed as 'sorcery' involves women, sexuality, and female wisdom about birth control including contraception and abortion.[85] Given the biblical emphasis on procreation, Brenner can understand how women who could regulate fertility would be perceived negatively as 'witches'.[86]

> In light of the predominant (and socially justified) procreation ideologies, such women do run the risk of being considered witches: they undertake to deal with matters of life and death; they seem to have damaged the social fabric by helping women to regulate their reproductive activities; their knowledge is dangerous to society and its beliefs – as evidenced by persecutions to woman healers in much later times.[87]

If the law against sorcery in Exodus applies to men and women, it does not construct gender. However, if a more literal reading of Exod. 22.17 [22.18] is adopted, the law is indeed directed exclusively against women and so constructs gender.

2. *Male reference: sorcery (Deut. 18.9-14)*. It is rare that a law is phrased in the feminine verbal form but applied generally, as seen in the previous law. It is more common that a law phrased in the masculine verbal form would be applied generally, which is the case for the laws on sorcery in Deuteronomy and the apostasy law in Exodus.

The law concerning sorcery in Deuteronomy, contrary to the version in Exodus, appears to address men and women. The same root is used (כשף) in the piel active participial form; the only difference is that the feminine singular participle is used in Exodus and the masculine singular form is used in Deuteronomy. Given that the masculine form is usually understood to include men and women, the law in Deuteronomy covers males and females. Furthermore, the rationale for the deuteronomic version of the prohibition is different from that in Exodus. Instead of merely

83. Brenner, *The Israelite Woman*, p. 75.

84. Brenner, *The Israelite Woman*, p. 77. Similarly, Phyllis Bird found that the Old Testament has more references to male practitioners of the occult than female ones. See Bird, 'The Place of Women in the Israelite Cultus', in *Missing Persons and Mistaken Identities: Women and Gender in Ancient Israel* (Minneapolis: Fortress Press, 1997), pp. 81–102 (101–102).

85. Athalya Brenner, *The Intercourse of Knowledge: On Gendering Desire and 'Sexuality' in the Hebrew Bible* (Leiden: E.J. Brill, 1997), p. 85.

86. Brenner, *The Intercourse of Knowledge*, p. 86.

87. Brenner, *The Intercourse of Knowledge*, p. 86.

targeting activities by females, the law now has broader theological implications, and the list of prohibited activities is expanded to include divination, soothsaying, and necromancy. Phillips defends the prohibitions covered in Deut. 18.9-14 as having been necessitated by Israel's covenant relationship with Yahweh.[88] He construes the law to indicate that 'men were only to be informed of what lay in the future as and when Yahweh decided', and such disclosure would then be 'by his own medium, his chosen prophet, and not by diviners typical of heathen religions'.[89]

With its broader application to males and females plus the longer list of prohibited activities, this law does not construct gender but it helps to define ancient Israel as a covenant community. As will be discussed in Chapter 3, the law on sorcery in Deuteronomy, in addition to the following laws on apostasy, help to shape the national identity.

3. *Male reference: apostasy (Exod. 22.19 [22.20] and Deut. 13.7-19 [13.6-18], 17.2-7).* Exodus 22.19 [22.20] forbids sacrificing (זבח) to other gods and specifies that anyone who does so is subject to the ban, that is, devoted to destruction. The verb form in Exod. 22.19 [22.20] is a qal participle in the masculine singular form, but it is translated inclusively. The comparable laws in Deuteronomy, though, do refer specifically to males and females. Furthermore, these laws in Deuteronomy expand the definitions of prohibited cultic activity and establish a legal procedure for determining guilt or innocence. The definition of apostasy is expanded in that just enticing others to worship other gods – whether it is one's own son, daughter or wife – is a crime (Deut. 13.7-12 [13.6-11]). Moreover, whole towns that have been enticed to follow other gods are to be put under the ban and remain a perpetual ruin (Deut. 13.13-19 [13.12-18]). Due process is accorded the town in that a complete investigation must be carried out, and the town is to be destroyed only if the charge of apostasy is proved (Deut. 13.13-16 [13.12-15]). Similarly, the procedural rights of a man or woman who has served and worshiped other gods are set forth in Deut. 17.2-7. Under this provision, allegations of apostasy must be thoroughly investigated and attested to by two or three witnesses and not just by one witness (Deut. 17.6). If the charge is true, the person is to be put to death by stoning so that the evil is purged from the community's midst (Deut. 17.5-7).

Patrick presents two reasons for these laws that advocate such drastic measures against individuals and whole towns if they deviate from the exclusive covenant with Yahweh. One reason suggested by Patrick is that they protect Israel's identity as the people of Yahweh, and the second reason he offers is that they instill individual responsibility for loyalty to Yahweh.[90] Under these laws, as Patrick observes, loyalty to Yahweh is something that 'overrides the organic ties of family and friendship'.[91] As a result, Patrick finds that the 'suppression of apostasy in Israel is an act of national self-preservation'.[92] In spite of its lofty aspirations, Patrick thought that

88. Phillips, *Deuteronomy*, p. 125.
89. Phillips, *Deuteronomy*, p. 125.
90. Patrick, *Old Testament Law*, pp. 107–108.
91. Patrick, *Old Testament Law*, p. 108.
92. Patrick, *Old Testament Law*, p. 107.

the law had the 'ring of utopian theory' since it was doubtful 'that Israelites would be willing to inform on family and friends or destroy a whole city'.[93]

Taken together, the laws against sorcery and apostasy, even if impractical, provide information about the seriousness of cultic orthodoxy: Israelites are not to worship other gods. These laws in Exodus and Deuteronomy, then, do not construct gender but they construct aspects of a national identity, as will be discussed in Chapter 3.

3. *Exclusive Laws*

In contrast to the preceding section which surveyed the rationales scholars have suggested for the inclusive laws, the following section covers comparable rationales for the exclusive laws. Exclusive laws on women in the BC and DL are those that treat women differently from men. Laws are exclusive if they only apply to females, exclude females by implication, or if they determine a female's treatment based on her relationship to a male. Because the laws in the last of these three categories constitute what are considered 'the family laws' in Deuteronomy, Steinberg, Pressler and Burnette-Bletsch have each considered most of these laws in their work.

A. *Exclusive Laws that Apply Only to Women*

These exclusive laws are those that prescribe or proscribe treatment that applies only to a female. Specifically, such laws address a particular type of injury to a (pregnant) woman and a particular type of action by a woman (grabbing a man's genitals).

1. *Injury to a pregnant female (Exod. 21.22-25).* Basically, Exod. 21.22-25 provides that causing a pregnant woman to miscarry will result in the one responsible paying a fine; if she then dies, *lex talionis* applies and the death penalty is warranted. In the circumstances described in the law, the injury to the woman is a third party injury because it is caused while two men are fighting. This law covers a particular type of injury to a female because no comparable law covers third party injury to a male or to a female who is not pregnant.[94]

Paul, in his analysis of the ancient Near Eastern parallels[95] as well as the biblical laws, determines that in all of these laws 'a pecuniary settlement for the loss of the fetus' is allowed.[96] Paul concludes that since the law in Exodus permits a monetary settlement, rather than mandating the death penalty for a homicide, 'a fetus is not considered to be a human being'.[97] Furthermore, in that same discussion,

93. Patrick, *Old Testament Law*, p. 108–109.

94. Exod. 21.18-19 does cover injury caused to one of the two men in a fight.

95. Paul cites the following cuneiform laws: LH 209–214; MAL(A) 21, 50–52; HL 17–18; LL d–f; SLEx 1'-2'. His abbreviations for the law codes have been changed to be consistent with those listed in Roth, *Law Collections*, p. xiv.

96. Paul, *Studies*, p. 71.

97. Paul, *Studies*, p. 71.

he suggests that the amount of the monetary settlement is 'based on the estimated age of the embryo', as seen in an ANE parallel, HL 17.

Consistent with the understanding that a miscarriage has resulted, Exod. 21.22-25 in the NRSV reads as follows:

> When people who are fighting injure a pregnant woman so that there is a miscarriage, and yet no further harm follows, the one responsible shall be fined what the woman's husband demands, paying as much as the judges determine. If any harm follows, then you shall give life for life, eye for eye, tooth for tooth, hand for hand, foot for foot, burn for burn, wound for wound, stripe for stripe.

Just the same, questions have arisen concerning the harm caused to the fetus. Some scholars, like Paul, interpret the circumstances to describe primarily a miscarriage,[98] whereas other scholars interpret the phrase to mean more specifically a premature birth.[99] Consequently, as opposed to the language in the NRSV, Exod. 21.22-25 in the NIV reads as follows: 'if men who are fighting hit a pregnant woman and she gives birth prematurely, but there is no serious injury...' The NIV, however, does include a marginal note after the word 'prematurely' to indicate the alternate translation: 'or she has a miscarriage'.[100]

At the very least, these different interpretations indicate that causing a pregnancy loss of this sort warrants some punishment; it is the form of that punishment – monetary compensation alone or talionic penalty – that varies.[101] Consequently, from the perspective of this study, the law on injury to a pregnant woman indicates the value of offspring, the responsibility for which is given in these laws as a whole to both men and women.

Arguably, gender constructions are implied in the law on injury to a pregnant woman because of the mother's subordinate status in the household. Phillips, in his introduction to an article on family law in preexilic Israel, described family law as the sole responsibility of the male head of the household where women, children, and slaves are subordinate.[102] He then referred to Exod. 21.22-25 as the kind of law that provided evidence of that subordinate status because, under the law's provisions, it is the husband and not the wife who seeks legal relief and receives

98. See, for example, Martin Noth, *Exodus* (OTL; London: SCM Press, 1962), p. 170; Ronald E. Clements, *Exodus* (Cambridge: Cambridge University Press, 1972), pp. 135–36; and Walter Brueggemann, 'Exodus' (*NIB* I; Nashville: Abingdon Press, 1994), pp. 675–982 (864).

99. See, for example, Umberto Cassuto, *A Commentary on the Book of Exodus* (trans. Israel Abrahams; Jerusalem: Magnes Press/The Hebrew University, 1967), p. 275.

100. Marshall proposes a different interpretation based on the degree of injury. In the case of premature birth and/or non-permanent injury, compensation is an appropriate settlement; but if the infant dies or there is permanent injury to the mother or child, talion law applies. Marshall, *Israel and the Book of the Covenant*, p. 126. Burnette-Bletsch, noting the absence of any distinction between permanent and non-permanent injury in the ancient Near Eastern parallels, finds Marshall's interpretation to be unpersuasive. Burnette-Bletsch, 'The Agrarian Family', p. 198.

101. Based on ANE parallels, Jackson suggests that, at an earlier stage of the law, substitution (corresponding action against the wife of the offender) was one of the remedies. Jackson, 'The Problem of Exodus XXI 22–5', *VT* 23 (1973), pp. 273–304.

102. Phillips, 'Some Aspects of Family Law in Pre-Exilic Israel', *VT* 23 (1973), pp. 349–61 (350).

financial compensation.[103] However, in Chapter 3, given this law and other laws that encourage procreation, this law is discussed as one of the inclusive laws that constructs fertility as a matter of national identity.

2. *Genital grabbing by a female (Deut. 25.11-12).* According to this law, if two men are fighting and the wife of one of them intervenes on behalf of her husband by seizing the genitals of the other man, her hand shall be cut off. As such, the law prohibits a type of behavior by a woman. It has been thought that the law mentions a female 'only because women were more likely to resort to this tactic; men, because of their greater strength, would rely on fisticuffs or wrestling'.[104] According to Nelson, the text suggests that the woman shamed the man.[105] Pressler, Phillips, and Frymer-Kensky, though, have offered three additional explanations for the law.

Pressler sees this as a breach of modesty – a married woman being in sexual contact with another man. For her, the law indicates that 'for a married woman to have sexual contact with a man other than her husband is abhorrent, even under extenuating circumstances'.[106] Phillips, assuming that permanent injury has been caused, suggests that the woman's offense is having ended the man's ability to procreate.[107] Similarly, Tigay, noting that this law follows the law on levirate marriage where a man has died childless, also concludes that the woman is punished because she risked the man's ability to father children.[108] The problem is that, unlike its Assyrian parallel MAL(A) 8, this law does not specify that any injuries to the male have occurred.

Frymer-Kensky sees the law on improper female behavior in symbolic terms. To her, the law represents the degree to which women became more subject in the DL to the public realm, which constitutes a 'diffused' form of male authority.

> A man's genitals – any man's genitals – are now sacrosanct. Women must not only follow the authority of their head of household: all men are now a privileged caste protected by the state, and their genitals, the emblem and essence of their manhood, are now sacrosanct. Concern for and allegiance to the males of one's family, even to one's husband, cannot be allowed to cause disrespect for maleness. Even the primary husband-wife bond, so protected by biblical law (including that of Deuteronomy), must bow to this diffused authority of 'maleness', which literally embodies the public realm.[109]

Even though the nature of the woman's crime is unclear, the seriousness of the offense is indicated by the punishment; this is the only Israelite law that prescribes

103. Phillips, 'Some Aspects of Family Law', p. 351. See also Gail Corrington Streete, *The Strange Woman: Power and Sex in the Bible* (Louisville, KY: Westminster/John Knox Press, 1997), p. 34.

104. Tigay, 'Excursus 24: Improper Intervention in a Fight', in Jeffrey Tigay (ed.), *JPS Torah Commentary: Deuteronomy* (Philadelphia: JPS, 1996), p. 486.

105. Nelson, *Deuteronomy*, p. 301.

106. Pressler, *Family Laws*, p. 75.

107. Phillips, *Ancient Israel's Criminal Law*, p. 95.

108. Tigay, 'Improper Intervention', p. 485.

109. Frymer-Kensky, 'Deuteronomy', in *Women's Bible Commentary*, p. 67.

corporal mutilation.[110] In Chapter 3, the nature of the offense in this law will be considered in two ways: she risked damaging the male's fertility, as proposed by Phillips and Tigay, and she touched another male, as proposed by Pressler. In the former case, this law contributes to the notion that fertility is an aspect of ancient Israelite national identity. In the latter case, by prohibiting activity by a female, it serves to construct gender.

B. *Exclusive Laws that Exclude Women by Implication: Cultic Participation (Exod. 23.17 and Deut. 16.16)*

In both Exodus and Deuteronomy, women are excluded by implication from the cultic requirement to worship in Jerusalem. Exod. 23.17 provides that three times a year all Israelite males must 'appear before the Lord God', and the same requirement appears in Deuteronomy 16.16. By implication, women are excluded from cultic participation here. The problem, though, is that the exclusion of women in Deut. 16.16 contradicts other laws in Deuteronomy which require the participation of all (Deut. 12.12, 18-19; 14.26-27; 15.20; 16.11, 14; 26.11). Various rationales have been offered for the apparent contradiction concerning the participation of women that appears within the deuteronomic laws. Patrick suggests that participation was mandatory for males but voluntary for females.[111] Phillips finds that the restriction in v. 16 is merely a vestige of the earlier form of the law in Exodus.[112]

It is believed that the deuteronomic revision of the laws, advocating the centralization of worship, had a tremendous impact on the cultic participation of women. At first glance, it would appear that the requirements set forth in Exod. 23.17 and Deut. 16.16 are identical, but they are not. The significance of that difference has been noted by Bernard Levinson.[113] In his work on these laws, he argues that the requirement for Israelite males to appear in Exod. 23.17 could have been fulfilled 'at any of the multiple altars or sanctuaries throughout Judah and Israel'.[114] That ability, however, is eliminated by the deuteronomic revision which is supposedly a restatement of the earlier law.[115] Consequently, that restatement shifts the site of compliance from local sanctuaries to the central one in Jerusalem.[116]

> There is no cultic access to Yahweh, the authors of Deuteronomy insist, but at the central sanctuary. That transformation asserts hegemony by the national and public cult over the local cult. The restriction of the site (and of sight) creates a religious monopoly that involves power and exclusivity. The very assertion that there is no cultus but the Jerusalem Temple implies that there is no valid religious law but the law of Deuteronomy.[117]

110. Phillips, *Deuteronomy*, p. 170; and Patrick, *Old Testament Law*, pp. 138–39. Obviously, such a sweeping statement seems questionable given the *lex talionis* formula, but the assumption here is that the phrases 'an eye for an eye', and so forth are 'poetic equivalences that were translated into monetary compensation'. Patrick, *Old Testament Law*, p. 77.

111. Patrick, *Old Testament Law*, pp. 115–16.

112. Phillips, *Deuteronomy*, p. 114.

113. Levinson, *Deuteronomy and the Hermeneutics of Legal Innovation*, pp. 90–91.

114. Levinson, *Deuteronomy and the Hermeneutics of Legal Innovation*, pp. 90–91.

115. Levinson, *Deuteronomy and the Hermeneutics of Legal Innovation*, p. 90.

116. Levinson, *Deuteronomy and the Hermeneutics of Legal Innovation*, p. 91.

117. Levinson, *Deuteronomy and the Hermeneutics of Legal Innovation*, p. 91.

The 'religious monopoly', to use Levinson's expression, that was created by the deuteronomic revisions had far-reaching consequences for women. Bird has suggested that women had roles in cultic practices but that participation diminished with the centralization of worship because its specialization of the priesthood was exclusively male.[118] In this way, the apparent contradiction between Deuteronomy 16.16 and the other passages in the DL concerning the participation of women takes on a new meaning. Deut. 16.16 neither reflects just an earlier tradition, as suggested by Phillips, nor indicates that female participation is voluntary, as mentioned by Patrick. Instead, the text serves as a reminder that although females must be physically present during the festivals, the degree of their participation in the cult is limited. Although the centralization of worship, as covered in Chapter 3, is related to the construction of a national Israelite identity, the issue of females and the degree of their involvement in the cultic practices of ancient Israel will be revisited in Chapter 4. More attention must be given to these laws that appear to be inclusive but would seem to have a disproportionately negative impact on women and so construct gender.

C. *Exclusive Laws that Treat Women Based on Their Relationship to Men*

This last category of exclusive laws covers those laws that prescribe or proscribe the treatment of a female according to her relationship to a male. These male/female pairings include the following: father/daughter, engaged man and woman, husband/wife, and deceased husband/widow.[119] These laws are most often cited in discussions on the treatment of women in biblical law and constitute the core of the laws that are considered to be the deuteronomic family law. Interestingly, only one of the ten laws that falls in this category appears in Exodus, namely, the law on intercourse with an unbetrothed virgin in Exod. 22.15-16 [22.16-17]. With this one exception, these family laws are found in the DL but not BC.

1. *Father and daughter: intercourse with an unbetrothed virgin (Exod. 22.15-16 [22.16-17] and Deut. 22.28-29)*. Exodus 22.15-16 [22.16-17] provides that if a man seduces a virgin who is not engaged to be married and has intercourse with her, he must give the brideprice for her and make her his wife. If her father refuses to allow the marriage, the man must still pay an amount equal to the brideprice for virgins. Deuteronomy's related law specifies that a man who rapes an unbetrothed virgin and is caught in the act has to marry the woman, pay the woman's father 50 shekels, and he is not permitted to divorce her as long as he lives (Deut. 22.28-29).

One question raised concerning these laws is the difference between them. One view is that the woman consents to intercourse in the law in Exodus but not the one

118. Bird, 'The Place of Women', in *Missing Persons and Mistaken Identities*, p. 93.

119. These family laws are presented in a logical order. With a hypothetical Israelite female in mind, these laws have been arranged according to the time period when this female would have 'encountered' the law. Therefore, the laws proceed in chronological order from her presence in her father's household, to her engagement and marriage, and then becoming a widow. The ability to arrange the laws in this manner demonstrates one of the ways in which laws can constitute a 'reality'.

in Deuteronomy. For example, Burnette-Bletsch interprets the verb in Exodus (פתה) to imply the female's consent, but that the verb used in Deuteronomy (תפש) implies force. In the latter case, therefore, she sees the inability of the man to divorce the woman as a way of providing her 'economic security in the absence of affection'.[120]

Pressler offers a different interpretation of these laws. She acknowledges that the laws' respective verbs do indicate seduction and coercion, but she observes that the female's consent or lack of it is not 'a material factor in the case'.[121] The reasons she cites for the insignificance of the woman's consent are (1) the laws' failure to clearly specify that difference as is done in the Middle Assyrian laws, and (2) the fact that the penalties in the two laws are basically the same.[122] As will be covered in Chapter 4, the laws on intercourse with an unbetrothed virgin are problematic for two reasons. One reason is that the consent of the female is not an explicit factor, and the other reason is that payment is to be made to the father which indicates that it is his injury rather than that of the female.[123]

2. *Engaged man and woman (Deut. 22.23-27).* If a man has intercourse with a woman who is engaged, his penalty is death. Whether the female is to be executed as well depends on whether she consented, and her consent is determined by the act's location. Her consent is implied if the act took place in the city, but it is not implied if the event occurred in the country. The reason stated in the text for this distinction is that if the rape happened in the country, even if the woman cried out, there may not have been anyone around who could intervene.

Burnette-Bletsch finds that this law on the betrothed woman may not represent actual practice, but she finds that the law is still significant because it 'at least attempts to distinguish cases based upon the presence or absence of female consent'.[124] She argues that this law 'views women as legal subjects with the ability to make choices', thereby invalidating 'claims by some scholars that sexual ethics in Israelite society primarily concerned one man's violation of another man's property'.[125] The problem, however, is that requiring the death penalty if the woman is

120. Burnette-Bletsch, 'The Agrarian Family', p. 203.

121. Pressler, *Family Laws*, p. 38. See also Patrick, *Old Testament Law*, p. 83; and Nelson, *Deuteronomy*, pp. 272–73.

122. Pressler, *Family Laws*, p. 39. Pressler cites here MAL(A) 55–56, two laws that distinguish between an unconsenting girl and a consenting girl, respectively. As for the similar penalties, she observes that both laws require the man who violates the unbetrothed girl to make a payment to her father and marry the girl.

123. It is acknowledged that women received more favorable treatment in the Talmud than in the letter of the biblical laws. For example, rabbis determined that the fine for rape is to be given to the injured female rather than to her father, and the forced marriage between the aggressor and the victim in Deut. 22.29 was eliminated. See Judith Hauptman, 'Rabbinic Interpretation of Scripture', in Athalya Brenner and Carole Fontaine (eds.), *A Feminist Companion to Reading the Bible: Approaches, Strategies and Methods* (FCB; Sheffield: Sheffield Academic Press, 1997), pp. 472–86.

124. Burnette-Bletsch, 'The Agrarian Family', p. 255.

125. Burnette-Bletsch, 'The Agrarian Family', p. 255.

engaged but not if she is single (Deut. 22.28-29) does indicate that this offense is more serious. Apparently, the rapist has to die because now the fiancé will not be the first to have sex with her.[126]

3. *Husband and wife*

a. *Newlywed exemption (Deut 24.5)*. Deut. 24.5 exempts a man who has recently married from military service for a full year. This law is supposedly an expansion of the exemption for a man who was engaged but had not yet married in Deut. 20.7, which Patrick refers to as the right to consummate a marriage.[127] Both Steinberg and Burnette-Bletsch interpret the year's exemption as providing time for procreation.[128] The issue of procreation as part of the Israelite national identity will be covered in Chapter 3.

b. *Bride accused of sexual immorality (Deut. 22.13-21)*. If a man marries a woman and, after having intercourse with her, slanders her by saying that the woman had not been a virgin, the woman's father and mother may produce evidence of her virginity to the elders at the city gate. If the parents do so, the man is fined 100 shekels of silver and the amount is given to the father. For having made a false accusation, the man must remain married to his wife and he forfeits the ability to divorce her. If his accusation is true, then the woman is to be stoned to death so that the evil is purged from their midst. The relevant issue here is whether this law confers upon the husband a right to have a wife who is a virgin.

Pressler finds that the law affirms the father's right to control the daughter's sexuality and indicates that the husband has a right to expect his wife to be a virgin.[129]

> Deut. 22.28-29 and Ex. 22.15-16 show that sexual intercourse between a man and an unbetrothed girl was not regarded as a capital offense. Apparently previous sexual activity becomes a capital offense if the girl then enters into a marriage with another man, who has the right to expect her to be a virgin.[130]

Gordon Wenham, however, argues that the absence of *bĕtûlîm* in v. 14 refers to the lack of menstrual blood in the first month following the wedding and not to the lack of hymenal blood.[131] According to Wenham, if the husband knows that his wife has not menstruated and becomes suspicious that she was pregnant before the wedding, the parents can 'rebut the accusation by producing evidence that the girl

126. Hauptman, 'Rabbinic Interpretation of Scripture', p. 474.

127. Patrick, *Old Testament Law*, p. 135.

128. Burnette-Bletsch, 'The Agrarian Family', pp. 270–71; and Steinberg, 'Adam's and Eve's Daughters', pp. 262–63.

129. Pressler, *Family Laws*, p. 31. Frymer-Kensky concurs: 'By the execution of the girl, the community of men reinforces the right of the fathers to demand that their daughters be chaste'. See Frymer-Kensky, 'Virginity in the Bible', in Matthews, Levinson and Frymer-Kensky (eds.), *Gender and Law*, pp. 79–96 (94).

130. Pressler, *Family Laws*, p. 31. See also Nelson, *Deuteronomy*, p. 271.

131. Gordon Wenham, '*Bĕtûlāh*: "A Girl of Marriageable Age"', *VT* 22 (1972), pp. 326–48.

was menstruating regularly when she was betrothed'.[132] As a result, Wenham finds that the law only provides the husband the right to expect that his wife is not pregnant (presumably by another man) when she marries him.

Pressler did not find Wenham's interpretation to be convincing.[133] More specifically, she disagrees with his translation of *bĕtûlāh* as 'a girl of marriageable age', rather than the traditional translation, 'virgin', and she finds the scenario that he posits to be 'implausible'.[134] In turn, Burnette-Bletsch thought that Pressler's critique of Wenham's approach was unpersuasive on the grounds that 'a retroactive claim over the wife's sexuality' would indicate 'a double standard in sexual mores extending far beyond a desire for legitimate offspring'.[135] Yet, that 'double standard' referred to does make sense if understood in terms of a male's unilateral right to control a female's sexuality – whether that female is a daughter or wife – and is evidence of the construction of gender.[136]

c. *Adultery (Deut. 22.22).* Pursuant to Deut. 22.22, if a man and a married woman have intercourse, both of them are to be executed to purge the evil from Israel. That the woman is subject to execution for adultery in this law has been seen by David Daube as a 'landmark in the struggle for women's rights'.[137] According to him, women were not 'persons' subject to adultery laws prior to this deuteronomic law.[138] Consequently, the 'price for personhood' is that the woman is covered under the law.[139] Pressler refutes such a position in her analysis of this law, finding that the language calling for the execution of both the man and the woman under 22.22 is due not to a deuteronomic innovation but to an underscoring of the gravity of the offense.[140]

In her consideration of Deut. 22.22-27, Pressler found that the penalties for intercourse with a married or betrothed woman depended on two important variables: the marital status of the female and whether she consented or not.[141] It would seem

132. Wenham, '*Bĕtûlāh*', p. 334.

133. Pressler, *Family Laws*, pp. 25–28.

134. Pressler, *Family Laws*, p. 27.

135. Burnette-Bletsch, 'The Agrarian Family', p. 242.

136. Burnette-Bletsch, 'The Agrarian Family', p. 242. Ironically, Burnette-Bletsch does perceive the injury here to be a matter of honor and shame. For example, she writes 'the fine imposed upon the husband functions as both a social deterrent and a sign of restored honor for the woman and her parents'. Burnette-Bletsch, 'The Agrarian Family', p. 244. But if the issue was the woman's pregnancy and not her virginity, what was the source of the shame brought to the parents? Was it only that they had allowed the daughter to become pregnant? Would this not imply that premarital encounters not leading to pregnancy were condoned? The only plausible interpretation of the shame brought to the parents is that they did not control their daughter's sexuality regardless of whether or not she had conceived.

137. David Daube, 'Biblical Landmarks in the Struggle for Women's Rights', *Juridical Review* 23 (1978), pp. 177–97 (178–79).

138. Daube, 'Landmarks'. Phillips reached the same conclusion in his work. See *Ancient Israel's Criminal Law*, pp. 110–11.

139. Daube, 'Landmarks', p. 179.

140. Pressler, *Family Laws*, pp. 33–35.

141. Pressler, *Family Laws*, pp. 31–32. See also Steinberg, 'Adam's and Eve's Daughters', pp. 255–57 and Burnette-Bletsch, 'The Agrarian Family', pp. 247–48.

that, if married, the woman's consent is not a determining factor because the law makes no such reference specifically. However, Pressler contends that the factor of consent applies by inference from the laws concerning the betrothed female.[142]

The rationales proposed for the harsh penalty for adultery vary. Steinberg finds that the execution of both the man and the woman for adultery (v. 22) is due to their 'having disrupted the family unit to which the woman belongs, and for having brought shame to their family name'.[143] Burnette-Bletsch dismisses the law on adultery as 'a statement of values held by the biblical redactors rather than actual social practice'.[144] Given non-legal texts such as the story of David and Bathsheba which indicate 'a more tolerant attitude towards sexual ethics', Burnette-Bletsch finds that it 'invalidates the claim that Israel's double standard on adultery necessarily results in a lower social position for women'.[145]

Pressler sees these laws on adultery, given that they only prohibit extramarital intercourse by the wife, as a means of protecting the male head of the household's control of his wife sexuality and his right to 'be certain that his sons were his own'.[146] In this study, the law on adultery and the resultant male control of female sexuality are among the topics on the construction of gender that will be covered more fully in Chapters 3 and 4.

d. *Primogeniture (Deut. 21.15-17)*. Under these provisions, if a man has two wives and prefers the second one, that man must honor the inheritance rights of the firstborn son even if that son is the son of the first wife and not the second one. One of the issues addressed with this law has been whether the first wife is the primary beneficiary of its provisions. Alexander Rofé, who considers this law among those in the BC and DL that concern women, suggests that the law is a reform measure.[147] At a point when the father had freedom in making his bequests, Rofé asserts that the law limits the father's control over his inheritance by prohibiting arbitrary bequests based solely on the man's preference for one wife over another.[148] Pressler, though, does not think that this law particularly concerns women. Pressler finds that, because the birthright of the chronologically first-born son is protected, the prohibition 'applies to any attempt by the father to arbitrarily transfer the rights of the first-born to a younger son'.[149]

142. Pressler, *Family Laws*, p. 32. See also Burnette-Bletsch, 'The Agrarian Family', p. 248.

143. Steinberg, 'Adam's and Eve's Daughters', p. 254.

144. Burnette-Bletsch, 'The Agrarian Family', p. 253.

145. Burnette-Bletsch, 'The Agrarian Family', p. 253.

146. Pressler, *Family Laws*, pp. 42–43.

147. Alexander Rofé, 'Family and Sex Laws in Deuteronomy and the Book of Covenant', *Henoch* 9 (1987), pp. 131–60 (135, 150). In her consideration of this law, Burnette-Bletsch mentions the contrast between the dictates of this law and the practices described in both the Genesis narratives and the historical traditions where, for example, neither David nor Solomon was the firstborn son. Given that discrepancy, she notes that the principle of the firstborn's inheritance rights 'may not have been universally followed' and that the drafters of the law may have been 'attempt[ing] to impose this principle in the face of popular resistance'. Burnette-Bletsch, 'The Agrarian Family', pp. 226–27.

148. Rofé, 'Family and Sex Laws', p. 153. Rofé then infers that arbitrary bequests for other reasons such as the situation with a rebellious son would still be possible.

149. Pressler, *Family Laws*, pp. 15, 17.

While the law on primogeniture provides some protection for the firstborn son and (indirectly) for his mother, in essence, it affirms the father's ability to transfer his property to the next generation. This ability to transfer property, as will be discussed in Chapter 3, is a form of generational privilege.

e. *Incest (Deut. 23.1 [22.30])*. The only provision possibly relating to incest in the BC or DL is that which enjoins a man from marrying his stepmother (or a woman associated with his father) in Deut. 23. More accurately, though, this is 'a marriage law' that 'protects the integrity of the extended family in a polygamous context by blocking a son's inheritance of his father's wives'.[150]

The breadth of this prohibition only becomes apparent when compared to those in the cuneiform laws. The Law of Hammurabi prohibits marriage only with the father's principal wife (as opposed to a secondary wife or a concubine) and then that principal wife must have had children with the deceased husband.[151] Similarly, the comparable Hittite law (HL 190) prohibits pairings only between a man and his stepmother while the father is still alive. In contrast to both of these laws, the restrictions in Deut. 23.1 [22.30] apply whether the father is dead or alive and cover any woman associated with the father.

Steinberg finds that the law's purpose is to protect the father's marriage: 'the law upholds the sanctity of the marriage between a man and a woman against the sexual interests of all others – especially the sons of the man'.[152] This is a plausible rationale, but it only makes sense while the father is alive, and the law has no such qualification. As indicated by Nelson and Steinberg, this prohibition clearly involves the relationship between the father and the son. In other words, the act of a son marrying a stepmother dishonors the father. This means that the dictates of Deut. 23.1 [22.30] relate to a generational distinction between father and son.[153] Such a prohibition, then, is one of the privileges of the father as the male head of the household and will be discussed accordingly in Chapter 3.

f. *Restriction of remarriage (Deut. 24.1-4)*. According to this law, if a man divorces his wife, she marries another man, and that husband dies or divorces her, then the first husband may not remarry her. The law continues with a reference to the woman having been defiled and a characterization of the remarriage as abhorrent to the Lord and an event that will bring guilt upon the land. Few laws have caused as much confusion over meaning as this one. The following are only two of the rationales proposed for the law.[154] One rationale is that it protects the woman in her second marriage from pressure by the first husband to return to

150. Nelson, *Deuteronomy*, p. 277.

151. LH 158. See also Lafont, *Femmes, Droits et Justice*, pp. 222–25.

152. Steinberg, 'Adam's and Eve's Daughters', p. 259.

153. Phillips agrees that Deut. 23.1a prohibits an heir from inheriting women associated with his father but he also proposes that Deut. 23.1b prohibits homosexual relations between a father and a son, based on similarities between that second half of the verse and Gen. 9.20-27. See, Phillips, 'Uncovering the Father's Skirt', *VT* 30 (1980), pp. 38–43, reprinted in Phillips, *Essays on Biblical Law* (JSOTSup, 344; Sheffield: Sheffield Academic Press, 2002), pp. 245–50.

154. For summaries of the discussion, see Nelson, *Deuteronomy*, pp. 287–88; and Pressler, *Family Laws*, pp. 45–62.

him,[155] and another is that it precludes the former husband from exploiting the woman financially.[156]

Pressler, based on the interpretation of Patrick Miller and Tikva Frymer-Kensky, argues that this law should be understood as a prohibition similar to that of adultery.[157] She thinks that the restored marriage 'apparently was seen as making the second marriage adulterous after the fact' which poses the 'threat of pollution' in the Deuteronomic view.[158] Underlying the 'threat of pollution', according to her, is the fear that such occurrences blur family boundaries and risk the integrity of a man's lineage.[159] Following Pressler's reasoning here means that the law against remarriage is understood to protect patrilineal kinship patterns and minimize questions about the paternity of any children.

4. *Deceased husband and widow: levirate marriage (Deut. 25.5-10)*. The widow of a deceased man who has no sons is not to remarry outside of the family. The deceased man's brother is to marry her and their firstborn becomes the deceased brother's heir so that his name will not be 'blotted out' of Israel. If the brother refuses, the widow may shame him before the town elders by removing his sandals and spitting in his face. Ideally, this arrangement known as a levirate marriage serves two purposes: it perpetuates the lineage of the deceased and it provides a means of support for the widow.[160] Between those two purposes, however, one question that arises is whether the law is meant to primarily benefit the widow or her deceased husband.

One view is that the law offers advantages to the widow by enabling her to remain in the household with which she was familiar rather than forcing her to relearn 'the subsistence tasks and interpersonal dynamics' of a new kinship unit.[161] Pressler, though, sums up well another view of this law's purposes. Although the law was also 'aimed at protecting the widow and ensuring the orderliness of the succession of property', she concludes that 'the overriding concern of Deut. 25.5-10 is the perpetuation of a "name" for the deceased man'.[162] As Nelson writes, 'it is important to note that the law makes no direct mention of inheritance, economic matters, or the protection of the widow...[w]hatever benefits the widow may receive are not mentioned'.[163]

155. Reuven Yaron, 'The Restoration of Marriage', *JSS* 17 (1966), pp. 1–11.

156. Raymond Westbrook, 'The Prohibition of Marriage in Deuteronomy 24.1–4', in Sara Japhet (ed.), *Studies in Bible* (*Scripta Hierosolymitana*, 31; Jerusalem: Magnes Press, 1986), pp. 387–405.

157. Pressler, *Family Laws*, pp. 60–62; Patrick D. Miller, *Deuteronomy* (Interpretation; Louisville, KY: John Knox Press, 1990), p. 164; and Tikva Frymer-Kensky, 'Law and Philosophy: The Case of Sex in the Bible', *Semeia* 45 (1989), pp. 89–102.

158. Pressler, *Family Laws*, p. 61.

159. Pressler, *Family Laws*, p. 61.

160. Pressler, *Family Laws*, pp. 63–64.

161. Burnette-Bletsch, 'The Agrarian Family', p. 279.

162. Pressler, *Family Laws*, p. 73.

163. Nelson, *Deuteronomy*, pp. 297–98.

In spite of some possible advantages to the childless widow, the law does restrict her behavior, by stipulating that she cannot marry outside of the family, even when her relationship with a male, her husband, has technically ended. In other words, this law, and others like it, result in a female being under the control of her father, and then her husband where her husband's control (or that of his family) continues even after his death.

5. *Female war captive (Deut. 21.10-14)*. This text describes a process for marrying a woman who is captured during a war and brought back to an Israelite man's household.[164] Pressler convincingly argued that the purpose of the law was not to prohibit rape on the battlefield, as previously thought, but to provide a legal procedure whereby an Israelite man could marry a foreign woman in circumstances under which the usual contractual arrangements could not be made.[165] Furthermore, Steinberg found that the detailed procedures, which limited male prerogatives by specifying that the woman must be given a full month to mourn and could not be sold at a later point in time, provided the woman with social legitimation in the Israelite community.[166]

Of great interest is the month's period of time that is specified and the rituals that are to be performed before that time: shaving her head, paring her nails, and changing her attire. Pressler sees these procedures 'as ways to facilitate the assimilation of the woman, a foreigner, into an Israelite household'.[167] As a result of this procedure, the woman has a new status: 'she is no longer a servant who might be bought or sold, but the exact nature of her new status is not precisely defined by the text'.[168]

Recognizing that the woman might have been married before her capture, Washington proposes that a month's waiting period is long enough to ensure that the woman is not pregnant.[169] Consequently, the paternity of any children later conceived would be assured.[170] Burnette-Bletsch thought that Washington's explanation for the one-month waiting period was 'probably legitimate in part' but it did 'not account for the rituals performed during the prescribed waiting period'.[171] She argues that these rituals such as discarding her foreign garments transform the woman 'not only from a foreigner into an Israelite, but also from property into a wife'.[172] In this respect, both Washington and Burnette-Bletsch have identified

164. It is usually presumed, but not stated in the law, that the woman is a foreigner and not an Israelite. For this reason, this provision is being considered apart from those in the preceding section that reflect the life of a hypothetical Israelite woman.

165. Pressler, *Family Laws*, pp. 9–12.

166. Steinberg, 'Adam's and Eve's Daughters', pp. 247–48.

167. Pressler, *Family Laws*, p. 12.

168. Burnette-Bletsch, 'The Agrarian Family', p. 225.

169. Washington, 'Violence and the Construction of Gender in Deuteronomy 20–22', p. 206.

170. Washington, 'Violence and the Construction of Gender in Deuteronomy 20–22', p. 206.

171. Burnette-Bletsch, 'The Agrarian Family', p. 224.

172. Burnette-Bletsch, 'The Agrarian Family', p. 224.

important purposes for the month's waiting period and the rituals required. On the whole, these provisions appear to ritualistically mark a woman as belonging to the household of an Israelite male and ensure his paternity of any children born to the woman.

4. *Conclusions*

As mentioned in the beginning of this chapter, Steinberg and Burnette-Bletsch found that gender-roles in the biblical laws were symmetrical but Pressler found that the laws outlined asymmetrical gender-roles. Their different opinions are, in part, based on a failure to distinguish between laws that treated men and women alike (inclusive laws) and those that treat men and women differently (exclusive laws). As a result, their conversation provides a perfect vehicle for demonstrating the substantive contribution that gender theory and its notion of polarized attributes for men and women can make to the analysis of biblical laws.

Specifically, Steinberg, who examined male/female relationships in the family setting as found in Genesis and the DL, found that men and women had symmetrical and interdependent relationships. For example, she found that social standing for both men and women came through marriage and that, even though the private domain is clearly the realm of female activity, the public domain is not marked as the superior one.[173] Steinberg's emphasis on marriage as the means of acquiring status can be seen in her discussion of Deut. 22.28-29. There, she states that requiring the rapist to marry the woman confers social legitimation upon the woman by making her a wife.[174]

In her work on women in the deuteronomic family laws, Pressler credits Steinberg with having introduced the notion that women should not be studied in isolation but in relationship to men and in the context of the family.[175] From that common point of departure, the opinions of the two scholars on these laws diverged. Pressler found that the laws served the interests of a patriarchal hierarchy and ascribed subordinate positions to females. Moreover, Pressler, thought that, in order for Steinberg to see such interdependence, she exaggerated the degree of symmetry in the treatment of men and women in the family laws and disregarded asymmetrical treatment.[176]

Like Steinberg, Burnette-Bletsch identified an emphasis on interdependence in the family unit in her work on the agrarian family in ancient Israel. As a result, she objects to Pressler's depiction of women having a subordinate role in these laws.

173. Steinberg, 'Adam's and Eve's Daughters', pp. 232, 235–36.

174. Steinberg, 'Adam's and Eve's Daughters', p. 258.

175. Pressler, *Family Laws*, p. 6.

176. Pressler, *Family Laws*, p. 6. Pressler's example of Steinberg exaggerating symmetry and disregarding asymmetry is based on Deut. 22.13-21. Steinberg had incorrectly referred to both the husband and the accused bride being put to death under the law if they perjured themselves. Steinberg, 'Adam's and Eve's Daughters', p. 253. In fact, the death penalty is required only for the accused bride.

Burnette-Bletsch refers to the marriage laws as merely 'suggest[ing] the social ideals of premarital virginity and marital fidelity for females'.[177] She finds that Pressler's consideration of these laws as examples of gender asymmetry is 'a sweeping overstatement', because of 'the selectivity of biblical law and its complex relation to social reality'.[178] Burnette-Bletsch reaches her conclusions based on considerations of the biblical narratives where, she argues, for example, that the death penalty is not exacted for adultery.[179] Furthermore, Burnette-Bletsch finds gender parity between the mother and father in the laws and, if an undeniably harsh punishment is to be meted out according to the law, she dismisses it as not representing social reality, as she did with the reference to adultery.[180]

The difference in the opinions reached by Steinberg, Pressler, and Burnette-Bletsch on asymmetrical/symmetrical gender roles can be explained according to the distinction made here between inclusive and exclusive laws. Steinberg and Burnette-Bletsch focus their analyses on the laws that are defined as 'inclusive'. For example, both Steinberg and Burnette-Bletsch point to parity in the laws concerning parental authority (Deut. 21.18-21) and procreation (Deut. 24.5) to support their conclusions.[181] Therefore, these two scholars find male and female roles to be interdependent and symmetrical.

The existence of such inclusive laws, however, should not prevent the recognition that exclusive laws also exist. Such exclusive laws mandate that a woman could be killed for lack of virginity (Deut. 22.13-21) when the absence of virginity is not an offense for a male.[182] Correspondingly, Pressler, who focuses on the laws that are defined as 'exclusive' since they treat women and men differently, finds women's roles to be asymmetrical and subordinate.

Gender theory, in addition to providing a rationale for the different conclusions reached by Steinberg, Pressler, and Burnette-Bletsch, can offer still another insight. As Burnette-Bletsch has developed the conversation, there seems to be an assumption that male/female roles in these laws are either symmetrical or asymmetrical, but such an assumption is false.[183] Based on an understanding of varying degrees of privilege, it is evident that a greater degree of complexity results. A woman may be treated in both interdependent and subordinate ways under the same laws depending on whether she is slave or free, foreign or Hebrew, married or single. For example, a married woman may be subordinate to her husband but have a more complementary role with her husband with respect to their children or slaves.

177. Burnette-Bletsch, 'The Agrarian Family', p. 352.

178. Burnette-Bletsch, 'The Agrarian Family', pp. 352–53.

179. Burnette-Bletsch, 'The Agrarian Family', p. 353. Burnette-Bletsch fails to mention that adultery only refers to the marital status of the female. As a result, she ignores an obvious example of gender asymmetry.

180. Burnette-Bletsch, 'The Agrarian Family', pp. 352–54.

181. Burnette-Bletsch, 'The Agrarian Family', pp. 270–71, 343–46, 362; and Steinberg, 'Adam's and Eve's Daughters', pp. 250, 262–63.

182. Steinberg, 'The Deuteronomic Law Code', p. 168.

183. See Pressler, 'Wives and Daughters' in Matthews, Levinson and Frymer-Kensky (eds.), *Gender and Law*, pp. 141–72.

Indeed, female identity is constructed in such a way that, depending on that female's class, age, and marital status, symmetrical and asymmetrical relations with males are suggested simultaneously. Furthermore, as will be argued more extensively in Chapters 3 and 4, even inclusive laws that appear to construct symmetrical roles, upon close examination, construct gender differences also.

Chapter 3

THE CONSTRUCTION OF IDENTITY IN THE BC AND DL

1. *Introduction*

Chapter 3 will consider the embedded ideologies of the laws on women in the BC and DL again. However, the objective now is to show that one of the laws' functions is to construct identity. Assuming the perspective of the free, privileged, adult male who is the head of a household, these laws construct identities for other groups who are not free (slaves and debt slaves), not privileged (the marginalized) and not male (females). More precisely, this chapter will show that the inclusive laws construct the identities of class, generation, and nationality, whereas the exclusive laws construct the identity of gender.

This next survey will be different from the one in the preceding chapter in two ways. One difference is that the earlier survey was sometimes synchronic, that is, it discussed the laws' values or rationales with reference to specific sociohistorical contexts. Here, through a non-historical analysis, the laws are considered independently of particular social contexts. The second difference pertains to the chapter's underlying concern. In the preceding chapter, the concern to be addressed was whether the law constructed gender or not. As demonstrated, a law was exclusive and constructed gender if men and women were treated differently, but it was inclusive if men and women were treated in the same manner. The primary focus in this chapter, though, is the way in which the inclusive laws and the exclusive laws construct their respective identities.

Based on the following analysis, multiple identities for any one hypothetical individual can be created from the different identities that are constitutive of inclusive and exclusive laws. For example, one individual could be an Israelite (national identity), free (class identity), and the male head of a household (generational identity). Another individual suggested by the laws could be an Israelite (national identity), debt slave (class identity) and female (gender). Each of these identities constructed by the inclusive and exclusive biblical laws of the BC and DL will now be discussed in turn.

2. *The Construction of Identity: The Inclusive Laws of the BC and DL*

Since the inclusive laws construct the identities of class, generation, and nationality, the following section on identities and the inclusive laws is divided accordingly.

A. *Class Identity*

For the purposes of this study, a class is 'an aggregation of persons in a society who stand in a similar position with respect to some form of power, privilege, or prestige'.[1] In the BC and DL, several classes, consisting of the free, slaves, debt slaves, and the marginalized, can be delineated by their relative amounts of wealth (or their lack thereof).[2]

1. *Slaves and debt slaves*[3] *(Exod. 21.2-11, 20-21, 26-27, 28-32; Deut. 15.12-18).* As noted in the previous chapter, the laws concerning the goring ox in the BC (Exod. 21.28-32) are different in some important respects from their cuneiform parallels in the LE and LH. One of those differences is that the ox must be stoned in the biblical version, and that difference has been attributed to the high value placed on human life.[4] Even though a high value is placed on human life, clearly the value placed on the life of a slave is not as high as that of a free person. Notably, the owner of the ox is to be killed if the goring nature of the ox was known and the owner failed to restrain the animal (Exod. 21.29).[5] Yet there is no such corresponding provision if the person gored is a male or female slave. If a slave is the victim, the ox is still to be stoned but the owner only has to pay thirty shekels of silver to the slaveowner. The life of the owner is never at stake if a slave is involved. Paul finds that the combination of financial compensation and the stoning of the ox indicates 'the ambiguous status of the slave'.[6] This ambiguity results from the slave's consideration as a human being but, contrary to the rule, his or her life can be assigned a specific monetary value.[7] Indeed, Paul identifies Exod. 21.32 as the only example in the BC where a specific sum for a penalty is recorded.[8]

Because women are mentioned in each scenario of the goring ox provisions, the law does not serve to construct gender. Moreover, Pressler argues that slave owners in ancient Israel could have been male or female.[9] Even if gender is not con-

1. Gerhard E. Lenski, *Power and Privilege: A Theory of Social Stratification* (Chapel Hill: The University of North Carolina Press, 1984), pp. 74–75.

2. Marshall, *Israel and the Book of the Covenant*, pp. 139–40.

3. The same word (עבד) in the Hebrew text can be translated as 'slave' or 'debt slave' but these terms refer to different categories of individuals. Specifically, Clements found that, since the deuteronomic law on the release of slaves, as well as the older law in Exodus, only apply to Hebrews, the law did not 'take into account' those slaves of 'alien origin' who might have been prisoners of war or victims of kidnapping and 'whose servitude was assumed in most cases to be permanent'. Clements, 'Deuteronomy', *NIB* II, pp. 405–406. It is worth noting that in Lev. 25.39-46, the law specifically provides that Israelites are to be debt slaves, to be released at the time of the jubilee, and the other categories of slaves are to come from the foreign and resident alien populations.

4. Greenberg, 'Postulates', pp. 15–16.

5. Note that the life of the negligent owner may be redeemed and the death penalty thereby avoided (Exod. 21.30). Unlike the payment that can be made for the slave, the payment here is to buy back his own life and not to compensate for the loss of the person (the slave) who was killed.

6. Paul, *Studies*, p. 83.

7. Paul, *Studies*, p. 83; and Patrick, *Old Testament Law*, p. 78.

8. Paul, *Studies*, p. 83.

9. Pressler, 'Wives and Daughters', p. 166. Pressler cites Gen. 16.1-15; 21.1-13; 29.24, 29; and 1 Sam. 25.42 as references to maidservants owned by women.

structed, the law does serve to construct class differences between those who are enslaved and those who are free. As Bernard Levinson observed in his work, the sequence in the law that refers to the death of a male or female adult, the death of a male or female minor, and the death of a male or female slave, reflects a 'principle of organizing legal paragraphs in a sequence that reflects social rank, from higher to lower', that is seen in both biblical and ancient Near Eastern laws.[10] Therefore, instead of the law of the goring ox indicating just an 'ambiguous status'[11] of the slave as Paul stated, it indicates an inferior one.

In the same way, the laws concerning the striking of a slave in Exod. 21.20-21 and 26-27 are gender inclusive but serve to construct class boundaries.[12] Specifically, Marshall found that these laws 'reinforce the social order and to some extent protect the property and rights of the owners'.[13] To be sure, there are repercussions if an owner causes some types of physical harm to a slave but, as in the case of the goring ox, the life of the owner is never at stake. Phillips has suggested that community limitations on a slaveowner's ability to kill with impunity a slave, a person without legal status, stemmed from self-interest: if the person could do that to a slave, that person might do the same thing to a free Israelite.[14] Although Phillips characterizes the slaveowner here as 'vicious' and 'a danger to the community, and must therefore be punished,'[15] he fails to note that the life of the slaveowner is never in jeopardy under the law.

As for the release of debt slaves in Exod. 21.2-11 and Deut. 15.12-18, scholars have noted that the release of these servants into an economically underprivileged group in the seventh year of service or after permanent physical injury would be a decidedly mixed blessing.[16] To help ensure the survival of the released debt slave, the law requires that the owner provide him or her with some basic provisions (Deut. 15.12-15). At the same time, in the subsequent verses (Deut. 15.16-17), it is recognized that the debt slave may want to remain with the owner, presumably after having decided that 'he could not hope to make a better life on his own'.[17]

Niels Peter Lemche provides reasons why the debt slave could not survive on his or her own in the context of ancient Israel. He emphasizes the importance of the lineage system (the extended family system), not only for survival in the ancient Near East, but as the primary means of settling disputes. Lemche finds that the lineage system, headed by a chosen leader, resolved a wide range of matters,

10. Levinson, *Deuteronomy and the Hermeneutics of Legal Innovation*, p. 142.

11. Paul, *Studies*, p. 83.

12. These laws on punishing slaves, however, may also construct boundaries based on the reasons leading to servitude. For example, Marshall considers these laws to pertain only to Israelite debt servants. Marshall, *Israel and the Book of the Covenant*, p. 119. Whereas Boecker, noting that 'there is no express mention of slaves by debt' as in Exod. 21.2-22, finds that Exod. 21.20-21 and 21.26-27 apply not just to debt slaves but to slaves in general. Boecker, *Law and the Administration of Justice*, p. 162.

13. Marshall, *Israel and the Book of the Covenant*, p. 122.

14. Phillips, 'Some Aspects of Family Law', p. 358.

15. Phillips, 'Some Aspects of Family Law', p. 358.

16. Marshall, *Israel and the Book of the Covenant*, p. 122.

17. Fewell and Gunn, *Gender, Power, & Promise*, pp. 99–100.

including murder.[18] So instead of any state system, Lemche concludes that matters were resolved at the level of the local village (where the majority of the population lived).[19] Lemche argues that the released debt slaves and other marginalized groups who fell outside of the lineage system for whatever reasons would need to have a patron to survive and to redress any wrongs done to them. In this way, the law of release would not effectively change the status of former debt slaves.

> The difference from proper debt-slavery may have been marginal and probably hardly recognized at all, and the terminology would most likely be the same. As is well known, the Hebrew word *ʿebed* (the Akkadian counterpart is *wardum*), normally translated as 'slave', also means 'dependent', i.e. a person in dependence of another person. [...] Whatever it was, simply to survive, a tie must be established between the poor and the rich, between the client and the patron.[20]

Based on Lemche's analysis of the ancient Near Eastern context, then, even the law of release in Deut. 15 can be understood as maintaining class distinctions between rich and poor in a patronage system. Even though Deut. 15.12-18 does not construct gender because the text expressly covers both males and females, it does construct class differences. Those same class differences are evident in Exod. 21 because that text affirms a form of slavery as an institution, permits an owner to physically discipline a slave, and places a lower valuation on the life of a male or female slave than that of a free person.

2. *The marginalized: the widow, orphan, and stranger (Exod. 22.21-23 [22-24]; Deut. 24.17-22).* Class differences are also constructed through the laws on the widow, orphan, and stranger – groups that are devoid of the economic support of a privileged Israelite male.[21] Initially, it seems that the laws in the DC on tithing (Deut. 14.22-29; and 26.12-15) and gleaning (Deut. 24.17-22) would, if implemented, eliminate the economic hardships of these groups.[22] If that were the case,

18. Lemche, 'Justice in Western Asia', p. 1705.

19. Lemche, 'Justice in Western Asia', p. 1706. For Lemche, this process of local dispute resolution explains why written laws in the ancient Near East are so scarce; such laws were simply not needed.

20. Lemche, 'Justice in Western Asia', pp. 1711–12.

21. The widow is not just a woman whose husband has died. She is also a woman whose sons or her husband's family are not willing or able to support her. Bennett, *Injustice Made Legal*, p. 37. The orphan may be an orphaned daughter because her ability to inherit her father's property was limited (Num. 27.7-11) whereas the orphaned son could have inherited the father's estate (Deut. 21.15-17). See Theophile James Meek, *Hebrew Origins* (Toronto: University of Toronto Press, rev edn, 1950), p. 78. The stranger (*gēr*) is an immigrant who is accepted within the Israelite community but maintains a distinctive ethnic or cultural identity. Bennett, *Injustice Made Legal*, p. 48; and Rolf Rendtorff, 'The *Gēr* in the Priestly Laws of the Pentateuch', in Mark G. Brett (ed.), *Ethnicity and the Bible* (Leiden/New York: E.J. Brill, 1996), pp. 77–88.

22. Lohfink, 'Poverty', p. 44. Lohfink distinguishes between the 'poor' (*'ebyôn* and *'ānî*) and the *personae miserae*. The former category consists of landowners who struggle with indebtedness (and may consequently work as day laborers), whereas the latter category consists of individuals, including levites and slaves, who do not possess landed property. Nevertheless, Lohfink finds that the eradication of poverty for both groups is an objective of the BC and DL. See also his article,

then, these laws would eliminate class distinctions. There is every reason to believe, however, that in their socioeconomic context, these laws were of minimal help to the widow, orphan, and stranger.

For example, the law presumes that the widow will be supported by her son(s), and if there are no sons, the law of levirate marriage (Deut. 25.5-10) would apply. The problem is that these provisions have fatal flaws which might preclude their effectiveness. In his work on levirate marriage, Eryl Davies presents at least one strong reason why the deceased's brother would not have been willing to carry out the levir's obligation. Specifically, by providing a son for the deceased relative, he would terminate his own ability to inherit the estate that he would have inherited in the absence of an heir.[23]

Furthermore, Davies points out that the law made it 'comparatively easy for the brother-in-law' to refuse the obligation by providing a ceremony in which the levir could formally renounce his duty and by not prescribing a penalty for his failing to fulfill the duty.[24] If the brother-in-law did refuse to cooperate, the property would still remain in the family since it would go to the nearest kinsman of the husband.[25] The only difference if the male relative refused to comply is that the widow could end up destitute. At the end of his series on levirate marriage, Davies surmises that 'the pleas of the prophets on behalf of the widow' are due to the fact that 'one of the most basic provisions legislating for her support (Deut. 25.5-10) may often, in practice, have been neglected'.[26] Whether because of a failure of the practice of levirate marriage or an inability of the sons to support the widow economically, she could become a part of the marginalized group known as the *personae miserae*.

The failure of the levirate marriage process to provide for a widow may not be an aberration. Harold Bennett contends that the laws on gleaning and tithing would have failed to support the economically marginalized as well.[27] After analyzing the pertinent laws on tithes and other forms of public support (Deut. 14.22-29; 16.9-12, 13-15; and 26.12-15), as well as the timing of such offerings, Bennett asks a crucial question: 'Where did they obtain food and other provisions between the period for the distribution of the triennial tithes and the celebration of cultic pilgrimages?'[28] Furthermore, Bennett argues that, given the payments that local peasant farmers and herders had to make to others meant that the farmers could only provide for their households and had little, if any surplus to share with these

'Das deuteronomische Gesetz in der Endgestalt-Entwurf einer Gesellschaft ohne marginale Gruppen', *BN* 51 (1990), pp. 25–40.

23. Eryl W. Davies, 'Inheritance Rights and the Hebrew Levirate Marriage: Part 2', *VT* 31 (1981), p. 259.

24. Davies, 'Inheritance Rights, Part 2', p. 263. Patrick similarly observes that 'if the lawgiver had wanted to put legal force behind the practice of levirate marriage, he could have declared the humiliated brother ineligible to inherit'. Patrick, *Old Testament Law*, p. 138.

25. Davies cites Num. 27.8-11 to support his position. 'Inheritance Rights: Part 1', *VT* 31 (1981), p. 139.

26. Davies, 'Inheritance Rights: Part 2', p. 268.

27. Bennett, *Injustice Made Legal,* pp. 120–25.

28. Bennett, *Injustice Made Legal*, p. 120.

marginalized groups.[29] Similarly, the laws on gleaning (Deut. 24.19-22) propose that the marginalized find sustenance from the fruits and vegetables left in the fields. Yet, as Bennett notes, it is unlikely that the farmers, knowing that anything left would no longer be theirs, 'left huge amounts of vegetables and fruits in the fields and orchards'.[30]

Based on this discussion, Bennett concludes that the periodic, if not improbable, distribution of food described in the DC contributed to the dire circumstances of the marginalized, forcing them into 'exploitive economic arrangements' such as debt slavery and prostitution.[31] Consequently, his basic argument is that these laws 'exacerbated, not rectified, the plight of these types of persons'.[32]

Prior to Bennett's work, the contention had been that the laws concerning the widow, stranger, and orphan at least lessened the harsh effects of socioeconomic inequality on the marginalized. Nevertheless, there was also the recognition that these laws would not redress the socioeconomic disparities that led to their marginalized status in the first place. For example, Marshall found that the laws in Part II of the BC describe a society with increased social stratification and corresponding poverty among the landless marginalized groups.[33] He also found, however, that these laws do not eradicate social stratification, but 'are designed to alleviate the accompanying economic poverty'.[34] Similarly, Ashmore, in his analysis of the DL, found that its measures to protect the poor and marginalized only addressed the effects of the unequal distribution of wealth, not the causes of it.[35] To support his argument, Ashmore cites the *šěmiṭṭāh* law of Deut. 15.1-11 and the law of release in Deut. 15.12-18, which allow for periodic cancellation of debt but do not prohibit debt slavery or address the origin of the poverty or debt.[36]

In spite of the BC and DL's proclamations that oppression was not to occur and hardship was to be eradicated, the laws' corresponding provisions simply are not those that would have resulted in any redistribution of wealth. So even if Marshall, Ashmore and Bennett debate whether the biblical laws diminished the suffering of the marginalized or contributed to it, they all agree that these laws maintain rather than eliminate class differences. As a result, class distinctions are made in the BC and DL between free and privileged Israelites and those who are debt slaves, the poor, and the marginalized subgroup known as the *personae miserae*.

B. *Generational Identity (Exod. 21.15, 17; Deut. 21.15-17, 18-21, 22.13-21, 23.1 [22.30]).* Laws requiring respect for both one's mother and one's father appear in both the BC and DL (Exod. 21.15, 17 and Deut. 21.18-21). Plus, the mother is an active participant in the legal procedures outlined in the DL for the parents of the

29. Bennett, *Injustice Made Legal*, pp. 121–22.

30. Bennett, *Injustice Made Legal*, pp. 123–24.

31. Bennett, *Injustice Made Legal*, p. 120 n. 17.

32. Bennett, *Injustice Made Legal*, p. 106.

33. Marshall, *Israel and the Book of the Covenant*, pp. 145–46.

34. Marshall, *Israel and the Book of the Covenant*, p. 146.

35. James P. Ashmore, 'The Social Setting of the Law in Deuteronomy' (unpublished doctoral dissertation, Duke University, 1995), p. 182.

36. Ashmore, 'The Social Setting', p. 182.

accused bride (Deut. 22.13-21) and the parents of the rebellious son (Deut. 21.18-21). Yet Fewell and Gunn do not think that the mother and father have equal authority in these household matters. Instead, they see the mother's authority as derivative; it is based on the husband's authority. They suggest that although the mother has some authority within the family hierarchy, 'systemic power' resides in the father and the mother, as 'the man's woman to some extent symbolizes his power'.[37]

Because the women associated with the male symbolize his power, Fewell and Gunn determine that a son's act of having intercourse with his father's woman as in 2 Sam. 16.20-22 constitutes a usurpation of the father's authority.[38] This statement clearly makes Deut. 23.1 [22.30], which prohibits a son from marrying his stepmother (or one of his father's women), a matter of respect for the father's authority. Deut. 23.1 [22.30] then, along with Deut. 21.18-21 and Deut. 22.13-21, construct generational identity.[39]

Although the matriarch may exercise derivative power under the laws on parental authority, it is power nonetheless. Such power comes into sharper relief when compared to the relative absence of power held by an unmarried female or a female debt slave. From this perspective, a female does exercise some authority as a matriarch. In spite of the absence of a gender difference, then, a generational difference can still exist. Frymer-Kensky expresses the relationship between gender and generation as follows:

> In the biblical family, generation superseded gender. Wives were subordinate to husbands, and girls might have been under the control of their brothers, but both daughters and sons were subordinate to both mother and father.[40]

Another law outlining a difference between an older and a younger generation is the law of primogeniture (Deut. 21.15-17). Rofé argues that the law allows the father to make any bequest, even an arbitrary one, but not on the basis of a preference for one wife over another.[41] Pressler rejects Rofé's contention that the law of primogeniture is among a series of laws concerned primarily with women on the grounds that, although improving the son's finances would improve those of his mother, the 'law quite explicitly intends to protect the status of the eldest son'.[42]

37. Fewell and Gunn, *Gender, Power, & Promise*, p. 100.

38. Fewell and Gunn, *Gender, Power, & Promise*, p. 100. See also Ken Stone, *Sex, Honor and Power in the Deuteronomistic History* (JSOTSup, 234; Sheffield: Sheffield Academic Press, 1996), pp. 41–49.

39. That Deut. 23.1a [22.30a] concerns a son's respect for his father is recognized even by Phillips who has an otherwise unique interpretation of this law. See Phillips, 'Uncovering the Father's Skirt', *VT* 30 (1980), pp. 38–43. Usually Deut. 23.1b [22.30b] is considered an integral part of 23.1a [22.30a] but instead of interpreting 23.1b [22.30b] as a restatement of 23.1a [22.30a], Phillips finds that the second part of the law prohibits homosexual activity between a father and son. Phillips does think, though, that the purpose of the first part of the law is 'to engender further filial piety towards the father rather than to protect his wife', Phillips, 'Uncovering the Father's Skirt', p. 41.

40. Frymer-Kensky, 'Virginity in the Bible', p. 96.

41. Rofé, 'Family and Sex Laws', p. 153.

42. Pressler, *Family Laws*, p. 17.

Under either rationale, however, the law assumes that a father can make bequests to a son, thereby creating a generational privilege and, as a result, a generational distinction.

Such privileges of the male head of household indicate that a more nuanced definition of the term 'patriarchy' is needed. As his starting point, Jon Berquist defines ancient Israel as a patriarchal culture because of the male dominance that 'favored men over women in a variety of ways'.[43] He continues, though, by defining 'patriarchy' as a hierarchical system that, in turn, has three separate elements.[44]

> This hierarchy of the fathers indicates three separate elements within culture: first, that the culture is based on hierarchicalism, and thus systems of privilege exist to distribute goods and statuses differentially; second, that these systems privilege the fathers, or the society's men who as a group control the bulk of the society's resources; and third, that these systems privilege the fathers, or the society's older persons who have reached the age at which they are considered adults and form their own households.[45]

Consequently, the law of primogeniture as well as the other laws on household matters discussed here construct hierarchical differences and the difference of generation is one of them. A father has authority over his children; sons must respect the father's control over his women; and a father has the ability to make bequests. Without a doubt, a female does have some relative degree of authority over her children as a matriarch, but the generational benefits she receives as a wife are not the same as those received by her husband. As Berquist writes: '[p]atriarchy requires the privileging of age as well as gender, and in ancient Israel these patterns reinforced each other as men lived longer than women'.[46]

C. *National Identity*

A national identity that defines who the people of Israel are as a community, as distinct from other communities, is the final identity constructed by the inclusive laws of the BC and DL. The anthropologist, Fredrik Barth, identified the maintenance of cultural (or social) boundaries that distinguish one group from another as an important dynamic for any ethnic group.[47] To Barth, though, an ethnic group

43. Berquist, *Controlling Corporeality*, p. 133.

44. Berquist, *Controlling Corporeality*, p. 133.

45. Berquist, *Controlling Corporeality*, pp. 133–34. Berquist's recognition that patriarchy involves more than simply a valuing of males over females parallels Elisabeth Schüssler Fiorenza's concept of kyriarchy, that is, the rule of the masters. In her work, kyriarchy describes interlocking hierarchical systems that involve, among other things, sexism, racism, poverty, and colonialism. See Elizabeth Schüssler Fiorenza, *But She Said: Feminist Practices of Biblical Interpretation* (Boston: Beacon Press, 1992); and Schüssler Fiorenza, 'Introduction', in Schüssler Fiorenza and M. Shawn Copeland (eds.), *Violence Against Women* (*Concilium*; London: SCM Press, 1994), pp. vii–xxiv.

46. Berquist, *Controlling Corporeality*, p. 134. Similarly, Fewell and Gunn define patriarchy as 'a system of discrimination based on age (or generation) as well as gender'. See Fewell and Gunn, *Gender, Power and Promise*, p. 100.

47. Fredrik Barth (ed.), 'Introduction', *Ethnic Groups and Boundaries: The Social Organization of Culture Difference* (Boston: Little, Brown, 1969), pp. 9–38. See also Steven Grosby, *Biblical Ideas of Nationality: Ancient and Modern* (Winona Lake, IN: Eisenbrauns, 2002).

describes not just a biologically-determined group but an organizational category that is developed through 'systematic sets of role constraints'.[48] These 'role constraints', according to Barth, 'impl[y] a series of constraints on the kinds of roles an individual is allowed to play, and the partners he may choose for different kinds of transactions'.[49] Barth further suggests that such constraints 'tend to be absolute' and that 'the component moral and social conventions are made further resistant to change by being joined in stereotyped clusters as characteristics of one single identity'.[50]

Likewise, the inclusive laws function to construct a national identity by describing appropriate behavior and attitudes for an Israelite. In the following section, three specific characteristics are discussed which together constitute 'one single identity', that of being an Israelite. These three characteristics are: concern for the marginalized, uniformity in cultic practices, and fertility. Each of these characteristics applies to any Israelite regardless of class, age, or sex and, simultaneously, attempt to distinguish Israelites from other groups.

1. *Concern of the privileged for the poor and marginalized (Exod. 22.20-26 [21-27]; Deut. 14.22-29, 15.1-11, 16.9-15, 24.10-15, 17-22, 26.12-15).* The BC, to a lesser extent, and DL, to a greater extent, have humanitarian provisions that mandate compassionate treatment towards the poor and marginalized. One aspect of these laws concerning the widow, orphan, and stranger was discussed earlier in this chapter. The rationale for these laws is usually thought to be both a recognition of the enduring nature of poverty and an ethos that requires continuous generosity of the privileged towards those in need.[51]

An issue in the scholarly literature concerning these humanitarian provisions is whether these laws were motivated solely by theological values or dictated by the harsh economic circumstances of these groups. Weinfeld, noting that such humanitarianism was not emphasized in the BC, subscribes to the theory that the greater number of such laws in the DL is due to an emergent humanism.[52] Refuting Weinfeld, Ashmore found that the lack of emphasis in the BC was simply because stratification was not as severe a problem then and that the deuteronomic provisions resulted from the greater economic stratification after the development of a centralized state.[53] Bennett would concur that economic stratification was a factor but he would go further and suggest that the presumably humanitarian laws in the DL were 'a pretext' that allowed cultic officials 'to oversee the allocation of com-

48. Barth, 'Introduction', pp. 10, 17.

49. Barth, 'Introduction', p. 17.

50. Barth, 'Introduction', p. 17.

51. Jeffries M. Hamilton, '*Hā'āreṣ* in the Shemitta Law', *VT* 42 (1992), pp. 214–22; and Jon D. Levenson, 'Poverty and the State in Biblical Thought', *Judaism* 25 (1976), pp. 230–41.

52. Moshe Weinfeld, *Deuteronomy and the Deuteronomic School* (Oxford: Oxford University Press, 1972), pp. 283–84.

53. Ashmore, 'The Social Setting', p. 181. H. Eberhard Von Waldow reached the same conclusion in his article, 'Social Responsibility and Social Structure in Early Israel', *CBQ* 32 (1970), pp. 184–204. Marshall also identified social stratification as an underlying problem in the laws in Part II of the BC. Marshall, *Israel and the Book of the Covenant*, pp. 145–46.

modities and to guarantee an influx of grain, wine, and meat into their personal coffers'.[54]

It may not be possible to calculate with any precision the degree to which Deuteronomy's humanitarian provisions are the result primarily of theology, sociology or self-interest. Nevertheless, it is possible to identify at least one of the purposes served by promulgating such laws: the construction of a national identity. Specifically, Jeffries Hamilton relates these pertinent laws in Deuteronomy to a society's perception of itself as a just society.

> The laws in Deuteronomy insist that the justness of society with respect to those within its midst in special need of care stands at the center of its program for the ideal society and, conversely, that their care serves as a barometer of the justness of society.[55]

The presence of such compassionate laws in biblical law codes other than the one in Deuteronomy as well as in the Mesopotamian laws means that humanitarian concern and notions of justice were often related concepts. Indeed, Charles F. Fensham has written that, because laws on the protection of the widow, orphan, and the poor are found throughout the ancient Near East, they were 'not started by the spirit of Israelite propheticism or by the spirit of propheticism as such'.[56] Instead, these laws exist because protecting the marginalized is considered to be a necessary prerequisite for political success.[57] Another way of looking at what Hamilton and Fensham describe is that the protection of the marginalized was used as an indicator of a just society and a just society was thought to be more likely to succeed.

That the element of a national identity can be detected in these humanitarian laws is seen in the use of the motive clause: 'Remember that you were a slave in Egypt'. In the humanitarian provisions of Deut. 24.17-22, for example, that motive clause is found twice. To remind the population of their history is to remind them of who they are as a covenant community, and therefore shapes identity.[58] Because of its laws that are geared to the protection of the marginalized, the redactors are able to depict Israel as a just society in the same manner as its regional neighbors. At the same time, the laws convey that the Israelites, as well as the Israelite laws, are different from their neighbors and their laws in two ways. One difference is that the Israelite laws are not just 'civil laws' but are 'the blending of ritual and social

54. Bennett, *Injustice Made Legal*, p. 171.

55. Hamilton, *Social Justice and Deuteronomy: The Case of Deuteronomy 15* (SBLDS, 136; Atlanta: Scholars Press, 1992), p. 136.

56. Charles F. Fensham, 'Widow, Orphan, and the Poor in Ancient Near Eastern Legal and Wisdom Literature', *JNES* 21 (1962), p. 129.

57. Fensham, 'Widow, Orphan, and the Poor', p. 129.

58. Mullen argues that such narrative history was, in fact, developed during the postexilic period to shape community identity. In his work on the development of the Pentateuch, Mullen finds generally that the creation of a narrative account of a group's origins and history is a 'major part' of the community's boundary formation and that such 'remembered history' functions 'to make the past coincide with and support the self-identity of the group in its present situation'. Mullen, *Ethnic Myths and Pentateuchal Foundations*, p. 12.

obligations'.[59] Consequently, according to Pleins, these laws convey the message that 'social well-being is not simply a product of royal or judicial fiat but finds its deepest roots in the community's worship response to Israel's divine sovereign'.[60] Another distinctive feature of these laws, and thus the Israelites, Pleins contends, is that rather than merely 'claim to service the disenfranchised', as Near Eastern rulers did, these Israelite laws provide very specific legislation (such as tithing and gleaning) which, by all appearances, are meant to achieve that end.[61] In these ways, the laws serve to construct identity for the Israelites by distinguishing themselves from others.

2. *Cultic practices.* Deuteronomy's emphasis on humanitarianism and its laws calling for unity in cultic practices are described as 'the essence of Deuteronomy'.[62] Whereas the humanitarian regulations define who the Israelites are as a people, the cultic practices set forth more precisely who they are as a religious community. Correspondingly, the cultic practices advocated in the DL involve the centralization of the cult and the establishment of cultic orthodoxy. As inclusive laws that apply to all Israelites across class, gender, and age distinctions, they serve to create another aspect of community identity.

Although these cultic prescriptions and proscriptions are identified as deuteronomic reforms, some of these laws such as the ones against apostasy and sorcery appear also in the BC. Yet, as Levinson has pointed out, the cultic requirements of the BC that are incorporated in the DL are linguistically similar but radically different in meaning because, among other things, the locus of worship shifts from local shrines to the temple in Jerusalem.[63]

a. *Centralization of worship (Exod. 23.14-17; Deut. 12.1-7, 16.16-17).* The cultic laws in the DL advocate a faith devoted to one deity, Yahweh, and one sanctuary, the Temple in Jerusalem. With the centralization of worship, the nature of cultic duties as well as their designated location change. The annual festivals described in Exod. 23.14-17 that were presumably celebrated in local shrines are to take place in Jerusalem under Deut. 16.16-17.[64] By making Jerusalem the center for worship, an additional impact was that Passover was taken out of Israelite homes where it had been celebrated previously.[65] Finally, the local shrines are to be destroyed and the practices conducted there are to be discontinued (Deut. 12.1-4).

One of the most striking features of these laws on the centralization of worship is their inclusivity. Deuteronomy 12.7 states that the laws apply to the free Israelite male and his entire household. The list of those individuals covered under the laws

59. Pleins, *The Social Visions of the Hebrew Bible*, pp. 43–44

60. Pleins, *The Social Visions of the Hebrew Bible*, p. 44.

61. Pleins, *The Social Visions of the Hebrew Bible*, p. 44. See also Lohfink, 'Poverty', p. 44.

62. John W. Rogerson and Philip Davies, *The Old Testament World* (Englewood Cliffs, NJ: Prentice–Hall, 1989), pp. 246–47.

63. Levinson, *Deuteronomy and the Hermeneutics of Legal Innovation*, pp. 90–93.

64. Levinson, *Deuteronomy and the Hermeneutics of Legal Innovation*, pp. 90–91.

65. Shigeyuki Nakanose, *Josiah's Passover: Sociology & The Liberating Bible* (Maryknoll, NY: Orbis Books, 1993), pp. 86–90.

is more specific in Deut. 16.1-17 and includes sons, daughters, male and female slaves, widows, orphans, strangers, and Levites.[66]

The clear intent of the centralization measures in Deuteronomy is to extend their application to all Israelites whether male or female, old or young, slave or free, rich or poor. As such, the unity of cultic practices sought in the DL serves to construct the national identity of the ancient Israelite community.

b. *Cultic orthodoxy (Exod. 22.19 [22.20]; Deut. 13.7-19 [13.6-18], 17.2-7, 18.9-14, 23.18-19 [23.17-18]).* While the DL's provisions on the centralization of worship dictated where the Israelites would worship, the laws concerning cultic orthodoxy dictated what and how the Israelites would worship. To be precise, the deuteronomic reforms require monotheism, the worship of Yahweh only, and only through practices approved by the centralized cult. For Mullen, 'the ideal of complete and absolute obedience to Yahweh alone' allowed the deuteronomic materials to define the community 'in terms of the various ways in which devotion to this single deity distinguishes "Israel" from all other nations'.[67] By condemning certain practices, then, these laws convey the areas in which Israel is to be different from its neighbors. Specifically, apostasy, sorcery, and cultic prostitution are prohibited and the corresponding assumption is usually that ancient Israel's Canaanite neighbors engaged in all of them. Current research, however, enables us to question some of those traditional assumptions about the Canaanites.

First, apostasy is addressed in Exodus 22.19 [22.20] by forbidding sacrifices to other gods, and in Deut. 13.7-19 [13.6-18], 17.2-7 legal guidelines are provided for those accused of apostasy. If guilty, individuals are to be stoned and a whole town and its inhabitants are to be utterly destroyed and the town is never to be rebuilt (Deut. 13.11, 16-17 [13.10, 15-16]). These deuteronomic laws against apostasy may not have been carried out and, because females are specifically covered in them, they do not construct gender, but they do serve to construct an element of community identity: Israelites, both men and women, are to be faithful to Yahweh.

Although the apostate practices are thought to distinguish Israel from its neighbors, there may have been the need to condemn similar practices of those within the Israelite community itself. A detailed reconstruction of the development of ancient Israelite religion is beyond the scope of this study, but some explanation is warranted as to why monotheism was part of a reform movement. Scholars believe that the deuteronomic reform intended to stamp out what had been monolatrous practices. Under an Israelite system of monolatry, cultic diversity existed where Yahweh was acknowledged as the national patron deity, but other gods such as Baal and Asherah were still worshiped in both official and popular circles.[68] These prohibited practices, then, may have existed within the

66. The wife of the male head of the household is not specifically mentioned but she is assumed to be included by implication. See, for example, Eckart Otto, 'False Weights in the Scales of Biblical Justice?: Different Views of Women from Patriarchal Hierarchy to Religious Equality in the Book of Deuteronomy', in Matthews, Levinson and Frymer-Kensky (eds.), *Gender and Law*, pp. 128–46 (143); and Burnette-Bletsch, 'The Agrarian Family', p. 215.

67. Mullen, *Narrative History and Ethnic Boundaries*, pp. 55–56.

68. For a detailed analysis of the role of Asherah in the official cult of Yahweh, see Saul M.

Yahweh cult itself and were not just practiced by the Canaanites. Clearly, the ubiquitous nature of 'Yahweh-only' laws in the Hebrew Bible indicates that cultic diversity existed both before and after the deuteronomic pronouncements.

Second, sorcery is enjoined in Exod. 22.17 [22.18] and refers expressly to female sorcerers but the same prohibition in Deut. 18.9-14 is phrased more inclusively.[69] Scholars have thought that the condemnation of sorcery is, to some extent, the result of its association with outsiders.[70] For example, in his discussion of Exod. 22.17, Brueggemann wrote that sorcery was thought to be 'an attempt to manage and manipulate power that truly belongs only to God' and that it was 'used by foreign peoples who compete with, jeopardize, and seduce Israel away from its proper trust in Yahweh'.[71] Because of the perceived association with non-Israelites, the prohibition against sorcery and related activities can be said to function 'as markers of the ethnic boundary between the doomed nations' and the people of Israel.[72]

Third, the target of Deut. 23.18-19 [23.17-18] is usually thought to be sacred or cultic prostitution. Again, this prohibition has often been explained with reference to presumed ancient Near Eastern religious practices. In essence, foreign cultic personnel were thought to routinely engage in sexual acts to ensure the fertility of the land and their people. Given the lack of 'unambiguous evidence for any such rites', Robert A. Oden, Jr, in his analysis of ancient Near Eastern sacred prostitution, proceeded under the assumption that 'sacred prostitution ought to be investigated as an *accusation* rather than as a *reality*'.[73]

After analyzing the known resources and finding that no such widespread sexual activities existed, Oden determined that scholars have assumed the reality of such practices based on the Hebrew Bible.[74] Yet, Oden argues that the accusations had a purpose other than describing a historical reality. Based on the work of Fredrik Barth on ethnic groups and their boundary marking, Oden concludes that the accusations about sacred prostitution in the ANE 'played an important role in defining

Olyan, *Asherah and the Cult of Yahweh in Israel* (SBLMS, 34; Atlanta: Scholars Press, 1988). For more on the development of ancient Israelite religion, see Mark S. Smith, *The Early History of God: Yahweh and the other Deities of Ancient Israel* (Grand Rapids: Eerdmans, 2nd edn, 2002).

69. The masculine singular participle form is used and is considered to be inclusive by implication.

70. Some of the 'outsiders' excluded by this law may well have been Israelite women. In *The Israelite Woman*, Athalya Brenner mentions that some magical practices were incorporated into priestly activities and she cites as illustrations the red heifer ceremony (Num. 19) and the ritual cleansing of skin diseases (Lev. 13–14). She then observes that, because women were excluded from the official cult, 'men could and did perform some "magical" tasks within the framework of accepted religion, while women were forbidden to do so'. Brenner, *The Israelite Woman*, p. 70.

71. Brueggemann, 'Exodus', p. 867.

72. Nelson, *Deuteronomy*, p. 232. See also, Randall C. Bailey, 'They're Nothing but Incestuous Bastards: The Polemical Use of Sex and Sexuality in Hebrew Canon Narratives', in Fernando F. Segovia and Mary Ann Tolbert (eds.), *Reading From This Place, Vol. I: Social Location and Biblical Interpretation in the United States* (Minneapolis: Fortress Press, 1995), pp. 121–38.

73. Oden, *The Bible Without Theology*, p. 132 (italics in original).

74. Oden, *The Bible Without Theology*, p. 153.

Israel and Israelite religion as something distinctive'.[75] Basically, then, the cultic orthodoxy laws against apostasy, sorcery, and cultic prostitution function to shape aspects of the ancient Israelite identity.

In spite of these laws' apparent inclusivity, some features of gender construction may remain. For example, if women tend to be associated with worship practices that deviate from those approved by the official cult, then gender construction is implicated.[76] As mentioned earlier, the use of the feminine participle in the prohibition against sorcery in Exod. 22.17 [22.18] has been thought to suggest 'that women were more prone to this sort of action than men'.[77] Furthermore, Brenner has reclaimed the gender-related interpretation of this law so that it condemns certain actions of women pertaining to fertility and procreation.[78]

Even the law (supposedly) against cultic prostitution may have an underlying gender bias. As Bird argues, the use of the term *qdš* in Deut. 23.18 is 'by itself insufficient to establish either the existence of a class of male hierodules or the nature of their activity'.[79] Instead, 'it is evidence only for the author's view that an institution defined by its female form (*qdšh*), and in some way analogous to prostitution, was not to be tolerated in Israel in any form, female or male'.[80] From this perspective, the exclusion of males (*qdš*) and females (*qdšh*) from participation in the official cult is, in fact, a gender difference.[81] The construction of gender by these laws will be discussed more fully in Chapter 4.

3. *Fertility (Exod. 21.22-25, 22.18 [22.19]; Deut. 24.5, 25.5-12).* An emphasis on procreation for both males and females in both the BC and DL results in its constituting an element of Israelite identity. One of the laws that helps to develop this aspect of national identity is Exod. 21.22-25. This law mandates that if a man injures a pregnant woman while fighting, he must pay damages if she miscarries but is subject to the death penalty if the woman dies. Even though scholars do not agree on whether the *lex talionis* provision of Exod. 21.22-25 would apply in the case of a miscarriage alone, there is a consensus that some liability results from causing a pregnancy loss. In this way, the law encourages procreation.[82]

There is also a consensus that *lex talionis* applies if the mother dies – and this fact may make sense only if understood in light of the passage's fertility theme. If

75. Oden, *The Bible Without Theology*, p. 153.

76. For example, see Karel Van Der Toorn, *From Her Cradle to Her Grave: The Role of Religion in the Life of the Israelite and Babylonian Woman* (trans. Sara J. Denning-Bolle; Sheffield: Sheffield Academic Press, 1994), pp. 111–33.

77. Patrick, *Old Testament Law*, p. 84.

78. Brenner, *The Intercourse of Knowledge*, p. 85.

79. Bird, 'Male Cult Prostitute', p. 51.

80. Bird, 'Male Cult Prostitute', p. 51.

81. See Bird, 'The Place of Women in the Israelite Cultus', in *Missing Persons and Mistaken Identities*, pp. 81–102.

82. The importance of procreation in ancient Israel was necessitated by a high infant mortality rate, depopulation due to disease and agricultural demands, among other factors, and is reflected in the biblical narratives. See Meyers, 'The Roots of Restriction: Women in Early Israel', *BA* 41 (1978): pp. 91–103; and *Discovering Eve: Ancient Israelite Women in Context*, (New York: Oxford University Press, 1988), pp. 47–71.

the talionic provision usually addresses injuries caused with malice and intent to do harm as Paul contends,[83] its use in a law that specifies accidental, negligent action is unusual.[84] Nevertheless, capital punishment for a death caused accidentally may be warranted given the emphasis on fertility. The problem is that with the woman's death the possibility of her having other children with her husband and for the benefit of the community ends. As a result, a person who causes the loss of a wife's reproductive capabilities becomes subject to the death penalty because the loss is not limited just to her husband; it is a loss to the community as a whole.

Assuming that procreation is an underlying rationale in the Book of the Covenant permits a different interpretation of the prohibition against bestiality in Exod. 22.18 [22.19]. Several explanations have been proposed, three of which are mentioned here. Patrick suggests that the condemnation of sexual intercourse with animals is 'roundly condemned because it is an extremely degrading act that violates the image of God in humans'.[85] Marshall considers the prohibitions against sorcery and bestiality in Exod. 22.17-18 [22.18-19] together and proposes that both are associated with foreign practices and banned as potential threats to the status quo.[86] Lastly, Brenner understands the prohibition on bestiality to reflect biblical injunctions against violating the created hierarchical order which distinguishes between humans and animals and prohibits admixtures.[87] In an earlier work on incest, Brenner related the negative connotation of admixing in the Hebrew Bible to the sexual prohibitions against bestiality and homosexuality.[88]

> From the perspective of hierarchy and social control, both requiring the establishment of strict social boundaries, incest is a component among others – and not always the most important. I would also suggest that the moral horror expressed of homosexuality, transsexuality, and bestiality serves the same ideological purpose of avoiding mixtures in the interest of social order and stability. Thus incest and non-heterosexual practices are both constituents of a larger set of prohibitions.[89]

The similarity between the prohibitions against bestiality and homosexuality has also been identified by Fewell and Gunn.[90] They posit that the underlying rationale for both of these provisions is the notion 'that male seed is not to be wasted'.[91]

83. Paul, *Studies*, p. 74.

84. Paul asserts that the requisite intent to do harm exists in this scenario because the guilty parties were engaged in a fight, 'i.e. an unlawful act with intent to inflict injury'. Paul, *Studies*, p. 74. I find his interpretation unpersuasive. The injury to the female is accidental and the intent, if any, does not rise to the level of premeditation which, according to Exod. 21.12-14, is required for a capital crime. The requirement of premeditation for a capital crime seen in Exod. 21 is paralleled in Num. 35.9-34. See Peter Haas, '"Die He Shall Surely Die": The Structure of Homicide in Biblical Law', *Semeia* 45 (1989), pp. 67–88.

85. Patrick, *Old Testament Law*, pp. 84–85.

86. Marshall, *Israel and the Book of the Covenant*, p. 151.

87. Brenner, *The Intercourse of Knowledge*, p. 146.

88. Brenner, 'On Incest', in Athalya Brenner (ed.) *A Feminist Companion to Exodus to Deuteronomy* (FCB, 6; Sheffield: Sheffield Academic Press, 1994), pp. 113–38 (132–33).

89. Brenner, 'On Incest', pp. 132–33.

90. Fewell and Gunn, *Gender, Power, & Promise*, pp. 106–107.

91. Fewell and Gunn, *Gender, Power, & Promise*, pp. 106–107.

Consequently, these prohibitions imply that male seed should be used to procreate.[92] As expressed by Jon Berquist, a significant responsibility of the ancient Israelite male head of household was 'to maximize the household's fertility' by fathering children there.[93] In this way, Berquist found that a 'good' patriarch could 'creat[e] a household of increasing numbers and growing strength'.[94]

Another law in the DL that promotes male procreation is the newlywed exemption in Deuteronomy 24.5, which encourages a male to procreate by allowing him to remain with his wife for a full year.[95] Similarly, the law on a female's genital grabbing in Deut. 25.11-12 can be interpreted as one that protects a male's ability to have offspring. In other words, when a female intervenes in a fight to help her husband who is one of the combatants by grabbing his opponent's genitals, she may cause damage to the male's reproductive organs. Punishment is then required for her having risked damaging his reproductive abilities.[96] Indeed, it has been argued that this law follows the one on levirate marriage – where a man died without an heir and risked having his name blotted out as a result – because both laws underscore the importance of reproduction.[97] Based on these laws in the BC and DL, fertility is encouraged for both men and women as members of the Israelite community, and it forms part of the Israelite identity.

3. *The Construction of Gender Identity: The Exclusive Laws of the BC and DL*

In the previous section, national, class, and generational identities are shown to have been constructed by the inclusive laws of the BC and DL. In this section, the construction of gender identity will be analyzed through the exclusive laws. To discuss gender as a construction of these laws presumes that gender does not flow automatically from the perceived physiological differences between the sexes.[98] Instead, as defined in Chapter 1, gender – the ascribed differences between males and females – is something that males and females 'do'.

92. Berquist, *Controlling Corporeality*, p. 73. Interestingly, proscriptions against bestiality in Exod. 22.18 [22.19] and Deut. 27.21 use masculine singular active participles which are then translated inclusively as 'anyone' or 'whoever'. Yet the comparable passages in Lev. 18.23 and 20.15-16 specifically refer to males and females. It is at least possible then that these laws in Exodus and Deuteronomy are directed primarily at males. In the context of the BC and DL as a whole, though, these laws work to shape the behavior of males and females alike, i.e. both Israelite men and women are to procreate.

93. Berquist, *Controlling Corporeality*, p. 65.

94. Berquist, *Controlling Corporeality*, p. 65.

95. Steinberg, 'Adam's and Eve's Daughters', pp. 262–63; Burnette-Bletsch, 'The Agrarian Family', pp. 270–71.

96. Phillips, *Ancient Israel's Criminal Law*, pp. 94–95; and Tigay, 'Improper Intervention', pp. 484–85. If risking a male's fertility is the female's offense, the law should prohibit identical action if done by a man. Tigay suggests, however, that the law only mentions women because they were more likely to resort to this tactic; another man would use wrestling or fisticuffs.

97. Phillips, *Deuteronomy*, pp. 169–70.

98. Judith Lorber, *Paradoxes of Gender* (New Haven: Yale University Press, 1994), p. 17.

> Doing gender involves a complex of socially guided perceptual, interactional, and micropolitical activities that cast particular pursuits as expressions of masculine and feminine 'natures'.[99]

To consider 'doing gender' as the appropriate 'pursuits' for males and females means that the emphasis is placed on the behavior ascribed to each sex. In the context of these biblical laws, the appropriate behavior ascribed to females can be identified through gender theory as well as feminist legal theory.

A. *Gender Theory*

Gender theory focuses on polarization, i.e. the 'mutually exclusive scripts for being male and female'.[100] As defined in Chapter 2 of this study, the exclusive laws in the BC and DL are those laws that set forth treatment for a female which differs from that of a male under similar circumstances. This section will consider the majority of these exclusive laws which are the ones that prescribe or proscribe treatment based on a female's relationship to a male. The basis for this category of laws – that is, a female's relationship with a male – applies whether that male is her father or her husband. Nevertheless, the common element among the laws found here is her sexuality. In other words, one of the polarized attributes of being female in these exclusive laws is having her sexuality controlled by a male. In marriage, her sexuality is controlled by her husband; before marriage or betrothal, it is controlled by her father.

To review briefly the provisions in Deut. 22.22-29, the penalties for a male and female who have intercourse vary according to the female's marital status. If the female is single and has been raped, the man must marry the female and he cannot divorce her (Deut. 22.28-29).[101] Pressler correctly understands the penalty to imply that 'a raped woman or girl is damaged goods' because the law locates the injury in the reduction of her marriageability and thus opportunities for economic security.[102]

The implications of Deut. 22.28-29, however, extend beyond the circumstances of rape. Both Pressler and Steinberg found that the law on the accused bride in Deut. 22.13-21 conferred upon the husband the right to have a wife who is a virgin.[103] Interpreting these two laws together means that the husband has a right to a wife who has not had previous sexual experience – whether that experience occurred with or without her consent.

99. Candace West and Don H. Zimmerman, 'Doing Gender', in Judith Lorber and Susan A. Farrell (eds.), *The Social Construction of Gender* (Newbury Park: SAGE Publications, Inc., 1991), pp. 13–37 (14).

100. Sandra Lipsitz Bem, *The Lenses of Gender*, pp. 80–81.

101. The law on intercourse with an unbetrothed virgin in Exod. 22.15-16 [22.16–17] is the only law from the BC that prescribes or proscribes treatment based on a female's relationship to a male. It has been distinguished from the corresponding law in Deut. 22.28-29 on the grounds that the female presumably consented to the intercourse and that marriage is optional rather than mandatory. Pressler rightly argues that both laws are variations of the same fact situation: the violation of an unbetrothed girl. See Pressler, *Family Laws*, p. 40.

102. Pressler, 'Sexual Violence and the Deuteronomic Law', pp. 107, 112.

103. Pressler, *Family Laws*, 31; and Steinberg, 'Adam's and Eve's Daughters', p. 251.

As for the provisions of Deut. 22.22-27, if the female is betrothed when intercourse with another man occurs, the penalty is death for the male and, if she consented, she is to die as well. If the female is married, the penalty is death for both the male and female.[104] Pressler considers the law on intercourse with a betrothed woman to fall within the deuteronomic laws on adultery because she finds that adultery here refers to intercourse 'between a married or betrothed woman and a man other than her husband'.[105] On the whole, Pressler finds that these laws on adultery in Deut. 22.13-29 emphasize the husband's right to control his wife's sexuality, but his wife has 'no such reciprocal claim' to possession of her husband's sexuality.[106] Under these exclusive laws, it is clear that a female's sexual activity is to occur only within the bounds of marriage. By affirming that the laws intend a husband's control of his wife's sexuality, Pressler rightly notes that what is at stake in these laws is the continuity of the family and the husband's assurance 'that his sons were his own'.[107] In this way, these laws demonstrate that polarized sexual behaviors are ascribed to males and females and, thereby, reveal the contours of gender construction.

B. *Postmodern Feminist Legal Theory*

As demonstrated in the preceding section, an analysis of the biblical laws using gender theory uniformly looks for oppositional male and female attributes constructed by the laws. In contrast, feminist legal theory has followed three different trajectories. Liberal feminism has promoted traditional liberal values such as equality, individual autonomy, and self-fulfillment as the means to eradicate discrimination against women.[108] Another category of feminist legal theory struggles with contexts such as pregnancy, in which women may be equal to men but are also different from men.[109] Finally, there are feminist theorists who have appropriated

104. Generally, it is presumed that whether the married woman consented determines her punishment as in the case of the betrothed woman. See for example, Pressler, 'Sexual Violence and the Deuternomic Law', p. 107. The fact of the matter, though, is that the law does not provide any such exception for the married female. Moreover, Pressler argues that the law on a female's immodest behavior in Deut. 25.11-12 indicates that 'for a married woman to have sexual contact with a man other than her husband is abhorrent, even under extenuating circumstances'. Pressler, *Family Laws*, p. 75. If any sexual touching of another man by a married woman is thought to be abhorrent by the redactors, it is unlikely that her consent would be an exculpatory factor under the law of adultery.

105. Pressler, *Family Laws*, p. 33.

106. Pressler, *Family Laws*, p. 42. Furthermore, a husband's control of his wife's sexuality does not cease with his death. Both Pressler and Bird have noted that, even if a widow, any sexual activity by the female could be construed as an offense against her deceased husband's family. Bird, 'To Play the Harlot: An Inquiry into an Old Testament Metaphor', in *Missing Persons and Mistaken Identities*, pp. 219–38 (222); and Pressler, *Family Laws*, pp. 72–73.

107. Pressler, *Family Laws*, pp. 42, 114.

108. See Alison M. Jaggar, *Feminist Politics and Human Nature* (Totowa, NJ: Rowman & Allanheld, 1983), pp. 27–50, 173–206.

109. For critiques of equality and difference theories, see Robin West, 'Jurisprudence and Gender', *University of Chicago Law Review* 55 (1988), pp. 1–72; and Catherine A. Mackinnon, 'Dominance and Difference: On Sex Discrimination', in *Feminism Unmodified: Discourses on Life and Law* (Cambridge: Harvard University Press, 1987), pp. 32–45.

postmodern understandings of 'the body – what we eat, how we dress, the daily rituals through which we attend to the body' as a 'medium of culture'.[110] Under these circumstances, the body becomes 'the direct locus of social control' or a text that can be analyzed for ideological content.[111] In other words, even our sense of the human body is socially constructed, and variations in a culture's definition of the male versus the female body become discernible and significant. For example, the standard for the normal human body temperature as 98.6 degrees excludes most premenopausal women during the two weeks before ovulation each month when their body temperatures are below 98.6 degrees.[112] As a result, the body temperature that is assumed to be generic is in fact male.

An analysis using postmodern feminist legal theory, therefore, looks for images of the female body that the laws create as forms of legal discourse. The recognition that legal discourse is 'a site of political struggle over sex differences', according to Mary Jo Frug, results from the postmodern emphasis on language as constitutive of human experience.[113]

From this perspective, laws can provide information on aspects of the assigned female identity. In her analysis, Frug refers to this process as the law 'encod[ing] the female body with meanings'.[114] Specifically, she identifies the following qualities of the female body that legal rules create and reinforce: the female body submits to male authority, the female body is meant for sex with men, and the female body is meant for maternity.[115] Although Frug's qualities are derived from contemporary laws, they apply surprisingly well to biblical laws.

1. *The female body submits to male authority*. Gender theory and the exclusive laws of the BC and DL reveal that an important aspect of female identity is submitting her sexuality to male control. Some examples are that, before marriage, the woman's father is to control her sexuality so that when she marries, she is still a virgin. As articulated by Bird, 'a woman's sexuality was understood to belong to her husband alone, for whom it must be reserved in anticipation of marriage as well as in the marriage bond'.[116] Once married, she is not to have intercourse with any other man (Deut. 22.22). In fact, she is not to touch the genitals of another man, even if she does so to help her husband, and her hand is to be cut off if she does

110. Susan R. Bordo, 'The Body and the Reproduction of Femininity: A Feminist Appropriation of Foucault', in Alison M. Jaggar and Susan R. Bordo (eds.), *Gender/Body/Knowledge: Feminist Reconstructions of Being and Knowing* (New Brunswick: Rutgers University Press, 1989), pp. 13–33 (13).

111. Bordo, 'The Body and the Reproduction of Femininity', p. 13.

112. Bordo, *Unbearable Weight: Feminism, Western Culture, and the Body* (Berkeley: University of California Press, 1993), p. 34.

113. Mary Jo Frug, 'A Postmodern Feminist Legal Manifesto (An Unfinished Draft)', in Dan Danielsen and Karen Engle (eds.), *After Identity: A Reader in Law and Culture* (New York: Routledge, 1995), pp. 7–23 (8).

114. Frug, 'Legal Manifesto', p. 11.

115. Frug, 'Legal Manifesto', pp. 12–13.

116. Bird, 'To Play the Harlot: An Inquiry into an Old Testament Metaphor', in *Missing Persons and Mistaken Identities*, pp. 219–38 (222).

intervene on his behalf in this manner (Deut. 25.11-12). Finally, under the levirate law, her husband's control of her sexuality continues even after his death because, if he dies childless, she is to produce a son for him with one of the deceased husband's male relatives (Deut. 25.5-10).

In her work on women in the Bible, Gail Corrington Streete found that such all-encompassing control over a female is necessitated by the desire 'to circumscribe female fertility' and to establish biological paternity.[117] Then, Streete determined, by referring to Nancy Jay's work, that control over female sexuality is particularly important in contexts such as that of ancient Israel, where ethnic identity and survival depend on endogamy (marriage within the kinship group), patrilocality (residence with the husband's family), and partiliny (descent reckoned through the father's line).[118] Such control is less important to matrilineal groups, Jay observed, because membership can be determined by birth alone whereas '[p]aternity never has the same certainty, and birth by itself cannot be the sole criterion for patrilineal membership'.[119]

The laws themselves do not indicate fully the consequences of a female's non-compliance, but at least one biblical narrative might provide some insight. In Judg. 19, a woman removes herself from the authority of a male and is later gang-raped. According to J. Cheryl Exum, the sequence of these events in the woman's life (whom Exum names 'Bath-sheber') is not coincidental. Exum suggests that Bath-sheber dared to act autonomously and, as a result, she 'put herself beyond male protection' and so must be punished.[120]

> The men who ordinarily would be expected to protect her – her husband and their host – participate in her punishment because her act is an offense against the social order; that is, against the patriarchal system itself. In the end, the woman is raped by a mob and dismembered by her own husband. As narrative punishment for her sexual 'misconduct', her sexual 'freedom', she is sexually abused, after which her sexuality is symbolically mutilated.[121]

2. *The female body is meant for sex with men*. In her analysis, Frug can argue that the sexualization of the female body occurs directly in today's context through rules that support pornography and the entertainment industries 'that eroticize the female body'.[122] Such sexualization of the female body also occurs in the biblical laws but only indirectly. As a general principle, male sexual activity is proscribed in the biblical laws when it infringes upon the marital or parental rights of another

117. Streete, *The Strange Woman*, p. 6.

118. Streete, *The Strange Woman*, pp. 5–6. See Nancy Jay, 'Sacrifice as Remedy for Having Been Born of Woman', in Clarissa W. Atkinson, Constance H. Buchanon and Margaret R. Miles (eds.), *Immaculate and Powerful: the Female in Sacred Image and Social Reality* (Boston: Beacon Press, 1985), p. 290.

119. Jay, 'Sacrifice as Remedy', p. 290.

120. J. Cheryl Exum, *Fragmented Women: Feminist (Sub)versions of Biblical Narratives* (Valley Forge: Trinity Press International, 1993), p. 179.

121. Exum, *Fragmented Women*, pp. 179–80.

122. Frug, 'Legal Manifesto', p. 12.

male.[123] As a result, an Israelite male would be wise to avoid sexual encounters with the wife or daughter of a free Israelite male, yet intercourse with prostitutes, female slaves, and foreign women would not violate the law. By clearly penalizing some sexual encounters (those with a woman in the household of another privileged Israelite man) but not others, the BC and DL indirectly sexualize non-privileged females.

In this context, prostitution takes on new importance. Intercourse with the professional prostitute, 'who has no husband nor sexual obligation to any other male', violates no man's rights or honor and so is free from the sanctions otherwise imposed.[124] According to Bird, prostitution, rather than being a universal phenomenon, is characteristic of urban patriarchal society.[125] More precisely, prostitution is the result of gender asymmetry in patriarchal societies where men demand 'exclusive control of their wives' sexuality' while maintaining their 'sexual access to other women'.[126]

> The greater the inaccessibility of women in the society due to restrictions on the wife and the unmarried nubile women, the greater the need for an institutionally legitimized 'other' woman. The harlot is that 'other' woman, tolerated but stigmatized, desired but ostracized.[127]

An additional indication of the sexualization of non-privileged females is the absence of laws penalizing intercourse with female slaves in the BC or DL, especially when such laws do exist in the Sumerian and Babylonian law codes.[128] Similarly, intercourse with foreign women is not penalized. The presence of a law on the female war captive in Deut. 21.10-14 does not preclude intercourse with foreign women outside of marriage.[129] As Harold Washington noted, 'the law does not curtail men's rape and subsequent killing or abandonment of women during combat'.[130] That law only applies if an Israelite male wants to incorporate a foreign woman into his household. In these ways, the biblical laws sexualize the bodies of non-Israelite and economically marginalized females.

3. *The female body is meant for maternity*. Earlier in this chapter, procreation was mentioned as an aspect of Israelite national identity. The law concerning injury to a pregnant female was cited in that discussion because it requires compensation for a pregnancy loss and mandates the death penalty if the female dies as a result of the accidental injury (Exod. 21.22-25). In addition, the husband's right under the laws

123. Bird, 'To Play the Harlot', p. 222.

124. Bird, 'To Play the Harlot', p. 222.

125. Bird, 'The Harlot as Heroine: Narrative Art and Social Presupposition in Three Old Testament Texts', in *Missing Persons and Mistaken Identities*, pp. 197–218 (200).

126. Bird, 'The Harlot as Heroine', p. 200.

127. Bird, 'The Harlot as Heroine', pp. 200–201.

128. LU 8; LE 31.

129. Pressler, *Family Laws*, pp. 9–12. See also E. Neufeld, *Ancient Hebrew Marriage Laws* (London: Longmans, Green & Co., 1944), p. 78.

130. Washington, 'Violence and the Construction of Gender in Deuteronomy 20–22', in Matthews, Levinson and Frymer-Kensky (eds.), *Gender and Law*, p. 203.

to control his wife's sexuality ensured that when she did conceive, the offspring would be 'his own'.[131] Collectively, these and other laws encourage reproduction for the perpetuation of the free Israelite male's household.

In contrast, the laws of the ancient Near East in general and the biblical laws in particular do not appear to encourage the continuation of the household of a male slave. Although compensation for a pregnancy loss is provided for slave women in the Sumerian, Babylonian and Hittite law codes, no such compensation for members of other classes is provided in the biblical laws.[132] Furthermore, even when compensation is allowed in the ancient Near Eastern laws, it is probably to be received by the slave owner rather than the female slave's husband.[133] Payment to the slaveowner indicates that the child would have added to the workforce of the slave owner and so the loss is his and not that of the father (the male slave). Class differences therefore exist because the continuation of the household is a privilege extended under the biblical laws to free Israelites but not slaves.

From this analysis, variations in gender construction according to socioeconomic class become evident. Specifically, male control of female sexuality is the only construction that applies to both privileged and non-privileged women. Even then, the control experienced by a female slave would be qualitatively different from that experienced by a married free woman. The female slave would have her sexuality controlled not only by her husband but also by her owner.[134] As for the other constructions discussed here, the encouragement of maternity applies only to privileged women, whereas the sexualization applies only to non-privileged women. Given these differences in the concept of 'female', a more nuanced understanding of gender is warranted. Indeed, it seems more appropriate to speak of the construction of genders (plural) and not just the construction of gender (singular), based on variations in the treatment of women according to class and national identity.[135]

4. *The Legitimation of Identity*

In gender theory, attributes assigned to males and females are 'naturalized' or legitimated. Bem observes that this process of legitimation is done by defining any

131. Pressler, *Family Laws*, p. 42. See also Phillips, 'Another Look at Adultery', *JSOT* 20 (1981), pp. 3–25.

132. LL d-f; LH 209–214; HL 17–18.

133. G.R. Driver and John C. Miles, *The Babylonian Laws. Vol. 1* (Oxford: Clarendon Press, 1956), p. 415; and *The Assyrian Laws* (Oxford: Clarendon Press, 1935), p. 108. See also Westbrook, 'Mesopotamia: Old Babylonian Period', in Westbrook (ed.), *History of Ancient Near Eastern Law*, pp. 361–430 (422–23).

134. See Raymond Westbrook, 'The Female Slave', in Matthews, Levinson and Frymer-Kensky (eds.), *Gender and Law*, pp. 214–38.

135. Lorber and Susan A. Farrell (eds.), 'Preface', *The Social Construction of Gender* (Newbury Park: SAGE Publications, 1991), pp. 1–5 (1). In the next chapter, the argument will be made that, from the perspective of the male 'subject', the female becomes an object, the 'Other'. Even though the reification of the female as the 'Other' connotes a single identity that occludes differences among females, the analysis done in this study seeks to undermine that single identity, thereby revealing the multiplicity of embodied female experiences. As a result, nuances in the construction of gender according to class and nationality, as seen here, can and will be highlighted.

deviations from the approved behaviors 'as unnatural or immoral from a religious perspective or as biologically anomalous or psychologically pathological from a scientific perspective'.[136] Although Bem's statement describes a process utilized in the construction of gender identity, the same process of normalization occurs for all constructed identities. The purpose of normalizing any identity is to provide those collective qualities with an aura of authority that fosters their incorporation by the targeted individuals. Regarding the BC and DL, the behaviors indicated are legitimated by their placement within the Torah.

Specifically, the class, generational, national, and gender identities constructed are then legitimated by the placement of these laws within the biblical narrative. Because they appear 'in the context of Israel's experience in the encampment and covenant making at Sinai', they must be 'read through the norm of the Sinai covenant'.[137] In this context, placing the laws in the mouth of Moses provides them with a sense of authenticity and antiquity that the laws would not have otherwise. Moreover, biblical laws become proclamations of God's will.[138] As a result, the authority of these laws (and, it might be added, that of the identities derived from these laws) is based on the Sinai covenant.[139] To be precise, membership in God's covenanted community is contingent upon living in accordance with these laws.[140]

To encourage compliance, motive clauses have been included with many of the laws which 'remind their Israelite addressees of their redemption from slavery in Egypt and exhort them to act as those rooted in that story'.[141] Waldemar Janzen rightly proposes that the laws are expressions of divine will, and compliance is motivated as our response to the biblical story of redemption.[142]

By shaping character, biblical laws legitimate the identities contained within them by specifying who the reader is to be as a person of faith.

> Part of the function of the legal material in the Bible is precisely to keep the reader from 'getting on with the story'. It forces the reader to stop and consider who he or she is and what he or she does. It specifies who such a reader must be if he or she wants to read the text correctly.[143]

A result of a biblical law's ability to shape behavior, then, is the ability to legitimate and therefore shape identity.

136. Bem, *The Lenses of Gender*, p. 81.

137. Bruce C. Birch, *Let Justice Roll Down: The Old Testament, Ethics, and Christian Life* (Louisville, KY: Westminster/John Knox Press, 1991), p. 158.

138. Janzen, *Old Testament Ethics*, p. 59.

139. Birch, *Let Justice Roll Down*, p. 158.

140. Nanette Stahl, *Law and Liminality in the Bible* (JSOTSup, 202; Sheffield: Sheffield Academic Press, 1995), p. 22.

141. Janzen, *Old Testament Ethics*, pp. 60–61. Motive clauses may be explanatory, ethical, cultic, theological or historical in nature. See Gemser, 'The Importance of the Motive Clause', pp. 50–66.

142. Janzen, *Old Testament Ethics*, p. 62.

143. Harry P. Nasuti, 'Identity, Identification, and Imitation: The Narrative Hermeneutics of Biblical Law', *Journal of Law and Religion* 4 (1986), p. 23.

5. *Conclusions*

In the context of the Torah, the authority of these laws originates with the Sinai covenant. As Judith Plaskow points out, however, 'at the very moment when Israel stands trembling waiting for God's presence to descend upon the mountain, Moses addresses the community only as men'.[144] This study shows that, with respect to the BC and DL, Moses addresses only adult males and, even then, only those who are free and privileged. These laws assume those characteristics of their audience and construct identities for other groups based on that assumption.

Of these other identities, gender is the one that has 'master-status'.[145] In sociology, 'master-status' is the trait that overpowers any other traits that might contradict it.[146] One example of a master-status trait in the contemporary context is when an African-American attains a high professional standing.[147] The idea is that a dilemma arises when (presumably racist) European-Americans meet that person. Is the person to be treated as an African-American (low status) or a professional (high status)? The answer is that race is a master-status determinative that dictates how such encounters will develop.[148] In the BC and DL, gender is the master-status trait because it defines the degree of privilege an individual has under these laws. As seen in the chart provided in Appendix B, whether one is male or female is the crucial distinction made in the BC and DL.

Gender is such a critical trait in these laws that it underlies other traits such as nationality and class. In other words, concepts of nationality and class depend on varying privileges over women in the same class or nationality and those of a lower class or a different nationality. For that reason, as Gail Corrington Streete explains, any challenges to the male dominant/female subordinate gender paradigm is perceived as a threat that would undermine the integrity of the whole group.[149]

> Those who get 'out of place' threaten to subvert the entire social hierarchy of groups, especially groups like those represented in biblical literature that already perceive themselves as marginal and under threat from the outside. In such a society, the deviance of no subgroup appears as dangerous as that of women. 'Woman' as a category transcends the boundaries both of nation and class and is tied most closely to the anxiety-producing realm of reproduction. Upon 'woman' then the ultimate integrity of the groups is perceived to depend.[150]

144. Judith Plaskow, *Standing Again at Sinai: Judaism from a Feminist Perspective* (San Francisco: HarperSanFrancisco, 1990), p. 25.

145. Everett C. Hughes, 'Dilemmas and Contradictions of Status', *The American Journal of Sociology* 50 (1945), pp. 353–59.

146. Hughes, 'Dilemmas and Contradictions', p. 357.

147. Hughes, 'Dilemmas and Contradictions', p. 357.

148. Hughes, 'Dilemmas and Contradictions', p. 357. For a contemporary application of the 'master-status' concept, see Mary C. Waters, *Black Identities: West Indian Immigrant Dreams and American Realities* (Cambridge, MA: Harvard University Press, 1999).

149. Streete, *The Strange Woman*, pp. 13–14.

150. Streete, *The Strange Woman*, pp. 13–14.

That the BC and DL assume the perspective of free, privileged, Israelite males can be seen in the provisions that address the possible concerns of an individual who is able to own slaves and who has an ox that might gore someone.[151] Furthermore, if a hypothetical person is considered, this person has sufficient means to support his household as well as the economically marginalized members of the community and still attend the annual festivals. This person has property to transfer and sons to whom the property can be transferred. Indeed, the continuation of his household is so important that he is compensated if his wife suffers a pregnancy loss. Most importantly, though, this person is male. The laws confer upon him the right to a wife who is a virgin and the right to control the sexuality of his wife and daughters. The degree to which he controls his wife's sexuality is so great that she is not to touch another man's genitals – even if it is done to help her husband while he is in a fight – and his sons may not approach any of his women even after he dies.

Under these laws, a poor Israelite male has fewer privileges than a rich one. A poor male would probably not have slaves, and he might have inadequate finances to attend the annual festivals if they are in Jerusalem rather than at local shrines. Nevertheless, as an Israelite male, he still has protections for the continuation of his household through compensation in case of his wife's pregnancy loss, and he has control of the sexuality of his wife and daughter. A male debt slave has even fewer privileges than the poor Israelite male because he has less control of his wife and daughter who would be subject to the dictates of their owner.

For slaves, the laws affirm slavery, provide that they can be physically disciplined, and do not value the continuation of their households. For those who are economically marginalized, such as widows and the poor, the BC and DL require that they be dependent on someone with means for their livelihood.

As for gender, the most striking characteristic in the BC and DL is that female sexuality is to be controlled by a male. In the case of a free woman, that male is her father, fiancé, or husband. In the case of a female slave, her sexuality is also controlled by her owner. The laws also sexualize the bodies of women who are not under the control of free Israelite men, such as prostitutes and foreign women. Finally, the laws communicate that females are to continue the privileged Israelite male's household through procreation.

Without a doubt, a matriarch, as a free privileged Israelite female, has privileges compared to other females in these laws. A matriarch may have owned a slave, she was accorded the respect of her children, and she and her husband were charged with the disciplining of both male and female children. However, any notion that her privileges are identical to those of the patriarch is countered by two glaring omissions in these laws. As a result of these omissions, the matriarch may own a male or female slave, but the slaves have two privileges that she does not have. Specifically, the laws on striking a slave limit the privileged male's ability to physi-

151. Non-Israelites are referred to in these laws in two ways. Exod. 21.8 prohibits the selling of a female debt slave to foreigners, which means that the law assumes that foreigners exist with adequate resources to purchase slaves. Also, Deut. 21.10-14 describes the treatment of a female war captive who could be a foreigner of either privileged or non-privileged status.

cally harm a slave but no such limitation exists with respect to his own wife.[152] Similarly, the male and female slave are expressly mentioned among those in the Israelite household who are to attend cultic observances but the householder's wife is not. Because of these omissions, we are reminded that, even with some privileges, the matriarch's subordinate status within the patriarch's household remains.

As Patricia Hill Collins argues in *Black Feminist Thought*, 'privilege' should be defined relationally so that women, who can be members of dominant and subordinate groups simultaneously, are recognized as possessing 'varying amounts of penalty and privilege'.[153] As seen in this discussion and the relevant chart in Appendix B, such an analysis of relative 'penalty and privilege' enables a more nuanced analysis of the man/woman, married/single, Israelite/non-Israelite, and slave/free distinctions of biblical laws.

152. See Fewell and Gunn, *Gender, Power, & Promise*, pp. 100, 192 n. 5.
153. Patricia Hill Collins, *Black Feminist Thought* (New York: Routledge, 1990), p. 225.

Chapter 4

LAW, GENDER, AND VIOLENCE

1. *Introduction*

In this study, inclusive laws have been shown to construct identities that apply to both males and females, such as those pertaining to being an Israelite, a member of a specific socioeconomic class, and a particular age group. Inclusive laws, however, are not ostensibly involved in the construction of gender. Gender, as defined here, refers to the attributes that constitute culturally approved notions of 'masculinity' and 'femininity'.[1] Correspondingly, exclusive laws have been shown to construct the identity of gender – that is, the polarized patterns ascribed to males and females in a social system.

Because masculinity and femininity are oppositionally defined characteristics, if femininity is defined as female subordination, the corresponding characteristic is masculinity defined as male dominance. Since female subordination was identified in the previous chapter, it stands to reason that a male dominance gender role exists. Yet rather than just assume that male dominance is inscribed in these laws, the pertinent features of the BC and DL must be reviewed again to specifically identify the male dominance paradigm. Furthermore, in this chapter, the gender paradigm of male dominance/female subordination found in the BC and DL will be shown to constitute a form of violence against women. To begin our consideration of the construction of masculinity, the term 'masculinity' needs closer scrutiny.

2. *Gender Theory and the Construction of Masculinity in the BC and DL*

As mentioned in Chapter 1, male/female and man/woman are not synonymous terms. 'The categories of "male" and "female" are not categories of social life and sexual politics; the categories "men" and "women" are'.[2] Until now, this investigation has focused primarily on the construction of femininity in its analysis of gender from which the reader may have inferred that 'gender' refers only to females.

1. Current gender theory recognizes that the construction of masculinity and femininity vary according to race and class. Therefore, it is more accurate (but more cumbersome) to refer to the construction of masculinities and femininities. See R.W. Connell, *Masculinities* (Cambridge and Oxford: Polity Press, 1995), pp. 75–76; and Judith Lorber and Susan A. Farrell (eds.), 'Preface', *The Social Construction of Gender* (Newbury Park: SAGE Publications, 1991), pp. 1–5 (1).

2. R.W. Connell, *Gender and Power: Society, the Person, and Sexual Politics* (Stanford: Stanford University Press, 1987), p. 137.

Yet, because the respective attributes are set up as oppositional, gender in its fullest sense refers simultaneously to the characteristics ascribed to males as well as females.

Today, in the cultural setting of the West, 'men are commonly described as aggressive, assertive, independent, competitive, insensitive, and so on'.[3] In fact, these traits are associated with maleness to such an extreme that they are thought to be innate and inevitable, but they are not. Instead, these traits are part of 'the ideology of patriarchy' that 'justifies and naturalizes male domination'.[4] Because of the dichotomous logic on which gender construction is based, male domination necessarily implies female subordination. Of critical importance in gender theory is the fact that this pattern of male domination/female subordination is not seen universally, which reinforces the claim that those traits typically ascribed to men are socially and not biologically derived.

As argued by Peggy Sanday, male dominance/female subordination is not an inevitable human occurrence because it is found in some cultures and not others.[5] In her work as an anthropologist, Sanday distinguishes between two different types of 'scripts' for gender-role behavior: a script for female power that allows females to participate fully in community affairs, and a script for male dominance that does not. According to Sanday, whether a culture is more likely to follow one script as opposed to the other is determined by the degree of separation between the sexes in the division of labor. In turn, that degree of separation is determined by that culture's relationship to its natural environment. Sanday found that if the environment is perceived as a 'partner', the sexes have more common activities, but if the environment is seen as hostile, the sexes become separate from one another.[6] Basically, a pattern of male dominance/female subordination is more likely to result, Sanday argues, if the environment is considered to be hostile and the sexes have segregated spheres of labor.[7] In contrast, the cultures in which

3. Arthur Brittan, *Masculinity and Power* (Oxford: Basil Blackwell, 1989), pp. 3–4.

4. Brittan, *Masculinity and Power*, p. 4. However, Brittan recognizes that the search for 'an original and underlying basis for human behaviour' has not been abandoned. Brittan, *Masculinity and Power*, p. 6. In fact, he reports on the same page an emergence of the 'new evolutionists' who 'claim that there is no way in which [gender] can be seen as a social construction'. A recent example of such 'biological essentialism' is Steven Pinker's book, *How The Mind Works* (New York: W.W. Norton, 1997). Pinker argues that men and women are different and behave differently because of their different investments in reproduction. For example, men have greater sex drives so that they can reproduce; whereas women seek a male's affection, earning capacity, and so forth to make sure that they and their children will be financially supported. Pinker, *How The Mind Works*, pp. 473–82.

5. Peggy Reeves Sanday, *Female Power and Male Dominance: On The Origins of Sexual Inequality* (Cambridge: Cambridge University Press, 1981), pp. 15–16. Correspondingly, Sanday rejects Sherry Ortner's contention that female subordination is universal. Sanday, *Female Power and Male Dominance*, pp. 4–5.

6. Sanday, *Female Power and Male Dominance*, p. 7.

7. Sanday, *Female Power and Male Dominance*, p. 7. The anthropologist David Gilmore also noted the same relationship between the sexual division of labor, as a response to the environment, and the resulting definition of masculinity as male dominance. See David D. Gilmore, *Manhood in the Making: Cultural Concepts of Masculinity* (New Haven: Yale University Press, 1990).

female power is supported, Sanday noted, feature minimal leadership, group decision-making processes in which men and women participate equally, and cooperation is encouraged.[8]

Sanday's observations mean that the construction of masculinity does not have to be equated with the fostering of male domination. If the distinction between masculinity and male dominance is taken seriously, a new question emerges that must be addressed in our discussion of the BC and DL. Rather than proceed from critically unexamined assumptions, we must ask whether the BC and DL do indeed equate masculinity with male dominance. This next section of the study will show that male dominance, as well as female subordination, are the gender-role scripts of the BC and DL. To analyze laws in this manner, feminist legal theorists offer the methodology needed by formulating the question: 'Is the law male?'[9]

A. *The Law as Male: Support for Male Dominance*

Because it looks for the oppositional construction of male and female attributes, gender theory has been used effectively to analyze the polarized sexual politics, referred to as 'gender regimes', in contemporary institutions.[10] Such gender regimes are identifiable in institutions such as the family, the state, and even the 'street'.[11] With respect to the analysis of a law, gender theory works well primarily if there is a distinction between the treatment of men and women that exists on its face.[12] As will be seen in this section, though, a law can still construct gender

8. Sanday, 'The Socio-Cultural Context of Rape: A Cross-Cultural Study', *Journal of Social Issues* 37 (1981), pp. 5–27 (17). An additional difference identified by Sanday between the cultures with the male dominance versus the female power gender-role scripts was that male participation in parenting was lower in the former cultures. See Sanday, *Female Power and Male Dominance*, pp. 60–64. See also Mary Stewart Van Leeuwen, *My Brother's Keeper: What The Social Sciences Do (And Don't) Tell Us About Masculinity* (Downer's Grove, IL: InterVarsity Press, 2002), pp. 116–17. Even in today's cultural context, the degree of male participation in childrearing is an important factor in redefining gender roles. See Francine M. Deutsch, *Halving It All: How Equally Shared Parenting Works* (Cambridge: Harvard University Press, 1999).

9. Pursuant to gender theory, the more precise wording of the question would be 'Does the law support male dominance?' However, the criteria incorporated here come from scholars in the field of feminist legal theory. These scholars phrased the question using only the term 'male', but that term has been defined in this study as a biological rather than a sociological term. To be consistent with the work of those scholars, though, their phrasing of the question will be used in this section of the study.

10. Connell, *Gender and Power*, p. 120.

11. Connell, *Gender and Power*, pp. 119–42. According to Connell, sexual divisions of labor within the household are one indication of gender constructions in the family. An example of such division is that females are observed to tend to the inside of the residence, whereas the males handle the outside. Sexual division in the state is evident in public policies that regulate sexuality and limit the participation of women in the public sphere. Finally, differences in the occupations of men and women that can be observed on the street and the relative absence of females on streets after dark are some of the reasons that the 'street' is an institution that also constructs gender distinctions.

12. Examples of this classification of gender discrimination were prevalent at one time in our recent history. 'Women were denied the right to vote, own property, enter into contract, sue in their own names, serve on juries, have custody of their children, or engage in different types of employ-

differences in spite of the absence of any obvious distinctions. To enable this more nuanced analysis of gender construction in the law, feminist legal theory will be used.

Based on writings in feminist legal theory, three criteria can be proposed to determine if a law is male. These criteria are that the law systematically favors males and oppresses females, the law is neutral but has a negative effect on women, and the law embodies only the male experience.[13] Each of these factors applies to the biblical laws considered here. A finding that a law is male using feminist legal theory means that it establishes and maintains a pattern of male dominance in addition to female subordination.

1. *A law is male if it systematically favors men and oppresses women.* The BC and the DL systematically favor males because they confer upon males the right to control female sexuality. As discussed in Chapter 3, the implication of the laws concerning unlawful intercourse is that before her marriage or engagement, a female's sexuality is controlled by her father, and after marriage, it is controlled by her husband. Consequently, the husband is assured that his wife is a virgin and that the paternity of his children is unquestionable.[14] Furthermore, these laws ensure that a male will control female sexuality by forcing her to be economically dependent on him. By comparison, the Israelite female had fewer financial resources than those offered her ancient Near Eastern counterpart in parallel laws. The Mesopotamian laws, for example, include references to a married woman's dowry as her own property that could be inherited by her heirs.[15] Under specific circumstances, a married woman in Babylonia could initiate a divorce, claim her dowry, and return to her father's house.[16] Similarly, under some circumstances, Babylonian and Assyrian

ment'. Lynn Hecht Schafran, 'Is the Law Male?: Let Me Count The Ways', *Chicago-Kent Law Review* 69 (1993), p. 402.

13. These criteria have been adapted from those presented in the article by Sylvia A. Law and Patricia Hennessey, 'Is the Law Male?: The Case of Family Law', *Chicago-Kent Law Review* 69 (1993), pp. 345–58. The final criterion as discussed here does not appear in their article. According to Law and Hennessey, the third criterion refers to a law that is based on male moral reasoning. In his work on ancient Israel, Meir Malul has written that biblical sources, like other ANE sources, are 'male in emphasis, outlook, and orientation'. Malul, *Knowledge, Control, and Sex*, p. 347. Preferring to bracket questions of definition and categories concerning 'moral reasoning', the statement has been rephrased to fit the context of these biblical laws and examines their exclusively male outlook. Law and Hennessey also mention a fourth way in which a law may be male. Specifically, a law is male if a dichotomy exists between public and private worlds that are designated respectively as male and female. Law and Hennessey, 'Is the Law Male?', pp. 345–46. That the same dichotomy exists in the Hebrew Bible has been adequately noted already. For a survey of this and other issues in the development of feminist biblical criticism, see Exum, 'Developing Strategies of Feminist Criticism/Developing Strategies for Commentating the Song of Songs', in David J.A. Clines and Stephen D. Moore (eds.), *Auguries: The Jubilee Volume of the Sheffield Department of Biblical Studies* (JSOTSup, 269; Sheffield: Sheffield Academic Press, 1998), pp. 206–49.

14. Pressler, *Family Law*, pp. 42–43.

15. LH 162–164, HL 27, LNB 9–13. See also Westbrook, 'Mesopotamia: Old Babylonian Period', in Westbrook (ed.), *History of Ancient Near Eastern Law*, pp. 397–99.

16. LH 142. Various opinions have existed as to whether this law authorizes a married woman

laws gave a woman access to her own dowry and the use of a share of her husband's or father's estates.[17] No comparable laws appear in the BC or DL. Succinctly stated, the laws in the BC and DL favor males by enabling them to control the sexuality of their wives and daughters, and that advantage is reinforced by the absence of laws that would provide for women economically. The resulting economic disadvantages for females help to ensure their subordination to males.

By all appearances, the ways in which these laws favor man serve to oppress women. In an article defining oppression, Iris Marion Young identifies five different types in contemporary social movements: exploitation, marginality, powerlessness, violence, and cultural imperialism.[18] It is the category of powerlessness that aptly describes the treatment of women under these biblical laws that favor men. According to Young, powerlessness describes the situation in which 'people do not participate in making decisions that regularly affect the conditions of their lives and actions'.[19] Given the male control of female sexuality and financial resources, the BC and DL construct gender in such a way that female powerlessness arguably would result, and so they constitute a form of oppression.

2. *A law is male if it is neutral in form but has a disproportionately negative impact on females*. To argue that a law has a discriminatory impact presumes that a law is enforced. Indeed, this is the case in the current legal system with respect to laws alleged to have a discriminatory impact based on race and/or gender.[20] How-

to initiate a divorce. Yair Zakovitch, following Driver and Miles, found that this Babylonian law describes a situation that occurs prior to marriage, and so it does not constitute a divorce. Yair Zakovitch, 'The Woman's Rights in the Bible of Divorce', *The Jewish Law Annual* IV (1981), pp. 28–46 (35), n.15; Driver and Miles, *The Babylonian Laws*, pp. 298–303. See also Westbrook, *Old Babylonian Marriage Laws* (AfOB, 23; Horn.F. Berger, 1988), p. 81; and 'Mesopotamia: Old Babylonian Period', in Westbrook (ed.), *History of Ancient Near Eastern Law*, p. 387 n. 80. Zakovitch's position was contradicted in an article by E. Lipinski. Lipinski argues that a divorce is described there because the formula articulated by the female is tantamount to a declaration of divorce and implies that she has been living with her husband for some time. E. Lipinski, 'The Wife's Right to Divorce in the Light of an Ancient Near Eastern Tradition', *The Jewish Law Annual* IV (1981), pp. 9–27 (10–11). In agreement, M. Stol recognizes that the LH does permit a woman to divorce her husband for cause and acceptable grounds for a Babylonian woman obtaining a divorce was her husband's 'bad behavior'. M. Stol, 'Women in Mesopotamia', *JESHO* 38 (1995), pp. 130–31. By comparison, Deut. 24.1-4 indicates that the husband initiates the divorce, and no mention appears of the wife's ability to do so.

17. LH, 178–184; MAL(A) 26–27. In general, the legitimate sons of the deceased inherited his property automatically but a father could provide that his daughters receive an inheritance share 'alongside their brothers'. Similarly, a marital gift from a husband to a wife is frequently attested. Such a gift took effect after the husband's death and its 'purpose in all these cases was to maintain the wife during widowhood, it being anticipated that the property would eventually pass to the children of the marriage'. Westbrook, 'The Character of Ancient Near Eastern Law', in Westbrook (ed.), *History of Ancient Near Eastern Law*, pp. 1–90 (59–60, 62).

18. Iris Marion Young, 'Five Faces of Oppression', *The Philosophical Forum* XIX (1988), pp. 270–90.

19. Young, 'Five Faces of Oppression', p. 283.

20. In the contemporary American legal system, laws that are discriminatory in effect have been harder to challenge than those that have explicit gender and race biases. Law and Hennessey, 'Is the Law Male?', p. 345 n. 3.

ever, one of the basic assumptions of this inquiry is that the biblical laws discussed here may not have been enforced within a judicial system. At first glance, then, including this category here seems to be contradictory. But these laws could have had an impact outside of any legal process. First, these laws may express the redactors' condemnation of certain types of behavior engaged in predominantly by females, such as sorcery and apostasy. If so, by shaping notions of identity that excluded these activities, certain aspects of female behavior might have been controlled. Second, the laws could have been the basis for sanctioning through shaming, a sanction that may have been used to penalize deviant behavior in social as well as judicial contexts.[21] Because the laws could have had an impact both with or without applicable legal procedures, some attention must be given to the overwhelming evidence that females engaged in many of the practices targeted by the BC and the DL.

a. *Sorcery*. In Exod. 22.17 [22.18], female sorcerers are specifically condemned; therefore, a disproportionate impact on females is easy to recognize. Nevertheless, such an impact may exist even under the more inclusively phrased prohibition in Deut. 18.9-14 if women were more likely to practice sorcery. Karel van der Toorn makes just this argument.

> Juridically, a woman could only undertake an action against her husband or in-laws in extreme cases. Compared to her husband's rights, hers were scarcely protected. Many women did not wish to acquiesce in such a state of affairs and they set their minds on strategems to fend for themselves. One may imagine the following situation: a newly married woman seems to be no longer fertile after a first pregnancy. Not satisfied with one child, her husband takes a concubine. What must the first woman do with her anger over the humiliation; does she swallow it? Possibly. But she could also try to make her rival sick by means of spells, or deprive her husband of his potency by adding magical materials to his food. In other words, she became a sorceress.[22]

Later in the same discussion, van der Toorn makes his point more emphatically: 'curse and incantation are the weapons of the powerless'.[23] Indeed, he asserts that 'through witchcraft and sorcery women took revenge for their social subordination'.[24]

Athalya Brenner, too, finds that a female would have been more likely to use sorcery than a male but for a different reason than that proposed by van der Toorn. Brenner proposes that the sorcery proscribed in the biblical texts refers to female knowledge of birth control.[25] As mentioned earlier, Brenner argues that this asso-

21. Lyn Bechtel, 'Shame as a Sanction of Social Control in Biblical Israel: Judicial, Political, and Social Shaming', *JSOT* 49 (1991), pp. 47–76 (76). See also Victor H. Matthews, 'Honor and Shame in Gender-Related Legal Situations in the Hebrew Bible', in Matthews, Levinson and Frymer-Kensky (eds.), *Gender and Law*, pp. 97–112.

22. Van der Toorn, *From Her Cradle*, p. 113.

23. Van der Toorn, *From Her Cradle*, p. 116.

24. Van der Toorn, *From Her Cradle*, p. 116.

25. Brenner, *The Intercourse of Knowledge*, pp. 85–86.

ciation between what is deemed sorcery (or witchcraft) and female knowledge of fertility regulation is seen 'across cultures and times'.[26]

Nancy Bowen recently made the same association between a biblical condemnation of female activity and female medical knowledge. In her analysis of Ezek. 13.17-23 and its condemnation of female prophets, Bowen found that the language and imagery used there to condemn the activities of the female prophets is the same as that in Mesopotamian materials relating to pregnancy and childbirth.[27]

> The activities that Ezekiel ascribes to the female prophets thus share some of the same imagery as those various Mesopotamian incantations associated with childbirth. In particular they share the imagery of the binding and removal of knots or bands of cloth (13.18, 20, 21) and the use of grain and bread for ritual use (13.19).
>
> In addition to these references to magical practices associated with childbirth, there are other reasons for considering the possibility that these female prophets were engaged in some kind of ritual medical activity. According to the literature on medicine in the ancient Near East, health care and medicine were intertwined with theology.[28]

Whether due to their marital status (as argued by van der Toorn) or their medical knowledge (as proposed by Brenner and Bowen), females would have been more likely than males to engage in practices that would be deemed 'sorcery'. In this respect, the prohibitions against the practice of sorcery in the BC and DL – although neutral on their face – have a disproportionate impact on females. The laws on sorcery, therefore, are male.

b. *Apostasy*. It has been argued in this study that the laws condemning apostasy in the BC and DL are inclusive because they apply to males and females.[29] In Chapter 3, the argument was made that, as inclusive laws, the prohibitions against apostasy serve to construct a national Israelite identity. In spite of this apparent inclusivity, some scholars do believe that the establishment of the Yahweh-only cult had a disproportionately negative effect on the participation of women. Bird has even argued that female presence in the official cult became synonymous with 'heterodox practices'.[30] Likewise, Bowen has concluded that the condemnation of female participation in Ezek. 13.17-23 is associated with the establishment of cultic orthodoxy.

> For Ezekiel, the female prophets, along with some of their male counterparts, have no place in the priestly world of the new temple that he envisions. In his theology of the exile none of the former ways will survive YHWH's judgment. He is saying that this new situation of exile cannot be supported by old ideologies. But the functional aspect of this theology is that it restricts, or even eliminates, certain roles for women in the cult.[31]

26. Brenner, *The Intercourse of Knowledge*, p. 86.

27. Nancy R. Bowen, 'The Daughters of Your People: Female Prophets in Ezekiel 13.17-23', *JBL* 118 (1999), pp. 417–33 (423).

28. Bowen, 'Female Prophets', pp. 424–25.

29. Deut. 13.7-19 [13.6-18] and Deut. 17.2-7 are expressly inclusive. Exod. 22.19 [22.20] is implicitly inclusive.

30. Bird, 'The Place of Women', in *Missing Persons and Mistaken Identities*, p. 93.

31. Bowen, 'Female Prophets', pp. 432–33.

The apparent association of females with heterodox practices made by the biblical writers and observed by Bird and Bowen may have been warranted. Based on biblical references, scholars have recognized that women in ancient Israel practiced various religious rituals that were Mesopotamian in origin. Susan Ackerman, for example, has written about women in Judah during the sixth century BCE who worshiped the goddess called 'the Queen of Heaven' (Jer. 7.16-20; 44.15-19, 25).[32] As part of their worship, women baked cakes as offerings, and poured out libations and burned incense to her; all of which the prophet Jeremiah condemned. The Queen of Heaven worshiped in these practices is thought to be foreign in origin. To be precise, Ackerman sees the Queen of Heaven as 'a syncretistic goddess who combines the characteristics of both west Semitic Astarte and east Semitic Ištar'.[33]

Similarly, women are associated in Ezek. 8.14 with the cult of Tammuz which is Mesopotamian in origin.[34] Van der Toorn believes that women were drawn to the cult because it provided emotional satisfaction denied to them in official celebrations.[35] If women were more likely than men to be drawn to these rituals of foreign origin then they would be more likely than men to have been negatively affected by the condemnations of apostasy.

Clearly, female participation in the cult was limited directly as the result of measures to create cultic uniformity, but female participation was also limited by these measures indirectly. For example, Deut. 23.18-19 [23.17-18] prohibits the use of funds derived from prostitution in the cult. Because this proscription applies equally to males and females, it is an inclusive law that serves to construct Israelite national identity. But van der Toorn argues convincingly that this ban would have a disproportionate impact on women.[36] He suggests that women participated in cultic rituals by making vows, and these vows had to be accompanied by a monetary offering. Given the limited number of financial resources available to females, some may have resorted to prostitution to raise the necessary funds. The ban on using funds raised in this manner, when they had been accepted previously, would limit female participation in the cult indirectly.[37]

32. Susan Ackerman, '"And The Women Knead Dough": The Worship of the Queen of Heaven in Sixth-Century Judah', in Peggy L. Day (ed.), *Gender and Difference in Ancient Israel* (Minneapolis: Fortress Press, 1989), pp. 109–24 (110).

33. Ackerman, 'The Worship of the Queen of Heaven', p. 110.

34. Van der Toorn, *From Her Cradle*, pp. 116–17.

35. Van der Toorn, *From Her Cradle*, p. 116. Ackerman finds that the rituals for the Queen of Heaven and the cult of Tammuz are related. She bases her conclusion on the fact that the cakes baked as offerings for the Queen of Heaven are the staple food of Mesopotamian shepherds, and Tammuz is the patron shepherd of Mesopotamia. Ackerman, 'The Worship of the Queen of Heaven', p. 116.

36. Van der Toorn, 'Female Prostitution in Payment of Vows in Ancient Israel', JBL 108 (1989), pp. 193–205.

37. Phyllis Bird questions van der Toorn's analysis here for two reasons. First, he uses the term 'cultic prostitution' to include both 'occasional prostitution' to pay for vows and prostitution by cultic personnel as a source of temple income, and Bird finds 'this combination of practices under a cover term that lacks ancient attestation problematic'. Second, she argues that the extension of the prohibition to males becomes 'more enigmatic' if the rationale offered is 'in terms of the peculiar

Overall, the laws promoting cultic orthodoxy, including those laws against apostasy and sorcery in the BC and DL, condemn practices in which females are more likely to engage than males. As a result, these laws as constructed have a disproportionate impact on females and, therefore, are male.

c. *Centralization of worship*. The requirement to worship in Jerusalem mandated in Deuteronomy specifically applies to all Israelites regardless of age, class, and gender.[38] As covered in Chapter 3, this inclusive aspect of cultic participation serves to construct national Israelite identity. Nevertheless, this requirement would have a disproportionate impact on females. Specifically, the centralization of worship in Jerusalem had two important consequences: local shrines were to be destroyed (Deut. 12.1-4) and the Passover celebration no longer took place in Israelite households. These two changes could dramatically lessen the degree of cultic participation by women.

First, prior to centralization, the household had been an important locus of cultic activity, and the removal of cultic celebrations from the household would have adversely affected women. In her work, Carol Meyers describes the household as 'the dominant social unit' before the rise of the state, and the site of important religious activity.[39] Because the household was the primary realm for females,[40] a greater degree of participation by women could be anticipated in religious activity occurring within the household.

Likewise, the teraphim, cultic objects related to the ancient Israelite household, may have been associated with women. In general terms, van der Toorn connects biblical references to the teraphim with folk religion practiced before centralization.[41] Specifically, he finds that the teraphim, which he defines as statuettes that are usually affiliated with household gods, may well have played a role in the Israelite cult of honoring ancestors.[42] The most important feature of the teraphim for the purposes of this study is that 'the only two narrative references to teraphim in the Hebrew Bible place them in women's hands' (Gen. 31 and 1 Sam. 19)'.[43] With this relationship between the household, females, and cultic practices, the shift under the Deuteronomic Law away from the household to a centralized official cultic site would negatively impact women.

socioeconomic circumstances of women'. Bird, 'Male Cult Prostitute', p. 39 n. 8 and p. 42 n. 20. Since the objective of this study is to consider the laws as they appear in the biblical text and not to determine ancient Israelite practices based on these laws, Bird's objections to van der Toorn's argument are reasonable but not fatal.

38. Deut. 12.2-7, 16.1-17.

39. Meyers, *Discovering* Eve, pp. 161, 190.

40. Meyers, 'To Her Mother's House: Considering A Counterpart to the Israelite *Bêt 'Āb*', in Peggy L. Day, David Jobling and Gerald T. Sheppard (eds.), *The Bible and the Politics of Exegesis* (Cleveland: The Pilgrim Press, 1991), pp. 39–51.

41. Van der Toorn, *Family Religion in Babylonia, Syria and Israel: Continuity and Change in Forms of Religious Life* (Studies in the History and Culture of the Ancient Near East, VII; Leiden: E.J. Brill, 1996), pp. 206–235.

42. Van der Toorn, *Family Religion*, p. 225.

43. Bird, 'Israelite Religion and the Faith of Israel's Daughters: Reflections on Gender and Religious Definition', in *Missing Persons and Mistaken Identities*, pp. 103–122 (111). The women referred to here are Rachel and Michal respectively.

Second, the destruction of the local shrines would have a disproportionate impact on women. Women were thought to favor local sites because they were 'better suited to the general rhythms and exigencies of their lives than were the major communal rites and celebrations'.[44] Thus these biblical laws on sorcery, apostasy, and the centralization of worship, although inclusive and therefore neutral on their face, would tend to have a greater impact on females than males. These laws on the centralization of worship are therefore male.

3. *A law is male if it embodies only the male experience*. The biblical laws are presented in the narrative context of the Sinai covenant. As Plaskow has emphasized, in Exod. 19.15, Moses addresses the community only as men.[45] Most significantly, she notes that we do not know if women were there or what they heard because 'it was not their experience that interested the chronicler'.[46] To illustrate the manner in which only the male experience is encoded in the BC and DL, the topic of intercourse/rape in Deut. 22.22-29 will be reconsidered. As discussed in Chapter 3, the exclusive laws in the BC and DL essentially provide that a female's sexuality is to be controlled by her father before marriage and her husband after marriage. By implication then, if a man has sexual intercourse with a free woman who is not his wife, he is violating another man's rights. Consequently, in the constructs of the BC and DL, there is effectively no difference between consensual and forced intercourse, as that distinction would exist from the female's perspective. In comparison, there are cuneiform laws that expressly distinguish between forced and consensual intercourse.[47] The absence of such a distinction means that even if intercourse is forced upon the female, the sexual assault, for all intents and purposes, is against the man whose rights have been violated rather than the female. As a result, the notion of a sexual assault against a female does not exist in the BC and DL.[48]

Washington contends that the failure to acknowledge the notion of sexual violence against a female in these laws can be directly attributed to the construction of the masculine gender in the Hebrew Bible.[49] In his work on violence and the construction of gender, Washington found that the ability to exert violence in warfare is an important element of the definition of 'manhood' in the Hebrew Bible.[50] Correspondingly, the 'woman' becomes the 'one who succumbs to violence; hence men who are defeated in combat are reckoned as women'.[51] With this understanding of violence and the construction of gender, Washington turns his attention to the treatment of women in Deut. 22.

44. Bird, 'Faith of Israel's Daughters', p. 112.

45. Plaskow, *Standing Again at Sinai*, p. 25.

46. Plaskow, *Standing Again at Sinai*, p. 25.

47. See LE 26; MAL(A) 12, 55–56; LH 130. According to these provisions, when forced (non-consensual) intercourse has occurred, the woman is not subject to the death penalty even if she is married.

48. Washington, 'Violence and the Construction of Gender in the Hebrew Bible', p. 354; and Pressler, 'Sexual Violence and the Deuteronomic Law', pp. 109–10.

49. Washington, 'Violence and the Construction of Gender in the Hebrew Bible', p. 330.

50. Washington, 'Violence and the Construction of Gender in the Hebrew Bible', p. 330.

51. Washington, 'Violence and the Construction of Gender in the Hebrew Bible', p. 330.

Summarized briefly, the provisions in Deut. 22.22-29 provide that if the female is single and has been raped, the man must marry the female, and he cannot divorce her (Deut. 22.28-29). If the female is engaged when intercourse with another man occurs, the penalty is death for the male and, if she consented, she is to die as well (Deut. 22.23-27). If the female is married, the penalty is death for both the male and female (Deut. 22.22). As for adultery, Washington argues that these provisions demonstrate that 'adultery is defined as one male's violation of another man's right to possess a woman'.[52] Concerning violence against women, he finds that the deuteronomic laws do not prohibit sexual violence, but 'stipulate the terms under which a man may commit rape, provided he pays reparation to the offended male party'.[53]

On the basis of a relationship between violence and gender in these laws, Washington refutes Lynn Bechtel's analysis of the treatment of Dinah in Gen. 34.[54] In essence, Bechtel argues that rape is equated with force in contemporary definitions and, since the text does not refer to the use of force, Dinah may not have been raped by Shechem.[55] Washington thinks that Bechtel overlooks the obvious violence described in the text.

> Whatever light Bechtel's interpretation may shed on interactions among social groups with closely guarded corporate identities, this reading is not adequate to the brute fact of what happens to Dinah when she goes out, not to meet Shechem, but 'to visit the women of the region' (Gen. 34.1). Shechem sees (ראה) Dinah, takes her (לקח), then sexually penetrates and humiliates her (שׁכב and ענה, Gen. 34.2). Bechtel at once relates these events and denies them in her interpretation of Genesis 34.[56]

Furthermore, as pointed out by Pressler, 'the Deuteronomic laws suggest that the question of whether Shechem raped or seduced Dinah (Gen. 34) is moot' because the injury is to her father and brothers whose right to control her sexuality was violated.[57] Following the interpretations of Washington and Pressler means that Dinah may have consented but the fact of the matter is that her consent (or the absence of it) is irrelevant under the deuteronomic laws.

Given my own use of contemporary legal theory, I find commendable Bechtel's use of contemporary definitions of rape to elucidate biblical legal material. However, I have to conclude that her comparison is misdirected. She utilizes the contemporary definition of rape *per se* which traditionally requires a showing of force and a lack of consent. This comparison allows her to conclude that the sexual activ-

52. Washington, 'Violence and the Construction of Gender in the Hebrew Bible', pp. 353–54.

53. Washington, 'Violence and the Construction of Gender in the Hebrew Bible', p. 354.

54. Washington, 'Violence and the Construction of Gender in the Hebrew Bible', p. 357.

55. Lyn M. Bechtel, 'What If Dinah Is Not Raped', *JSOT* 62 (1994), pp. 19–36.

56. Washington, 'Violence and the Construction of Gender in the Hebrew Bible', p. 357. Similarly, Suzanne Scholz argues that Gen. 34.2 not only describes a rape but that the Hebrew verbs used and the order in which they are used emphasize Shechem's increasing use of violence against Dinah. Scholz, *Rape Plots: A Feminist Cultural Study of Genesis 34*, (Studies in Biblical Literature, 13; New York: Peter Lang Publishing, 2000), pp. 136–38.

57. Pressler, 'Sexual Violence and the Deuteronomic Law', p. 111.

ity in Gen. 34 is not a rape because Dinah may have consented.[58] Yet in the DL, the female's consent is not the determinative factor in establishing a sexual assault. Instead, the definition of illicit sexual activity in the DL depends on the female's relationship to a free Israelite male. As a result, any potential harm is based on the status of the female and not her consent.

In this respect, Bechtel's comparison to contemporary rape laws is misleading. She compares a context in which female consent is a determinative factor (the contemporary laws on rape) to one in which female consent is not a determinative factor (the relevant biblical laws). A more appropriate comparison here would be between two laws – contemporary and biblical – that define an illicit sexual activity according to the female's status. Such a comparison can be found in the contemporary laws on statutory rape, where because of the age of the person involved, consent is irrelevant. The difference between the treatment of illicit intercourse in Deut. 22 and in contemporary laws on statutory rape is that, in the contemporary law, the person's consent is irrelevant because of the person's age. In the biblical laws, consent is irrelevant because the person is a female. Obviously, a female who is raped considers the act to be a violation of her bodily integrity. The biblical laws discussed here, however, do not define the assault as one against the female. Consequently, these laws embody the male experience to the exclusion of the female one.

On the matter of rape in general, Sanday, in her anthropological work, found that the incidence of rape varies from one culture to another and that in a culture with an ideology of male dominance, females are more likely to be raped (a rape-prone culture) than in a culture that affirms female power and authority (a rape-free culture).[59] In his work on violence and the construction of gender in the Hebrew Bible, Washington relied on Sanday's analysis of rape-prone versus rape-free cultures.[60] Washington concluded that 'the prevalence of rape in biblical narrative suggests that ancient Israel might well be designated a rape culture'.[61] Most importantly,

58. Bechtel, 'Dinah', pp. 27–31.

59. Sanday, 'Rape and the Silencing of the Feminine', in Sylvana Tomaselli and Roy Porter (eds.), *Rape* (Oxford: Basil Blackwell, 1986), pp. 84–101. See also her article, 'The Socio-Cultural Context of Rape', pp. 5–27. My application of Sanday's work and its implications for the study of the Hebrew Bible contrast starkly with Carol Meyers' use of the same material. See Meyers, 'Procreation, Production, and Protection: Male-Female Balance in Early Israel', *JAAR* 51 (1983), pp. 569–93. Meyers uses Sanday's work to argue that women had somewhat more egalitarian relationships with men in the premonarchic highland environment of ancient Israel. She reaches this conclusion based on Sanday's findings that the most balanced societies are those in which men and women share nearly equally in subsistence tasks. Meyers, 'Procreation, Production, and Protection', p. 575. Finding that such a gender balance in tasks existed in that highland context, she concludes that interdependence characterizes male-female roles in the agrarian household. The difficulty with Meyer's interpretation is that Sanday also says that if women have higher status, then the corresponding culture is relatively rape-free. If ancient Israel, as evidenced in the laws and narratives mentioned in this discussion, constituted a male-dominant and therefore a rape-prone culture, then the accompanying subordination of females would undermine the possibility of interdependence as the pattern of male-female relationships in premonarchic Israel.

60. Washington, 'Violence and the Construction of Gender in the Hebrew Bible', p. 352 n.108.

61. Washington, 'Violence and the Construction of Gender in the Hebrew Bible', p. 353. Some

he sees clear evidence of a rape culture in the laws of Deut. 22.23-29. For him, 'the laws do not in fact prohibit rape; they institutionalize it and confirm men's control of women'.[62]

With the context of a rape culture in mind, the androcentric bias of those laws in Deut. 22.23-29 becomes even more obvious. First, the laws in Deut. 22.23-27 imply the female's consent to intercourse if the act took place in the city because it is presumed that, if she had cried out, she would have been rescued. However, the law overlooks the fact that the male involved might have used force. The force used actually could be in the form of a knife or other weapon, but even the threat of potential violence or harm could be sufficient to constitute force. In today's context, feminist scholars note that means of non-physical force are available to a rapist, 'including extortion, economic threats and deception'.[63] Without an allowance being made for the use of force in these laws, a betrothed female who has intercourse in the city with another man could be executed when her only 'crime' is having been raped.

Second, Deut. 22.28-29 on intercourse/rape with an unmarried (and unengaged) female provides that the man has to support her financially. The argument has been made that imposing such a financial obligation on the man serves as a deterrent to this type of behavior.[64] The likelihood that such a provision would actually deter a rape is small given that it applies only when the male is caught in the act. Few if any rapists are ever caught in the act, yet no law in the BC or DL allows for the rapist's punishment, as in MAL(A) §12, if witnesses can prove that the rape occurred.[65] These additional factors support Washington's conclusions that these laws are not meant to prevent rapes but function to legitimate male access to female sexuality.[66]

In addition to the Sanday article, Washington relied on an article by Dianne Herman in his analysis of ancient Israel as a rape culture.[67] Herman's article sketches out more fully the contours of today's rape culture in the United States, and it contains two insights of particular importance to this analysis of the BC and DL. First, Herman offers the following basic assumption of a rape culture, namely, that 'males are sexually aggressive and females are sexually passive'.[68]

of the biblical depictions of rape that Washington lists are the rape of Dinah (Gen. 34.2), Tamar (2 Sam. 13.11-15), and David's wives (2 Sam. 16.21-22).

62. Washington, 'Violence and the Construction of Gender in the Hebrew Bible', p. 353.

63. Dorothy Roberts, 'Rape, Violence, and Women's Autonomy', *Chicago-Kent Law Review* 69 (1993), pp. 359–95 (374). These same non-violent threats could have been effective in an ancient context, too.

64. Frymer-Kensky, 'Virginity in the Bible', in Matthews, Levinson and Frymer-Kensky (eds.), *Gender and Law*, p. 94.

65. A stronger but more ethically distasteful deterrent to rape is found in MAL(A) 55–56 which provides that the rapist's wife may be seized and raped.

66. Washington, 'Violence and the Construction of Gender in the Hebrew Bible', p. 353.

67. Dianne Herman, 'The Rape Culture', in Jo Freeman (ed.), *Women: A Feminist Perspective* (Palo Alto: Mayfield Publishing Company, 3rd edn, 1984), pp. 20–38, cited in Washington, 'Violence and the Construction of Gender in the Hebrew Bible', p. 356 n.123.

68. Herman, 'The Rape Culture', p. 20.

As presented by Herman, the problem with this concept of human sexuality is that, instead of characterizing healthy heterosexuality 'by loving, warm, and reciprocally satisfying actions', it connects sexuality with violence.[69] She argues that such a connection results from normal heterosexual relations in a rape culture being described as 'consisting of an aggressive male forcing himself on a female who seems to fear sex but unconsciously wants to be overpowered'.[70] Herman goes so far as to write that rape is the direct result of stereotypes that connect sexuality with violence.[71]

The same assumption that men are sexually aggressive and women are sexually passive has been noted in the Hebrew Bible. Steinberg, in her analysis of Deut. 22.23-27, finds that 'the man is always considered a consenting party', and 'the law does not entertain the possibility that he could have been coerced by the woman'.[72] The presumption here that men are always guilty but women are always innocent contributes to the notion that men are sexually aggressive but women are sexually passive.[73] Given the relationship Herman has identified between rape and cultures that construe sexuality in passive/aggressive terms, the presence of that pattern in the biblical laws indicates that they foster an ideology of male dominance.

A second insight from Herman's article stems from her discussion of a husband's reaction if his wife is raped. She finds that the husband may feel that the attack was an assault on his masculinity because he 'cannot protect, hold on to, and control his woman'.[74] The psychological damage of the wife's rape does not end there, because the husband may also feel that his wife willingly participated in the act or 'enjoyed the experience'.[75] In fact, one of the contemporary 'myths' about rape is that 'women secretly want to be raped'.[76] Male-oriented texts, then, may not acknowledge a woman's acts of resistance against rape. Specifically, Ken Stone

69. Herman, 'The Rape Culture', p. 21. Washington noted the same connection between violence and sexuality in the Hebrew Bible. See 'Violence and the Construction of Gender in the Hebrew Bible', pp. 330–31.

70. Herman, 'The Rape Culture', p. 21.

71. Herman, 'The Rape Culture', p. 34.

72. Steinberg, 'Adam's and Eve's Daughters', pp. 255–56. Similarly, in biblical narratives, David Carr has seen the same characterization of sexually aggressive males and sexually passive females in themes where 'men sow the seed of procreation' and 'women receive the seed and wives bear children who inherit the land'. David Carr, 'Gender and the Shaping of Desire in the Song of Songs and its Interpretations', *JBL* 119 (2000), pp. 233–48. Ken Stone, in his study of sexual imagery in the Deuteronomistic history, *Sex, Honor, and Power*, also concluded that the sexual acts depicted were all initiated by men and women are not portrayed as '*active initiators of sexual activity*'. Stone, *Sex, Honor, and Power*, p. 135 (italics in original).

73. There are no biblical laws that portray the woman as the sexual aggressor although there are biblical narratives to this effect. See, for example, Potiphar's wife (Gen. 39). In contrast, there are two ancient Near Eastern laws, LU 7 and MAL(A) 16 that describe a (married) woman as the one who initiated the unlawful sexual encounter. The woman's punishment varies between the two laws. In the Sumerian law, the woman is to be killed, but in the Middle Assyrian law, her punishment is determined by her husband. In both versions of the law, the man is not punished.

74. Herman, 'The Rape Culture', pp. 22–23.

75. Herman, 'The Rape Culture', p. 23.

76. Pamela Cooper-White, *The Cry of Tamar: Violence Against Women and The Church's Response* (Minneapolis: Fortress Press, 1995), pp. 85–86.

found in his study of sex in the Deuteronomistic History that 'there is little interest expressed in the possibility that the women may have tried to resist or fight off the sexual actions, some of which are extraordinarily violent'.[77]

Herman's profile of the husband involved may have a bearing on our understanding of the law on adultery in Deut. 22.22. That law does not exempt from punishment a married woman who has not consented to the act; but the law concerning the engaged woman does (Deut. 22.23-27). It is usually argued that the married woman's consent is required by inference from the subsequent laws on the engaged female.[78] In the context of a rape culture, though, it is not likely that such a requirement to show her consent would be implied. Given the information Herman provides, it is more likely that the husband would feel his wife somehow participated willingly even if she had not actually consented. Under laws that embody the male experience, then, her consent may simply be presumed.

Three criteria are suggested by feminist legal theory to indicate that a law is male: it privileges males, it disproportionately impacts females, and it embodies only the male experience. A finding of any one of these factors in a law would justify a conclusion that the law is male, but all three factors are present in the BC and DL. These laws are clearly male and as such they follow a gender-role pattern that supports and sustains male dominance.

On the whole, then, a culture's treatment of rape can provide a lens through which its notions of the masculine and the feminine can be evaluated. If masculinity is equated with male dominance and the subordination of females, as appears to be the case in the BC and DL, a rape culture is likely to exist. In such a culture, its law codes legitimate and organize rape as a practice. In the case of ancient Israel, though, these laws are neither the result of a democratic process nor do they necessarily represent generally held societal values.[79] Clearly, though, these laws express the ideology of male dominance/female subordination which lends credence to Washington's argument that ancient Israel may have been a rape culture.

Nevertheless, the objective of this study is not to reconstruct ancient Israelite society from these laws. Rather, the concern here is that, since these laws do construct gender, violence becomes integral to masculine and feminine identities – men can use force against women and women (and men) are conditioned to condone the use of that force. As Washington found, the association between violence and females in the biblical representations 'demonstrates that violence against a feminine object is elemental to normative masculinity'.[80]

77. Stone, *Sex, Honor, and Powe*r, p. 135.

78. Pressler, *Family Laws*, p. 32 and Burnette-Bletsch, 'The Agrarian Family', p. 248.

79. Because the redactors made sure that the laws were preserved, it can be assumed that they wanted them to have some type of influence in their cultural settings. Yet for these laws and their ideology of male dominance to have any influence at all, they may have had to fit within 'existing conceptual systems'. See Martha Albertson Fineman, *The Neutered Mother*, p. 21. If so, the pattern of male dominance/female subordination that is evident in the BC and DL probably reflects a similar conceptual system in some (male?) segments of Israelite society. However, it is also possible that these measures were an attempt to initiate a more patriarchal culture or that the pertinent 'conceptual system' was cultically rather than socially related.

80. Washington, 'Violence and the Construction of Gender in the Hebrew Bible', p. 331.

B. *The Repression of the Feminine: Law as Violence*

In the previous section, the BC and DL were shown to support the construction of masculinity as male dominance and that gender pattern is the corollary of the female subordination paradigm covered in the previous chapter. In this section, it is argued that these 'male' laws do not just allow violence against women to occur, but that they are a form of violence in and of themselves. The basis for this discussion is the classical critical theory of the Frankfurt School – specifically, the work of Theodor Adorno, Max Horkheimer, and Walter Benjamin. In addition, the work of the contemporary philosopher, Julia Kristeva, will be used. This discussion starts by tracing how the 'subordination of women' described under gender theory becomes the 'repression of the feminine' in classical critical theory.

1. *From the subordination of women to the repression of the feminine*. As mentioned previously, male traits such as aggressiveness and competitiveness that are thought to be inborn are, in fact, manifestations of a patriarchal ideology that 'sanctions the political and dominant role of men in the public and private spheres'.[81] By dominating the public sphere, men are able to control a culture's intellectual life, which means that the male perspective becomes standardized as 'knowledge'. Specifically, the modern field of philosophy known as 'epistemology', grounds the opposition between a universal knowing subject and a known object.[82]

Feminists have objected to this definition of knowledge because, in a historical context of gender construction based on male domination/female subordination, only men can be subjects and, therefore, knowers.[83] With only men as subjects and knowers, women become the objects and the unknowable.[84] Such a concept of knowledge is problematic because it allows men to treat women as the Other and correspondingly imposes an essential identity on women. Philosophically, to treat women as the Other becomes a larger issue than the treatment of females individually. Instead, the issue becomes one of the repression of 'Woman' or of 'the feminine'. Along these lines, the work of Theodor Adorno, a member of the Frankfurt School of critical theory, provides helpful insights into the problems incurred with a subject imposing an identity as 'Other' that results in the repression of the feminine.

In *Negative Dialectics*, Adorno rejected several of Hegel's formulations.[85] First, he argued that thinking is a process of imposing a single identity, and a thought or

81. Brittan, *Masculinity and Power*, p. 4.

82. See Susan J. Hekman, *Gender and Knowledge: Elements of a Postmodern Feminism* (Boston: Northeastern University Press, 1990), p. 9.

83. Hekman, *Gender and Knowledge*, p. 9.

84. In philosophical terms, women become unknowable either empirically or transcendentally. Women are unknowable empirically because they are associated with nature, whereas men are associated with reason and culture. See Genevieve Lloyd, *The Man of Reason: 'Male' and 'Female' in Western Philosophy* (Minneapolis: University of Minnesota Press, 2nd edn, 1993). Women are also considered unknowable because as 'Other' they have identities as transcendentally constructed 'objects'. See Hekman, *Gender and Knowledge*, pp. 73–104.

85. Theodor Adorno, *Negative Dialectics* (trans. E.B. Ashton; New York: Seabury, 1973).

a 'concept does not exhaust the thing conceived'.[86] Any concept of a 'totality is mere appearance'.[87] Second, Adorno concluded that Hegel's dialectics results in any contradictions being subsumed, when 'contradiction is non-identity under the aspect of identity'.[88] If we are to know an 'object', Adorno contends, any contradictions between reason (identity) and reality (the nature of the object) must be acknowledged. It is on the basis of this 'non-identity' of the subject and object, that Adorno developed his philosophy of 'negative dialectics'.[89]

The problem with the knowing subject imposing an identity on another person, Adorno found, is that the (male) subject then perceives the Other based on his own identity. Therefore, the subject never truly knows the Other. Instead, the subject merely seeks confirmation of the identity that he has imposed on the Other and any contradictory information offered by the Other is minimized or discounted.[90]

For Adorno, the process by which the subject reified an individual or a group into the conceptual object, and doing so by obscuring the fact that the difference between the subject and the 'object' is non-reducible, constitutes a form of violence.

> Idealism – most explicitly Fichte – gives unconscious sway to the ideology that the not-I, *l'autrui*, and finally all that reminds us of nature is inferior, so the unity of the self-preserving may devour it without misgivings. This justifies the principle of the thought as much as it increases the appetite. The system is the belly turned mind, and rage is the mark of each and every idealism.[91]

Based on Adorno's analysis, the process of the subject's determination of the identity of the Other as object is one that can be equated with 'devouring', and is filled with 'rage'. We can recognize, therefore, that the imposition of identity by the subject (privileged males) on the object (the Other) is a violent act because it renders impossible actual knowledge of the Other as different from the subject. Relating this analysis to the BC and DL, these laws not only subordinate females, they also impose a single constructed identity on all females that ignores similarities between males and females and differences between one female and another. As such, then, these laws constitute a form of violence.[92]

86. Adorno, *Negative Dialectics*, p. 5.

87. Adorno, *Negative Dialectics*, p. 5. Hegel's famous statement is that 'the Absolute alone is true'. G.W.F. Hegel, *The Phenomenology of Mind* (trans J.B. Baillie; London: George Allen & Unwin Ltd., 2nd edn, 1964), p. 133.

88. Adorno, *Negative Dialectics*, p. 5.

89. Susan Buck-Morss, *The Origin of Negative Dialectics: Theodor W. Adorno, Walter Benjamin, and the Frankfurt Institute* (New York: The Free Press, 1977), p. 63.

90. As a result, the groups that could be desginated as 'Other' vary. For example, because in today's setting the subject is always male and white and almost always Christian and privileged, the 'Other' could be non-Christians, women, people of color, or the poor.

91. Adorno, *Negative Dialectics*, pp. 22–23 (italics in original).

92. In her article on oppression, Iris Marion Young cites 'cultural imperialism' as one of its types. She defines 'cultural imperialism' as 'the experience of existing with a society whose dominant meanings render the particular perspectives and point of view of one's own group invisible at the same time as they stereotype one's group and mark it out as the Other'. Young, 'Five Faces of Oppression', p. 285. From another perspective, then, the designation of the feminine as Other constitutes oppression, hence, a form of violence.

Not only is the conceptual repression of the Other a form of violence, Adorno argues, but that repression makes actual physical violence against the Other more probable. Actual violence against the Other results from the complete (conceptual) identification of the designated group with the identity imposed on it by the subject. Collectively, as the Other, this group ceases to be considered human, and becomes 'a specimen'.[93] For Adorno, then, Auschwitz is an instance of 'identity' dynamic when Jews were targeted as the Other.[94]

Similarly, the theorist, Julia Kristeva, recognizes the dramatic separation of males and females that renders females the 'Other'.[95] Moreover, Kristeva places that gender pattern squarely within the monotheistic tradition of Judaism and Christianity.

> Monotheistic unity is sustained by a radical separation of the sexes: indeed, it is this very separation which is its prerequisite. For without this gap between the sexes, without its localization of the polymorphic, orgasmic body, desiring and laughing, in the *other* sex, it would have been impossible, in the *symbolic realm*, to isolate the principle of One Law – the One, Sublimating, Transcendent Guarantor of the ideal interests of the community.[96]

For Kristeva, the result of this 'radical separation of the sexes' is both the subordination of women and the repression of the feminine. As she writes, this monotheism 'represses, along with paganism, the greater part of agrarian civilizations and their ideologies, women and mothers'.[97] Furthermore, women, as Other, are outside of the male-defined and male-established symbolic order and can partici-

93. Adorno, *Negative Dialectics*, p. 362.

94. Adorno, *Negative Dialectics*, p. 362. The violent result of identity politics can be seen in the treatment of additional populations that have been designated as 'Other' by those who have the ability to do so. With respect to women, the witch hunts of an earlier era serve as an example. See Marsha Aileen Hewitt, *Critical Theory of Religion: A Feminist Analysis* (Minneapolis: Fortress Press, 1995), p. 84. A similar analysis could be made for African-Americans, and the occurrence of 'mass death' is the slave trade. That type of violence, though, is transformed in the contemporary era. Instead, African-American groups are subjected to 'disciplines', violence in the form of systemic discrimination that results in higher incarceration rates, among other things. For an analysis of the historical movement from state imposition of capital punishment to the 'disciplines', see Michel Foucault, *Discipline and Punish*.

95. Julia Kristeva, 'About Chinese Women', in Toril Moi (ed.), *The Kristeva Reader* (trans. Leon S. Roudiez and Sean Hand; New York: Columbia University Press, 1986), pp. 138–59.

96. Kristeva, 'About Chinese Women', p. 141 (italics in the original). Kristeva's dinstinction between the semiotic realm (feminine) and the symbolic realm (masculine) builds on the work of Jacques Lacan. For a detailed discussion of Kristeva's use of Lacan's psychoanalytic theory, see Martha J. Reineke, *Sacrificed Lives: Kristeva on Women and Violence* (Bloomington: Indiana University Press, 1997), pp. 17–48.

97. Kristeva, 'About Chinese Women', p. 141. For Kristeva, the fear underlying the construction of woman as Other is 'fear of the archaic mother' and 'her generative power' which 'patrilineal filiation' sees itself as having 'the burden of subduing'. Kristeva, *Powers of Horror: An Essay on Abjection* (European Perspectives; trans. Leon S. Roudiez; New York: Columbia University Press, 1982), p. 77. Because that fear is based on the potential of procreation and not its actuality, Kristeva uses the words 'the feminine', 'woman' and 'mother' as related, if not synonymous, terms.

pate in it only by 'childbearing and procreation in the name of the father'.[98] Based on Kristeva's analysis, then, the repression of the feminine and the emphasis on women procreating for the household patriarch, both of which were dynamics identified in the BC and DL, are related phenomenon.

Moreover, Kristeva relates the suppression of the feminine to violence, as does Adorno. In *Powers of Horror*, Kristeva considers 'defilement' to refer to that which is outside of the symbolic system and, because women are not part of the male symbolic system, they are associated with defilement.[99] As a result, Kristeva understands circumcision, as mandated in Leviticus, to be a ritual that 'concerns an alliance with the God of the chosen people' but it also functions to separate the son from the mother who is 'the other sex, impure, defiled'.[100] Kristeva then reiterates that 'symbolic identity presupposes the violent difference of the sexes'.[101]

Rather than being limited to the realm of religion, Kristeva sees the need for separation from the mother elsewhere. In the semiotic realm, as part of the human maturation process, the mother initially appears to the infant as indistinguishable from himself and this sameness triggers a later mimetic conflict because the infant must separate from the mother as he develops speech and moves toward becoming 'I', a subject in the symbolic realm.[102] Described another way, the cost of becoming a subject is through the sacrifice of the mother.[103] Using Kristeva's theory of sacrifice more generally, physical and emotional violence against women can be

98. Kristeva, 'About Chinese Women', p. 146. It is important to know that Kristeva refers to the 'symbolic' in two different ways – as the Symbolic Order itself (with an uppercase 'S') and as an element (the symbolic with a lowercase 's') within the Symbolic. As described by Kelly Oliver, 'the symbolic is the element within the Symbolic against which the semiotic works to produce the dialectical tension that keeps society going'. Kelly Oliver, *Reading Kristeva: Unraveling the double-bind* (Bloomington: Indiana University Press, 1993), pp. 9–10.

99. Kristeva, *Powers of Horror*, pp. 65, 112. Kristeva's understanding of defilement as a process that demarcates groups differentiated by class, gender, or age, is borrowed from the work of Mary Douglas. See Reineke, *Sacrificed Lives*, pp. 105–27.

100. Kristeva, *Powers of Horror*, p. 100.

101. Kristeva, *Powers of Horror*, p. 100. Kristeva's concept of circumcision as a sacrificial ritual that separates sons from their mothers parallels the work of Nancy Jay on the use of sacrificial rituals in patrilineal systems. See Nancy Jay, *Throughout Your Generations Forever: Sacrifice, Religion, and Paternity* (Chicago: University of Chicago Press, 1992).

102. Kristeva, *Powers of Horror*, p. 112. As for the development of a girl, the fact that the mother and child are of the same sex raises the issue of homosexual desire and that desire is later transferred to a male. Accordingly, Kristeva sees a process 'in which individuation is set against the demands of procreativity as well as constantly interacting with the allure of sameness – or homosexual desire, and in which heterosexuality implies a more or less successful transcendence of homosexual fixation'. Anne-Marie Smith, *Julia Kristeva: Speaking the Unspeakable* (Modern European Thinkers; Sterling, VA: Pluto Press, 1998), pp. 87–88. It is worth noting that Judith Butler finds Kristeva's 'body politics' problematic. Butler prefers Foucault's framework where concepts of sex and sexuality are the result of socially-constructed 'discourses' and not a presumed biological-determination. See Butler, *Gender Trouble*, pp. 79–92.

103. In *Violence and the Sacred* (trans. Patrick Gregory; Baltimore: The Johns Hopkins University Press, 1977), René Girard also used mimesis and sacrifice as significant themes in his work on sociocultural formation. For an excellent analysis of the similarities and differences between the work of Kristeva and that of Girard, see Reineke, *Sacrificed Lives*, pp. 65–104.

thought of as constituting a 'sacrificial economy' where women are sacrificed as the cost of maintaining (male) individual or collective connections to the symbolic realm.[104] Kristeva's work on gender, then, shows the connection between the repression of the feminine and violence against women, whereby the women are rendered sacrificial objects.

We have just seen that, by rendering groups, 'the Other', the conceptual repression of another group makes physical violence against that group more palatable. Specifically, the approaches of Adorno and Kristeva show us that the repression of the feminine in the male-oriented laws in the BC and DL foreshadows the violence against women referred to as a rape culture in those same laws.[105] Indeed, once male dominance in the BC and DL was found, a finding of a rape culture could have been anticipated. Again, the issue here is not primarily whether ancient Israel was, in fact, a rape culture. Instead, the underlying issue here, which will be covered in the next chapter, is the impact that such a paradigm has in today's context.

2. *From the repression of the feminine to the construction of masculinity.* As indicated in the previous section, the violence of the repression of the feminine is related to actual physical violence against women. In this respect, women suffer directly from imposed constructions of dominance/subordinate gender roles. However, an often overlooked fact is that the repression of the feminine also has a negative impact on men. This negative impact occurs because patriarchal ideologies of male dominance/female subordination are not biologically determined and must be constantly reinforced. Therefore, the resultant harm to males is the anxiety that stems from maintaining an oppositional difference between males and females as a social construction. In this section, using the analysis of Theodor Adorno and Max Horkheimer in their work, *Dialectic of Enlightenment*,[106] it will be seen that not only does the repression of the feminine work against both men and women, but that there is also an indication of the harmful effect of such repression in the biblical laws.

It is generally recognized that in the male-dominated Western culture, reason was initially set in opposition to and then valued over nature; and women, because of reproductive abilities, have been associated with nature.[107] In *Dialectic of Enlight-*

104. Reineke, *Sacrificed Lives*, pp. 11–12.

105. Washington, 'Violence and the Construction of Gender in the Hebrew Bible', p. 353.

106. Theodor W. Adorno and Max Horkheimer, *Dialectic of Enlightenment* (trans. John Cumming; New York: Herder & Herder, 1972).

107. Genevieve Lloyd, *The Man of Reason*, p. 2. Similarly, in his work on epistemological themes in ancient Israel and the ANE, Malul refers to the 'widely known homology between the earth or land and the woman' which asserts that 'the land is symbolically perceived to be female in nature and function'; and the woman and the land are to be somehow 'owned' by the male element. As a result, he considered this homology to indicate that 'to let the woman – as a woman – own land would seem self-contradictory'. Malul, *Knowledge, Control, and Sex*, pp. 357–58. According to Sanday's *Female Power and Male Dominance*, the association of females with nature is indicative of a male dominant/female subordinate gender-role pattern. Sanday reminds us, however, that male dominance is only one of two 'scripts' for male-female roles. Therefore, the script for male dominance seen in these biblical laws and Western civilization are not inevitable and need not exist.

enment, Adorno and Horkheimer explain the pattern of male domination/female subordination in Western civilization on the basis of women's classification as 'nature' and men's desire to overcome weakness and, correspondingly, nature that is a 'key stimulus to aggression'.[108] In this schema, the attributes associated with the feminine are nature, powerlessness, weakness, and domesticity. Correspondingly, the masculine, defined in dichotomous logic as the opposite of the feminine, means that men are strong, powerful, and associated with reason and culture. To Adorno and Horkheimer, the disturbing result of defining masculinity in this way is that men, who become estranged from nature and from their own selves, 'must always suppress their fear'.[109] In this regard, the repression of the feminine in a culture of male dominance harms men too because they must then suppress the natural aspects of being human within themselves that are considered feminine, namely, weakness, fear, powerlessness. Yet, additional attributes associated with feminine domesticity such as emotional expressiveness and the ability to nurture must also be repressed. The problem is that these suppressed qualities are not inherently different for males and females. To the contrary, these qualities are similar for both sexes.[110]

In the context of the BC and DL, the construction of masculinity as male dominance is evident. At the same time, we know from the discussion on classical critical theory that the repression of the feminine is an essential feature of the male dominance gender paradigm. Some evidence of a struggle to repress those human qualities should be evident in the biblical text – and it is. Specifically, Brenner, in her discussion of the law on cross-dressing in Deut. 22.5, concludes that it attests to 'anxiety' and 'uncertainty'.[111]

> A male sexual body may be primarily recognizable by its penis and ability to produce semen; a woman's sexual body is primarily defined by virginity (or its lack) and then menstruation. But penis and semen, virginity and menstruation and other sex-specific bodily attributes are not immediately apparent. They can be disguised or obliterated by clothing. 'There should not be a man's outfit on a woman, and a man should not wear a woman's garment, for all this is an abomination for Yhwh your god' (Deut. 22.5). This short passage betrays a concern, perhaps anxiety, about visible differences between the clothed male and female bodies: they should be clear-cut. The insistence on easily recognizable boundaries often signifies uncertainty about those same boundaries.[112]

108. Adorno and Horkheimer, *Dialectic of Enlightenment*, p. 248.

109. Adorno and Horkheimer, *Dialectic of Enlightenment*, p. 112.

110. Gayle Rubin, 'The Traffic in Women: Notes on the "Political Economy" of Sex', in Rayna Reiter (ed.), *Toward an Anthropology of Women* (New York: Monthly Review Press, 1975), pp. 157–210 (180).

111. Brenner, *The Intercourse of Knowledge*, p. 31.

112. Brenner, *The Intercourse of Knowledge*, p. 31. Later in her discussion, Brenner finds that the anxiety evident in this law on cross-dressing is anxiety 'about *male* sexual and social identity', and that the law is another expression of 'the safeguarding of male sexual autonomy…for it signifies male social supremacy'. Brenner, *The Intercourse of Knowledge*, p. 145 (italics in original).

The anxiety described by Brenner results from gender constructions with a male-dominant paradigm. Because the ascribed gender attributes of male dominance and the corresponding social authority must be continuously produced and reproduced throughout a given cultural system, anxiety occurs when blurring of those constructed boundaries seems to occur. A gender-role pattern of male domination, therefore, harms women by making violence against them more likely; but it also harms men. If Brenner's analysis of Deut. 22.5 is correct, such a pattern in the biblical texts can be seen to harm men by producing anxiety as they strive to perpetuate artificially created gender differences.[113]

3. *Conclusions*

The BC and DL, because they inscribe a patriarchal ideology that constructs masculinity as male dominance and, correspondingly, female subordination, are inherently a form of violence. In this respect, the problem with these laws is not only that they fail to recognize rape as a crime against the female, a fact that has been identified in earlier work. More importantly, these laws are problematic because they fail, through the repression of the feminine, to consider the female experience at all.

Although the BC and DL may or may not indicate that a rape culture actually existed in ancient Israel, the results of this study severely challenge the notion that the DL 'shows a particularly humanistic attitude towards women'.[114] That positive view of these laws has been expressed recently by Eckart Otto who asserts that 'the family laws in the Book of Deuteronomy had a progressive and protective attitude to the legal status of women' and that 'they were deeply concerned with the restriction of male predominance'.[115] Using a diachronic approach, Otto finds that these laws are an improvement in the legal status of women. To him, the law on the unbetrothed virgin in Deut. 22.28-29 protects women from divorce during a period of increased divorces during the Judean monarchy.[116] It is true that the law ensures that the woman is economically provided for by the male involved. But such a law also reinforces the notion that female sexuality is to be controlled by a male. In the same way, Otto finds that the law on the slandered bride in Deut. 22.13-21 protects women from unfair divorce.[117] Yet, as discussed in Chapter 2, this law effectively confers upon a man the right to a wife who has not had previous sexual experience. Similarly, Otto identifies the law on levirate marriage

113. In today's culture, the harmful effects of the male dominant/female subordinate pattern are all too obvious. With the recent number of violent attacks by schoolboys, the construction of masculinity that forces boys away from interpersonal support is being questioned. See William Pollack, *Real Boys: Rescuing Our Sons from the Myths of Boyhood* (New York: Harry Holt & Co., 1999); James Garbarino, *Lost Boys: Why Our Sons Turn Violent and How We Can Save Them* (New York: Free Press, 1999); and Dan Kindlon and Michael Thompson, with Teresa Barker, *Raising Cain: Protecting the Emotional Life of Boys* (New York: Ballantine, 1999).

114. Weinfeld, *Deuteronomy and the Deuteronomic School*, p. 291.

115. Otto, 'False Weights', p. 140.

116. Otto, 'False Weights', p. 133.

117. Otto, 'False Weights', pp. 134–37.

in Deut. 25.5-10 as one that provides women with legal standing in local court proceedings.[118] However, as noted in Chapter 3, if the male relative refuses to comply, he would still inherit his portion of the deceased's property, but the widow would be rendered destitute.

In finding that these laws intend to 'restrict male predominance', Otto's analysis fails to adequately acknowledge the degree to which that male predominance still exists in the laws. For example, there is a difference in the penalty prescribed for the male rapist in these laws that depends on whether the female involved is betrothed or unbetrothed. If she is unbetrothed, he is to marry her (Deut. 22.28-29), but if she is betrothed, the penalty is death (Deut. 22.25-27). As Judith Hauptman has pointed out, the female's injury is identical in both cases, so the determinative factor appears to be the injury inflicted upon the betrothed male.[119] The rapist has to die because the betrothed male has suffered a loss for which he cannot be compensated, namely, 'that he will no longer be the first to have sex with her'.[120] Hauptman's analysis here serves as a fine example of the manner in which the male perspective is encoded in the biblical laws. Instead of restricting male predominance as Otto contends, these laws on women in the DL reinforce it.

To consider the female experience in the BC and DL, as proposed in this discussion, means that traditional interpretations of these laws as humanitarian in nature must be questioned. That questioning then offers an opportunity for change. As expressed by Walter Benjamin, another member of the Frankfurt School, the questioning of traditional thought creates a tension that is 'the sign of a Messianic cessation of happening, or put differently, a revolutionary chance in the fight for the oppressed past'.[121] In this study, however, both the present and the past are of concern.

It is proposed here that the biblical laws' gender-role pattern of male dominance, one that is prevalent and affirmed today, creates a sociocultural atmosphere in which actual physical violence against women becomes predictable. As articulated by Marion Iris Young, physical violence and the threat of physical attack constitute one of the 'five faces of oppression' because such violence is systematized and legitimated in ways that serve to maintain sexist (as well as racist and heterosexual) privilege.[122] Given the detrimental effects of the dominance/subordination gender paradigm, as shown in the next chapter, it is clear that our notions of gender as well as our usual interpretations of these texts must be reconsidered.

In fact, to minimize the detrimental effects of the dominance/subordination paradigm, the 'Other' must be re-conceptualized. For that task, Kristeva may offer us crucial guidance. In her analysis of the biblical story of Ruth, Kristeva gives an interpretation of the narrative that envisions the re-integration of the 'Other'.[123] She

118. Otto, 'False Weights', pp. 138–40.

119. Hauptman, 'Rabbinic Interpretation of Scripture', p. 474.

120. Hauptman, 'Rabbinic Interpretation of Scripture', p. 474.

121. Walter Benjamin, 'Theses on the Philosophy of History', in Hannah Arendt (ed.), *Illuminations: Essays and Reflections* (New York: Schocken Books, 1986), pp. 262–63.

122. Young, 'Five Faces of Oppression', p. 287.

123. Kristeva, 'Ruth the Moabite', in *Strangers to Ourselves* (trans. Leon S. Roudiez; New York: Columbia University Press, 1991), pp. 69–76.

emphasizes that Ruth, David's ancestor, is not only a foreigner, but a Moabite and as such she is a descendant of incest. She then writes, 'foreignness and incest were thus at the foundation of David's sovereignty', where the 'conception of sovereignty [is] based on the rejected, the unworthy, the outlaw'.[124] In Kristeva's psychoanalytical framework, the significance of the 'outsider' within the tradition is that 'the assimilated foreigner works on the faithful himself from the inside', which results in the believer having to identify with that outlaw who is part of his own identity.[125]

> If David is *also* Ruth, if the sovereign is *also* a Moabite, peace of mind will then never be his lot, but a constant quest for welcoming and going beyond the other in oneself.[126]

In this way, Kristeva shows us that 'the inner, unconscious wound of the individual must first be understood before it is possible to establish effective measures for addressing estrangement on a social level'.[127] Consequently, the healing of that 'unconscious wound' is integral to changing the polarized constructions of 'masculinity' and 'femininity'.

124. Kristeva, 'Ruth the Moabite', p. 75.

125. Kristeva, 'Ruth the Moabite', pp. 75–76.

126. Kristeva, 'Ruth the Moabite', p. 76 (italics in the original).

127. Morny Joy, Kathleen O'Grady, and Judith L. Poxon (eds.), 'Editors' Introduction to "The Chosen People and the Choice of Foreignness"', in *French Feminists on Religion: A Reader* (New York: Routledge, 2002), pp. 150–52 (150). Iris Marion Young, too, found that the use of violence to maintain privilege 'must be traced to unconscious structures of identity formation which project onto some groups the fluid, bodily aspect of the subject that threatens the rigid unity of that identity'. Young, 'Five Faces of Oppression', p. 287.

Chapter 5

IMPLICATIONS

1. *Dominance/Subordination and Violence Against Women Today*

The argument has been made that the male dominant/female subordinate gender paradigm, given its suppression of the feminine, is inherently a form of violence against women. The additional argument, explored more fully in this chapter, is that the inherent violence of that gender paradigm makes actual violence against women more likely. Although the connection between the male dominance paradigm and actual violence against women may appear at first glance to be strained, that very connection has been established in both historical and contemporary contexts. To support the arguments made here, a brief discussion of the connection between dominance/subordination and violence against women in both of these contexts is warranted.[1]

A. *Dominance/Subordination: Historical Contexts*

The connection between the male dominance/female subordination gender paradigm and symbolic violence can be seen as early as the first-century of the common era. Pieter Botha suggests that the first-century world was one where 'magic' is not merely 'in' the environments of the Old Testament and New Testament but 'magical beliefs and practices *constituted* much of the world in which the ancients *lived*.[2] He goes on to describe a 'magical formulary' from that ancient context where the client is instructed to make two figures of wax or clay – a male one that

1. As a Christian and an African-American, as well as for the sake of brevity, I will only discuss the connection between Christianity, the male dominance paradigm, and violence against women in the United States. However, similar investigations can and should be done for other religious traditions and national settings. See, for example, Barbara Swirski, 'Jews Don't Batter Their Wives: Another Myth Bites the Dust', in Barbara Swirski and Marilyn P. Safir (eds.), *Calling the Equality Bluff: Women in Israel* (Elmsford, NY: Pergamon Press, 1991), pp. 319–27; Naomi Graetz, *Silence is Deadly: Judaism Confronts Wifebeating* (Northvale, NJ: Jason Aronson Press, 1998), Warren Rosenberg, *Legacy of Rage: Jewish Masculinity, Violence, and Culture* (Amherst, MA: University of Massachusetts Press, 2001); Mary John Mananzan, and others (eds.), *Women Resisting Violence: Spirituality for Life* (Maryknoll, NY: Orbis Books, 1996); Adrien Katherine Wing (ed.), *Global Critical Race Feminism: An International Reader* (New York: New York University Press, 2000); and Sheila Meintjes, Anu Pillay and Meredeth Turshen (eds.), *The Aftermath: Women in Post-Conflict Transformation* (New York: Zed Books, 2001).

2. Pieter J.J. Botha, 'Submission and Violence: Exploring Gender Relations in the First-Century World', *Neotestamentica* 34 (2000), pp. 1–38 (6) (italics in the original).

is armed with a sword and one female figure that is kneeling with her arms tied behind her back.[3]

> The formulary instructs that specific magical words should be written on particular parts of the female figure and then, using thirteen copper nails, to pierce various body parts saying, 'I pierce [the various body parts] of so-and-so, so that she will think of no one except for me, so-and-so alone'.[4]

Botha, while acknowledging that some scholars think that such 'love magic' may only be 'constructive symbolism' or 'therapy for a troubled person', assesses those practices differently by recognizing that 'violence (or the menace of violence) is a strategy of intimidation in the service of (male) domination'.[5]

> To allow *any* violence, even simulated, symbolized or ritualized, just makes it that much easier to accept *actual* violence; to not only live with it, but to condone it and to allow it to thrive.[6]

Botha traces the subordination of women in this time period to a worldview that understands the structure of reality to be like 'a huge vertical chain' with 'higher beings and properties' situated above 'lower beings and properties'.[7] Botha finds that, under 'the chain of being' women are conceptually placed in secondary and subordinate positions throughout their lives.[8] More importantly, though, he proposes that 'the great chain "metaphor" operates not merely to characterize the nature of the levels of "reality" but in fact to *create* them'.[9]

> Consequently, consider the *embodiment* of that ancient point of view. It is not simply a matter of men having 'authority' over women. This 'authority' had a distinct and powerful *materiality*: 'real' humans with 'proper' bodies above 'inferior', not fully humans with 'improper' bodies.[10]

In classical Christianity, the subordination of women was based, among other things, on those supposedly 'improper bodies'. Based on Aristotelian biology, Scholastic theology deemed females to be 'misbegotten males' and Augustine's position was that women, as imperfect humanity, 'cannot represent Christ who is perfect humanity'.[11] Women's subordinate status was justified by referencing specific biblical texts as well. One way of doing so is based on the hierarchical structure of patriarchy and the parallels made between the Lord's relationship over man and that of man over woman.

3. Botha, 'Submission and violence', p. 7.
4. Botha, 'Submission and violence', p. 7.
5. Botha, 'Submission and violence', pp. 8, 16.
6. Botha, 'Submission and violence', p. 18 (italics in the original).
7. Botha, 'Submission and violence', p. 18.
8. Botha, 'Submission and violence', p. 19.
9. Botha, 'Submission and violence', p. 19 (italics in the original).
10. Botha, 'Submission and violence', p. 19 (italics in the original).
11. Rosemary Radford Ruether, 'The Western Tradition and Violence against Women', in Joanne Carlson Brown and Carole R. Bohn (eds.), *Christianity, Patriarchy, and Abuse: A Feminist Critique* (New York: Pilgrim Press, 1989), pp. 31–41 (32).

> The term 'lord' (*dominus*) was used simultaneously for God as Lord of the world, the aristocracy as masters of the lower classes, and finally the male head of household as lord of his wife, children, and servants. The oft-repeated metaphor, drawn from St. Paul, that the woman has no head of her own, but her husband is her head as she is his body, summed up the subjugated status of woman.[12]

Furthermore, in First Timothy 2.12-14, female subordination is justified on the basis of Eve's actions in Gen. 3.

> I permit no woman to teach or to have authority over a man; she is to keep silent. For Adam was formed first, then Eve; and Adam was not deceived, but the woman was deceived and became a transgressor (NRSV).

Citing this text, Rosemary Radford Ruether states that traditional Christian theology adopted this reading of the 'Fall' so that Eve 'was disproportionately responsible for sin'.[13] As Ruether concludes, '[w]oman's subordinate status, therefore, not only reflects her original inferior nature but also is a just punishment for her guilt in causing evil to come into the world, thereby leading to the death of Christ'.[14] In the same article, Ruether connects these views on the subordination of women to actual violence against women in the witch hunting that develops in the late Middle Ages.[15] She points out that the targets of these hunts were usually women who were not appropriately subordinate. The women 'most likely to be regarded as the town witches', she writes, were 'marginal women, women who did not fall under "proper" male authority, women who talked back and led their lives independently'.[16] In effect, then, witch hunts can be understood as demonstrating the use of violence to keep women in a subordinate status.

The rationales for female subordination seen in the earliest stages of the history of Christianity – her lower place on the 'chain of being', her inferior body, and her responsibility for sin – remained prevalent in sixteenth-century England.[17] Based on this relationship of dominance and subordination, 'the use of violence was accepted as a necessary means of maintaining order in hierarchical relationships, both within and outside the household'.[18] England, like other European countries at that time, had legal codes which 'allowed husbands to inflict what was called "moderate correction" on their wives, besides beating children and servants when they

12. Ruether, 'The Western Tradition', pp. 31 and 41. The scriptural references here are to 1 Cor. 11.3 and Eph. 5.22-28.

13. Ruether, 'The Western Tradition', p. 32.

14. Ruether, 'The Western Tradition', p. 32. See also Ruether, *Sexism and God-Talk: Toward a Feminist Theology* (Boston: Beacon Press, 1983), pp. 94–99.

15. Ruether, 'The Western Tradition', p. 36. For a feminist analysis of witch-hunting using Kristeva's work, see Reineke, *Sacrificed Lives*, pp. 128–60.

16. Ruether, 'The Western Tradition', p. 36. Two other theories concerning witch hunts noted by Ruether here are that they were 'an effort to reduce an excess marginal female population or an effort by the rising medical profession to eliminate its popular rivals'.

17. Anthony Fletcher, *Gender, Sex & Subordination in England 1500–1800* (New Haven: Yale University Press, 1995), pp. xvi–xvii and p. 286.

18. Fletcher, *Gender, Sex & Subordination*, p. 192.

found it necessary'.[19] Some minimal guidelines for 'correcting' did exist: 'that the violence should not draw blood and that if a stick was used it should be no thicker than a man's thumb, the original source of the idea of a rule of thumb'.[20]

In his work on female subordination in England from 1500 to 1800, Anthony Fletcher observed that over time, although patriarchal ideologies remained entrenched, the expressions of patriarchy and the rationale for subordination changed. Such shifts, although they took place in England, are significant because of the influence that they continue to have on constructions of gender outside of England, including those in the United States. One change that occurred during the eighteenth century 'was a deliberate rhetorical displacement of family violence on to the lower classes' with wife-beating being viewed 'as a special mark of the inferiority and animality of the poor'.[21] As a result, 'what actually happened in respectable families' was 'being veiled in silence'.[22] The most important change, though, was the development during the Enlightenment of 'modern secular patriarchy'.[23] Secular patriarchy constructs gender differences in dichotomous rather than hierarchical terms and the subordination of women is attributed to their being 'the fair sex'.[24] According to Fletcher, women actively participated in the development of this new gender rationale because it 'told them something positive about themselves' whereas their prior subordination 'was based upon misogynistic assumptions about them that were entirely negative'.[25] Secular patriarchal ideologies supplemented rather than replaced traditional religiously-based patriarchal notions so that women's subordination was supported by both the church and the state.

One of the key features of secular patriarchy was that gender roles for boys and girls could be inculcated through dichotomous educational patterns. As a result, upper and middle class boys received 'a social training' that involved 'breaking with motherly apron-strings, schooling and further education at university and sometimes abroad'.[26] Yet comparable girls received 'a moral training' that prepared them for marriage and took place primarily at home.[27]

From Fletcher's work, it is possible to discern two lasting effects of this gender shift that began in seventeenth-century England – one that affects males and one that affects females. As for males, the effect of removing boys from their mothers, the process of 'breaking with motherly apron-strings', was that 'maternal influence was seen as dangerous, even pernicious', and boys, who were subjected to an 'enforced repression of emotional spontaneity', developed what has been referred to

19. Fletcher, *Gender, Sex & Subordination*, p. 192.

20. Fletcher, *Gender, Sex & Subordination*, p. 192. It was only in the nineteenth century, starting in 1829 in England and 1871 in Alabama and Massachusetts, that wife-beating was made illegal. R. Emerson Dobash and Russell Dobash, *Violence against Wives: A Case against Patriarchy* (New York: The Free Press, 1979), p. 63.

21. Fletcher, *Gender, Sex & Subordination*, p. 201.

22. Fletcher, *Gender, Sex & Subordination*, p. 201.

23. Fletcher, *Gender, Sex & Subordination*, p. 295.

24. Fletcher, *Gender, Sex & Subordination*, pp. 291, 412.

25. Fletcher, *Gender, Sex & Subordination*, p. 296.

26. Fletcher, *Gender, Sex & Subordination*, p. 295.

27. Fletcher, *Gender, Sex & Subordination*, pp. 370, 376.

as the 'male wound'.[28] That 'male wound' and corresponding difficulties with intimacy, in turn, have been associated with male patterns of violence and promiscuity.[29] Concerning females, the new 'cult of womanhood' meant that 'women were desexualized', their 'sphere of activity' was limited, and these restrictions have 'lain like a pall, in so far as it has been successfully inculcated, across many women's lives'.[30]

B. *Dominance/Subordination: Contemporary Context*

Violence against women, such as wife-beating, existed in earlier periods of time. Consequently, the surprising element in today's context is not that such violence exists but the frequency with which it occurs. Using the definition that appears in the work of James Poling, 'male violence toward women'

> encompasses physical, visual, verbal, or sexual acts that are experienced by a woman or girl as a threat, invasion, or assault and that have the effect of hurting her or degrading her and/or taking away her ability to control contact (intimate or otherwise) with another individual.[31]

To understand the depth of violence against women in today's context, some statistics are needed. The following are national statistics on domestic abuse[32] and rape[33] which are only two forms of gendered violence.[34]

28. Fletcher, *Gender, Sex & Subordination*, pp. 339–40. For the concept of the 'male wound' here, Fletcher cites the work of L. Hudson and B. Jacot, *The Way Men Think* (London, 1991), pp. 118–35.

29. Fletcher, *Gender, Sex & Subordination*, p. 340. In this same paragraph, Fletcher writes: 'The chronological coincidence between the adulthood of the first generations who had experienced this kind of training in large numbers and the demand for commercial sex of one kind or another is temptingly plausible as an historical connection'. See also James N. Poling, *Understanding Male Violence: Pastoral Care Issues* (St. Louis, MO: Chalice Press, 2003), pp. 107–108.

30. Fletcher, *Gender, Sex & Subordination*, pp. 412–13.

31. Poling, *Understanding Male Violence*, p. 9.

32. Some advocates avoid using the terms 'domestic violence' and 'spousal abuse' because they do not communicate the overwhelmingly gendered nature of such violence. Studies show that '95 to 98 per cent of battered spouses are women'. Cooper-White, *The Cry of Tamar*, p. 108. According to recent U.S. Department of Justice statistics, 85 per cent of victimizations by intimate partners were against women. See U.S. Dept. of Justice, *Intimate Partner Violence*, NCJ 178247 (May 2000).

33. The definition of rape under common law involved the use of force and the absence of the woman's consent. Since 1974, some state statutes have been enacted which replace the term 'rape' with 'sexual assault'. As defined, 'sexual assault' recognizes that both males and females can be assaulted and consolidates laws on rape, statutory rape, incest and other related offenses. Linda Brookover Bourque, *Defining Rape* (Durham: Duke University Press, 1989), pp. 97, 110–11. As Cooper-White notes, under such statutes, the use of force or threat of force constitutes an 'aggravated' sexual assault. She also mentions that '[m]arital rape has only recently been recognized in some states as a crime comparable to other rapes; [i]n twenty-nine states it is a lesser offense, and in two states it is still not a crime at all'. Cooper-White, *The Cry of Tamar*, p. 81.

34. For an excellent discussion of the different forms of violence against women, including sexual harassment and clergy abuse, see Cooper-White, *The Cry of Tamar*.

- Domestic violence is the leading cause of injury to women, producing more injuries than muggings, stranger rapes, and car accidents combined.[35]
- In the United States, 1,247 women and 440 men were killed by an intimate partner (current or former spouse, boyfriend or girlfriend) in 2000. In recent years, an intimate partner killed about 33 per cent of female murder victims and 4 per cent of male murder victims.[36]
- In the case of rape or sexual assault, two-thirds of the victims were related to or acquainted with their assailant.[37]
- One out of three women will be raped in her lifetime in this country.[38]

As theorists have grappled with these statistics, some traditional 'myths' about male violence have been shattered. Notably, rape is neither the result of 'uncontrollable' male biological urges nor an act of sexual passion.[39] Most rapes are committed, not by a stranger, but by someone known or related to the woman, and 'the vast majority of rapes are same-race crimes'.[40] As for battering, one of the challenged 'myths' is the notion that it is rare. To the contrary, battering is not committed by only 'a few sociopathically violent men' and it 'cuts across all lines of education, class, color, sexual orientation, and religion'.[41]

> Violence (against women) has come to be seen as a socially-produced and often socially-legitimated cultural phenomenon, rather than the 'natural' expression of biological drives or an innate male characteristic.[42]

From this perspective, then, violence against women can be conceptualized as a purposeful act. Succinctly put, rape functions to assert and maintain the patri-

35. Schüssler Fiorenza, 'Ties That Bind: Domestic Violence Against Women', in Mary John Manzanan *et al.* (eds.), *Women Resisting Violence: Spirituality for Life* (Maryknoll, NY: Orbis Books, 1996), pp. 39–55 (40). See also Susan Brooks Thistlewaite, 'Every Two Minutes: Battered Women and Feminist Interpretation', in Letty M. Russell (ed.), *Feminist Interpretation of the Bible* (Philadelphia: Westminster Press, 1985), pp. 96–107.

36. U.S. Department of Justice, *Intimate Partner Violence, 1993–2001*, NCJ 197838 (February 2003).

37. Suzanne E. Hatty, *Masculinities, Violence, and Culture* (Sage Series on Violence against Women; Thousand Oaks, CA: Sage Publications, 2000), pp. 4–5.

38. Cooper-White, *The Cry of Tamar*, p. 80.

39. Cooper-White, *The Cry of Tamar*, p. 84. See also Bourque, *Defining Rape*, pp. 59–76.

40. Cooper-White, The Cry of Tamar, p. 88. In the United States, it is virtually impossible to discuss 'myths' about rape without discussing constructions of race and class. See Angela Y. Davis, *Women, Race, and Class* (New York: Random House, 1981). For thorough discussions of 'acquaintance rape', see Peggy Reeves Sanday, *Fraternity Gang Rape: Sex, Brotherhood, and Privilege on Campus* (New York: New York University Press, 1990) and *A Woman Scorned: Acquaintance Rape on Trial* (New York: Doubleday, 1996). See also Leslie Francis (ed.), *Date Rape* (University Park, PA: The Pennsylvania State University Press, 1996).

41. Cooper-White, *The Cry of Tamar*, p. 110. For a concise review of the theoretical treatments of battering, see Dobash and Dobash, *Violence Against Wives*, pp. 20–30. See also bell hooks, 'Violence in Intimate Relationships: A Feminist Perspective', in *Talking Back: Thinking Feminist, Thinking Black* (Boston, MA: South End Press, 1989), pp. 84–91.

42. Anne Edwards, 'Male Violence in Feminist Theory: An Analysis of the Changing Conceptions of Sex/Gender Violence and Male Dominance', in Jalna Hanmer and Mary Maynard (eds.), *Women, Violence, and Social Control* (Atlantic Highlands, NJ: Humanities Press International, 1987), p. 26.

archal authority of males over females.[43] Correspondingly, it can be said that battering 'is the domestic counterpart of rape' and it 'reflects a defense of patriarchal authority'.[44]

In spite of these shocking statistics on violence against women, churches, for the most part, have not seriously challenged that violence or the dominant/subordinate paradigm that shapes it.[45] The traditional (conservative) Christian view, and the one that is most embedded in the national (sub)conscious is that 'male violence is a sign of the breakdown of God's natural hierarchy of the headship of men over women and children'.[46]

> Violence occurs, in this view, when the natural hierarchy of men over women and children is threatened and needs to be reestablished. Male violence is unfortunate because some men are too immature to know how to assume their rightful place at the head of the family without resorting to violence, and because many women have been led by womanism and feminism into rebellion against the leadership of men, which makes violence inevitable as men rightfully enforce their dominance.[47]

Without a doubt, this view asserts that violence is a way of disciplining or punishing women and thereby maintains a relationship between the male dominance ideology and violence against women as argued in this study. Yet there are several other problems with this understanding of battering that merit attention. First, women's movements are held solely responsible for any rebellion against patriarchal authority. However, a strong factor in greater independence for women is and has historically been rising economic incomes.[48] Second, this traditional view of male violence ignores the pervasive nature of the problem because it only addresses the issue of wife-beating. As Stark and Flitcraft observed, 'the fact that at least half of the women who are battered are single, separated, or divorced suggests a broader "property right" than was afforded in traditional societies based on blood or kin'.[49]

Third, the traditional view has an underlying construction of masculinity that sees men in one of two categories – those who rape women and those who protect the 'fair sex' – but the distinction between these categories is not as sharp as it might seem.[50] Although the subordination of women may be based on their being 'the fair sex' (a newer and more positive image) rather than 'the inferior sex', (an older and more negative image), what are referred to as 'pedestal values' do not

43. See Angela Davis, *Women, Class and Race*, p. 7. Cited in Cooper-White, *The Cry of Tamar*, p. 83.

44. Evan Stark and Anne Flitcraft, *Women at Risk: Domestic Violence and Women's Health* (Thousand Oaks: Sage Publications, 1996), pp. 30–31.

45. Poling, *Understanding Male Violence*, p. 16.

46. Poling, *Understanding Male Violence*, p. 16.

47. Poling, *Understanding Male Violence*, p. 16.

48. See, for example, Dobash and Dobash, *Violence Against Wives*, pp. 34–40. For a detailed consideration of the inherent tensions between patriarchy and capitalism, see Stark and Flitcraft, *Women at Risk*, pp. 31–42.

49. Stark and Flitcraft, *Women at Risk*, p. 36.

50. Susan Griffin, 'Rape: The All-American Crime', *Ramparts* 10 (September 1971), pp. 21–35 (30).

reflect 'positive feelings for women, as myth would have us believe', because they 'spring from intolerance and are associated with very hostile and violent attitudes towards women'.[51]

Finally, but most significantly, this traditional view blames the female for the male's violence. Such a view is so deeply entrenched in our society that women who have been battered or raped will take responsibility for what has happened to them. Some of the myths that have been debunked about women and violence are those such as 'She asked for it' or 'I provoked him'.[52] To make matters worse, those to whom these women go for help often blame them in subtle ways, too, resulting in what is called 'the dual impact of trauma'.[53]

The traditional perspective, though, does consider the woman's degree of submissiveness (or its lack) to determine whether violence occurs. Research indicates, however, that it is the structure of a hierarchical relationship itself that is a more reliable indicator. In his work on the common features of family abuse, violence against women and male and female children, David Finkelhor identified two features of importance here – and neither one involves the woman's degree of submissiveness.[54] First, he found that family abuse is 'not simply aggression committed by one family member against another', but it was 'more precisely the abuse of power'.[55] In other words, 'abuse tends to gravitate toward the relationships of greatest power differential' which usually means in the case of child abuse, for example, that the father (the one with the most power) abuses the child with the least power.[56] Correspondingly, he suggests that 'in families where a woman has less power by virtue of not being in the labor market, by virtue of being excluded from participation in decision making, and by virtue of having less education than her husband, she is at higher risk of abuse'.[57] As could be expected, Finkelhor found evidence that violence is more common in families that 'are more patriarchically organized'.[58]

Similarly, another common feature noted by Finkelhor is that, although the abuser is the one who has power in the family system, he perceives himself to lack or to have lost power. Under these circumstances, abuse is carried out to compensate for a sense of powerlessness as measured by 'masculine ideals in our society'.[59]

51. Diana Scully, *Understanding Sexual Violence: A Study of Convicted Rapists* (Perspectives on Gender, 3; Boston: Unwin Hyman, 1990), p. 165. See also Fletcher, *Gender, Sex & Subordination*, p. 412.

52. Cooper-White, *The Cry of Tamar*, pp. 85–86, pp. 110–11.

53. Stark and Flitcraft, *Women at Risk*, pp. 157–91.

54. David Finkelhor, 'Common Features of Family Abuse', in David Finkelhor, Richard J. Gelles, Gerald T. Hotaling and Murray A. Straus (eds.), *The Dark Side of Families: Current Family Violence Research* (Beverly Hills: Sage Publications, 1983), pp. 17–28 (18).

55. Finkelhor, 'Common Features of Family Abuse', p. 18. See also Poling, *The Abuse of Power: A Theological Problem* (Nashville: Abingdon Press, 1991), pp. 23–33.

56. Finkelhor, 'Common Features of Family Abuse', p. 18.

57. Finkelhor, 'Common Features of Family Abuse', p. 18.

58. Finkelhor, 'Common Features of Family Abuse', pp. 21–22.

59. Finkelhor, 'Common Features of Family Abuse', p. 19. Additional indications of the harm caused by such ideals to boys and men are, for example, higher suicide rates, lower educational

Feelings of powerlessness for poor or working class men may stem from their inability, in American capitalism, to exercise any control over someone else; whereas professional/managerial men may feel frustrated when their exercise of public power is blocked in any way.[60] That sense of powerlessness in the face of life's realities demonstrates how patriarchal norms harm men who, in turn, harm their loved ones.

Other studies have confirmed the connection that Finkelhor made between male dominance and violence against women. One study found that men who batter women 'generally have very strict traditional ideas about gender roles and a "woman's place"' and 'they are anxious to prove their own masculinity'.[61] Similarly, another study concluded that men who rape women 'identify with traditional images of masculinity and male gender role privilege; they believe very strongly in rape stereotypes, and for them, being male carries the right to discipline and punish women'.[62] Although these traditional patriarchal values are cultural values that are shared broadly, the researcher noted, 'sexually violent men are more extreme in their beliefs'.[63]

Such research confirms the conclusions that feminists in the field of religion have reached. The 1989 book, *Christianity, Patriarchy, and Abuse*,[64] by its title, makes the connection between patriarchy (the male dominance paradigm), Christianity, and violence against women in the contemporary context. In her article in that volume, Karen Bloomquist begins with the statement that 'sexual violence is viciously intertwined with patriarchy'.[65]

> Violence against women can be seen as the outgrowth of patriarchal social constructs that define the relationship between women and men as one of subordination and domination.[66]

completion rates and higher rates of alcoholism than for girls and women. See the statistics cited by Van Leeuwen in *My Brother's Keeper*, pp. 20–21.

60. Karen Bloomquist, 'Sexual Violence: Patriarchy's Offense and Defense', in Joanne Carlson Brown and Carole R. Bohn (eds.), *Christianity, Patriarchy, and Abuse: A Feminist Critique* (New York: Pilgrim Press, 1989), pp. 62–69 (63).

61. Cooper-White, *The Cry of Tamar*, p. 119. See also, Cheryl A. Kirk-Duggan, *Misbegotten Anguish: A Theology and Ethics of Violence* (St. Louis, MO: Chalice Press, 2001), pp. 96–102. However, females are not only victims of battering. Females also hit males but males, unlike females, do not suffer from the pattern of injury and entrapment referred to as the 'battering syndrome'. Stark and Flitcraft, *Women at Risk,* pp. 166–67.

62. Scully, *Understanding Sexual Violence*, p. 165.

63. Scully, *Understanding Sexual Violence*, p. 165. It must be acknowledged that, in the United States, violence against women is 'located within our larger (and seemingly uncontrollable) violent society' where force is used 'as a primary tool of persuasion and reaction – a tendency revealed in everything from the Gulf War to the war on drugs (or guns or poverty or whatever – the relevant word being "war")'. Martha Albertson Fineman, 'Preface', in Martha Albertson Fineman and Roxanne Mykitiuk (eds.), *The Public Nature of Private Violence: The Discovery of Domestic Abuse* (New York: Routledge, 1994), pp. xi–xviii (xvi).

64. Joanne Carlson Brown and Carole R. Bohn (eds.), *Christianity, Patriarchy, and Abuse: A Feminist Critique* (New York: The Pilgrim Press, 1989).

65. Bloomquist, 'Sexual Violence', p. 62.

66. Bloomquist, 'Sexual Violence', p. 62.

Bloomquist explains that connection based on patriarchy's valuing of male control over females which means that '[i]f one's identity is rooted in exercising control over another, one is tempted to go to any lengths to assure or reassert that control'.[67] Although male violence against women is a complex phenomenon and no one rationale is conclusive, hierarchical patriarchal norms certainly aggravate the problem because they confer upon men 'an *entitlement* to abuse'.[68] Therefore, the dominance/subordination paradigm constitutes a form of (symbolic) violence against women and it has the potential within itself for actual male violence against women – a potential that is realized all too often in today's context.[69]

2. *Biblical Interpretation in a Culture of Violence Against Women*

Washington, while acknowledging that 'biblical accounts of sexual assault are literary constructs, not historical reports', has written that 'the prevalence of rape in biblical narratives' means 'that sexual assault and coercion were considered commonplace in ancient Israel' and he suggests that 'ancient Israel might well be designated a rape culture'.[70] We may not be able to determine whether ancient Israel actually was a rape culture. However, given the statistics on rape, we know that the United States today is one. In a rape culture, Washington noted, 'laws do not in fact prohibit rape; they institutionalize it and confirm men's control of women'.[71] That very same observation has been made about such laws in the United States.

67. Bloomquist, 'Sexual Violence', p. 62.

68. Bobbie Groth, 'Lessons from the Spiritual Lives of Men Who Work in the Movement to End Violence Against Women and Children', *Journal of Religion and Abuse* 2 (2000), pp. 5–31 (italics in the original).

69. I am not contending that the hierarchical dominance of the male in a patriarchal family constitutes violence in such a way that even consensual sex between a married man and woman becomes an instance of rape. See Catherine MacKinnon, *Feminism Unmodified*; and *Towards a Feminist Theory of the State* (Cambridge, MA: Harvard University Press, 1989). For an analysis of MacKinnon's work as a theoretical resource in current discussions of violence against women, see Traci C. West, *Wounds of the Spirit: Black Women, Violence, and Resistance Ethics* (New York: New York University Press, 1999), pp. 91–121, 131–33. Instead, the argument is that the power differential between men and women in the dominant/subordinate gender paradigm confers upon men the *possibility* of using actual violence to maintain their control. Even though that hierarchical gender paradigm may even make violence against women more likely, that violence is not inevitable. Hence, the Pentecostal movement, used here as an umbrella term that also includes charismatic and conservative evangelical churches, is the fastest growing expression of Christianity globally, emphasizes a strict patriarchal hierarchy, and bars women from leadership roles. Nevertheless, women appear to have a sense of empowerment. Women 'have been enabled to institute a family discipline, sanctioned and effectively policed by the church community' that tends to re-domesticate the men by calling for an end 'to the long-tolerated double standard of sexual morality' and such a 'shift towards gender equality will be tolerated so long as women are not seen to be publicly exercising formal authority over men'. Bernice Martin, 'The Pentecostal Gender Paradox: A Cautionary Tale for the Sociology of Religion', in Richard K. Fenn (ed.), *The Blackwell Companion to Sociology of Religion* (Blackwell Companions to Religion, 2; Oxford: Blackwell Publishers, 2001), pp. 52–66 (54).

70. Washington, 'Violence and the Construction of Gender in the Hebrew Bible', p. 353.

71. Washington, 'Violence and the Construction of Gender in the Hebrew Bible', p. 353.

> Attempts to stop rape through legal deterrence fundamentally chose to persuade men not to rape. They thus assume that men simply have the power to rape and concede this primary power to them, implying that at best men can secondarily be dissuaded from using this power by means of threatened punishment from a masculinized state or legal system. They do not envision strategies which will enable women to sabotage men's power to rape, which will empower women to take the ability to rape completely out of men's hands.[72]

Part of the problem is that, although laws criminalizing rape exist, most rapes are not reported to the police and, even if prosecution results, rape convictions are rare.[73] To make matters worse, rape is not the only form of violence against females. Battering, sexual harassment, as well as the sexual abuse of children also occur. Consequently, the United States is more than a rape culture, it is one in which male violence, primarily against females, is endemic. It is in this context that the process of biblical interpretation must be considered.

> More than 25 per cent of the members of the typical congregation have experienced male violence, either as survivors of child abuse or as adult survivors of rape, battering, and psychological abuse.[74]

Until recently, the cultural context in which the Bible was interpreted was not thought to be an important, or even a valid, factor. As the scholars who participated in the Bible and Culture Collective knew, 'historical criticism brackets out the contemporary milieu and excludes any examination of the ongoing formative effects of the Bible'.[75]

> The pervasive modern emphasis on the objective recovery of the ancient context in which biblical texts were produced had the double effect of obscuring the significance of the Bible in contemporary Western culture and of turning the Bible into an historical relic, an antiquarian artifact.[76]

In recent years, however, the notion of an 'objective' approach to biblical criticism has been challenged and more attention is being given to 'flesh and blood'

72. Sharon Marcus, 'Fighting Bodies, Fighting Words: A Theory and Politics of Rape Prevention', in Judith Butler and Joan W. Scott (eds.), *Feminists Theorize the Political* (New York: Routledge, 1992), pp. 385–403 (388).

73. According to recent federal government statistics, over sixty per cent of completed and attempted rapes of females were not reported to the police and 'the closer the relationship between the female victim and the offender, the greater the likelihood that the police would not be told about the rape or sexual assault'. U.S. Department of Justice, *Rape and Sexual Assault: Reporting to Police and Medical Attention, 1992–2000*, NCJ 194530 (August 2002). As for criminal prosecution, 'no suspect is even apprehended in a majority of cases, and of those, only one-fifth to one-half go to trial, and only approximately 10 per cent of *those* are convicted'. Cooper-White, *The Cry of Tamar*, p. 80 (italics in the original).

74. James Poling, *Understand Male Violence*, p. 14. Poling mentions here that 'these statistics do not diminish with social class, race, religion, or faithful church attendance, although they do correlate with gender (women are more frequently victims than men)'.

75. George Aichele and others, *The Postmodern Bible* (New Haven: Yale University Press, 1995), p. 1.

76. Aichele and others, *The Postmodern Bible*, p. 2.

readers and their different social locations – that is, their cultural contexts.[77] The first volume of the New Interpreter's Bible offers evidence of this trend because it includes essays on interpreting the Bible as women, African-Americans, Hispanic-Americans and so forth.[78] Considering 'real' readers and their particular ethnic and socioeconomic contexts raises new questions and allows new meanings of biblical texts to emerge. After the findings of this study, one of the cultural contexts for biblical interpretation that needs to be explored, along with these other ones, is the current culture of violence against women. Do new questions of the biblical text emerge as the dominant/subordinate gender paradigm's role in male violence against women and children is taken into account? Which traditional interpretations are contested as a result?

For example, Tikva Frymer-Kensky, finding that the Hebrew Bible narratives present images of men and women who have substantially the same goals, attitudes, and strategies, describes the Bible as having a 'gender-free concept of humanity'.[79] At the same time, though, she found that 'male privilege' was assumed to be 'fundamental to human social structure' and that 'male dominance was assumed'.[80] Clearly, if the ideology of male dominance is identifiable, then, gender is being constructed. Moreover, the narratives she references are those that usually involve women (and men) working for the survival and strengthening of the Israelite community. As Gail Corrington Streete asserts, 'in Judaism and Christianity alike, the connection between women, wisdom, and sexuality is negative when it challenges the prerogatives of the men who constitute communal religious authority, positive when it supports them or maintains a subordinate position'.[81] When women work toward communal goals, the women and their actions are affirmed but that does not mean that patriarchal authority is undermined in any way.

In *Reading the Women of the Bible*, Frymer-Kensky writes that 'the biblical view understood that women were powerless and subordinate without being inferior'.[82] Based on our earlier discussions, though, we know that it is that subordinate status itself which is potentially harmful. Physical harm to women results because of the power differentials accorded men under the dominant/subordinate paradigm and the abuse of power that can occur. In other words, women do not have to be labeled as 'inferior' explicitly before the dominant/subordinate paradigm becomes problematic.

77. See Fernando F. Segovia, '"And They Began to Speak in Other Tongues": Competing Modes of Discourse in Contemporary Biblical Criticism', in Fernando F. Segovia and Mary Ann Tolbert (eds.), *Reading from This Place (Vol. 1): Social Location and Biblical Interpretation in the United States* (Minneapolis: Fortress, 1995), pp. 1–32. For a summary of these developments in biblical scholarship, see also Scholz, *Rape Plots*, pp. 5–8.

78. *NIB* I (Nashville: Abingdon Press, 1994), pp. 150–87.

79. Frymer-Kensky, *In the Wake of the Goddesses: Women, Culture and the Biblical Transformation of Pagan Myth* (New York: Faucett Columbine, 1992), pp. 121, 143.

80. Frymer-Kensky, *In the Wake of the Goddesses*, pp. 120, 128.

81. Streete, *The Strange Woman*, pp. 166–67.

82. Frymer-Kensky, *Reading the Women of the Bible: New Interpretations of Their Stories* (New York: Schocken Books, 2002), p. xvi.

Similarly, Hyun Chul Paul Kim uses the complementary roles for men and women in the stories of Miriam and Deborah to model partnerships between men and women in ministry today.[83] However, oppositional gender dynamics are not totally absent from these narratives. When Miriam and Aaron complain to Moses in Num. 12, Miriam is punished but her brother Aaron is not. Likewise, as Mieke Bal tells us, in Judges, men kill women and women kill men but the women killed are powerless and the men killed are powerful and the females who kill live as independent women but the females killed 'are somebody's property'.[84]

It may be true that the Bible did not create patriarchy.[85] The issue in a context of male violence against women, though, is the way in which the Bible has been used historically and is used today to maintain patriarchy's hierarchical ideologies and structures. In this context, biblical interpretation becomes an ethical issue as the actual consequences and possible consequences of patriarchal interpretations become abundantly clear.[86]

The ethical aspects of biblical interpretation and violence against women in biblical texts were issues addressed by J. Cheryl Exum in her article, 'The Ethics of Biblical Violence Against Women'.[87] In that article, she proposes a 'threefold interpretive strategy' for dealing with rhetorical violence against women in the prophetic literature. This strategy involves recognizing the differing claims made upon male and female readers, exposing 'prophetic pornography' for what it is, and identifying competing discourses.[88] Although her proposed strategy focuses on the interpretation of texts such as Ezek. 16, Hos. 1–3, and Isa. 3, that contain (metaphorical) descriptions of specific violent acts against women, it works well, with only minor adjustments, as a strategy for interpreting any biblical text in a cultural context of male violence against women.

First, Exum wants us to recognize that these prophetic texts make different claims upon male and female readers. Male readers, she writes, can identify with and defend 'a righteous and long-suffering God for punishing a wayward and

83. Hyun Chul Paul Kim, 'Gender Complementarity in the Hebrew Bible', in Wonil Kim, Deborah Ellens, Michael Floyd and Marvin A. Sweeney (eds.), *Reading the Hebrew Bible for a New Millennium: Form, Concept, and Theological Perspective* (Harrisburg, PA: Trinity Press International, 2000), pp. 263–91.

84. Mieke Bal, *Death & Dissymmetry*, p. 26.

85. Frymer-Kensky, *Reading the Women of the Bible*, p. xiv.

86. On the ethics of biblical interpretation, see Schüssler Fiorenza, 'The Ethics of Interpretation: De-Centering Biblical Scholarship', *JBL* 107 (1988), pp. 3–17 and *Rhetoric and Ethic: The Politics of Biblical Studies* (Minneapolis: Fortress Press, 1999); Daniel Patte, *Ethics of Biblical Interpretation: A Reevaluation* (Louisville, KY: Westminster/John Knox Press, 1995); and Stephen Fowl, 'The Ethics of Interpretation or What's Left Over After the Elimination of Meaning', in David J.A. Clines, Stephen E. Fowl and Stanley E. Porter (eds.), *The Bible in Three Dimensions: Essays in celebration of forty years of Biblical Studies in the University of Sheffield* (JSOTSup, 87; Sheffield: Sheffield Academic Press, 1990), pp. 379–98. See also John Collins, 'The Zeal of Phineas: The Bible and the Legitimation of Violence', *JBL* 122 (2003), pp. 3–21.

87. J. Cheryl Exum, 'The Ethics of Biblical Violence Against Women', in John W. Rogerson, Margaret Davies and M. Daniel Carroll R. (eds.), *The Bible in Ethics: The Second Sheffield Colloquium* (JSOTSup, 207; Sheffield: Sheffield Academic Press, 1995), pp. 248–71.

88. Exum, 'Ethics of Biblical Violence', pp. 265–69.

headstrong nation'.[89] If females adopt the male point-of-view, however, we must 'read these texts against our own interests' and that means 'acceptance, if not of guilt, then at least of the indictment of our sex that these texts represent'.[90] In response, Exum encourages the identification of the gender-related 'rhetorical strategies' in these texts and how they 'affect what is at stake for female and male readers'.[91] That same identification process would work well when interpreting the biblical laws discussed here. For example, the law on levirate marriage is explained even today from a male perspective within its historical context, that is, as a means of providing for the widow. Yet a female, if given the opportunity to shape her own perspective today, would probably prefer to inherit her husband's estate or seek legitimate employment. Pointing out the difference in these perspectives would serve to undermine the exclusively male outlook of these texts which contributes to male dominance and so help to develop both male and female 'resisting readers'.[92]

Second, Exum encourages us to 'expos[e] prophetic pornography for what it is' rather than offer the rationalizations that 'the violence is metaphoric and presented with a theological justification'.[93] In the same way, explicit expressions of violence against women must be identified, as they already have in books such as *Texts of Terror*. Yet *Texts of Terror* does not include a discussion of Dinah's rape and that omission may communicate that rape is not an act of 'terror'.[94] Although probably warranted for other reasons, that omission becomes a significant one in the context of a culture of male violence against women where rape is already normalized.[95]

One way of underscoring the obscene nature of a violent biblical text is to draw out the parallels between the male violence described in that text and male violence today. Such a creative method was used in two recent articles on male violence against women in Ezekiel. For example, in his article, Jan William Tarlin portrays Ezekiel, whose priestly and prophetic body was once defined 'by its purity, dignity, and wholeness', as becoming the 'shattered male subject' in the text.[96] Tarlin then argues that the violence against females in the text marks Ezekiel's return to a type of male subjectivity.

89. Exum, 'Ethics of Biblical Violence', p. 249.

90. Exum, 'Ethics of Biblical Violence', pp. 249–50. See also Judith Fetterley, *The Resisting Reader: A Feminist Approach to American Fiction* (Bloomington: Indiana University Press, 1978). On a comparable process whereby African-Americans are trained to read biblical texts against our own interests, see Randall Bailey, 'The Danger of Ignoring One's Cultural Bias in Reading Biblical Texts', in R.S. Sugirtharajah (ed.), *The Postcolonial Bible* (Sheffield: Sheffield Academic Press, 1998), pp. 66–90.

91. Exum, 'Ethics of Biblical Violence', p. 266.

92. Exum, 'Ethics of Biblical Violence', p. 266.

93. Exum, 'Ethics of Biblical Violence', p. 266.

94. Scholz, *Rape Plots*, p. 3 n. 5.

95. For an analysis of the silence surrounding Dinah's rape, even by feminist writers, and its consequences, see Julie Ann Pfau, 'Dinah is Still Silent: Trauma and the Unrealized Potential of Midrash' (unpublished masters thesis, Emory University, 2002).

96. Jan William Tarlin, 'Utopia and Pornography in Ezekiel: Violence, Hope, and the Shattered Male Subject', in Timothy K. Beal and David M. Gunn (eds.), *Reading Bibles, Writing Bodies: Identity and the Book* (New York: Routledge, 1997), pp. 175–83 (181).

> In Chapters 16 and 23, and in the oracles against the nations, Ezekiel identifies with Yahweh to become a super-male: pumping himself up in his all-sufficiency by gleefully inflicting extravagant violence on women, on foreign 'others', and on the very community to which the prophet/priest and his God are bound by covenant (since the women of chapters 16 and 23 are figures meant to represent Yahweh's people).[97]

Basically, Tarlin relates the violence against women in the text to Ezekiel's sense of estrangement and powerlessness. In other words, Ezekiel can be thought of as re-establishing some sense of self by demonstrating his violent control over others, the very same dynamic that was discussed earlier in Finkelhor's work. Finkelhor found that, although family abuse was an abuse of power, the men who abused did so to compensate for a sense of powerlessness.[98] Showing how violence against women is an aspect of patriarchal constructions of masculinity, both in ancient texts and the world around us, will hopefully result in more responsible interpretations of these texts.

Similarly, in her discussion of Ezek. 16, Linda Day drew parallels between the text and violence against women today.[99] She described the current understanding of the three-stage cycle of domestic abuse and found corresponding states in the text. Specifically, the first phase is when the tension builds (vv. 1-26), the physical violence actually occurs in the second phase (vv. 27-41), and, in the third phase, the batterer expresses his remorse, behaves in a kind manner, 'often showers her with gifts and attention', and assures her 'that she will not again have to suffer such an incident' (vv. 42-63).[100] Consequently, Day is able to expose a violent pattern in the texts, as Exum suggests, and elucidate its present manifestation in our culture. The work of Tarlin and Day, therefore, demonstrates how biblical interpretation can provide insights into patriarchal ideology and the mechanisms of male violence in the Bible and in our contemporary context.

For the third part of her interpretive strategy, Exum suggests that we look for competing discourse(s).[101]

> This involves looking for places where attempts to silence or suppress the woman's rival discourse – a discourse that threatens to subvert the dominant prophetic patriarchal discourse – are not completely successful.

97. Tarlin, 'Utopia and Pornography', p. 182. See also S. Tamar Kamionkowski, *Gender Reversal and Cosmic Chaos: A Study on the Book of Ezekiel* (JSOTSup, 368; London: Sheffield Academic Press, 2003).

98. Finkelhor, 'Common Features of Family Abuse', pp. 18–19.

99. Linda Day, 'Rhetoric and Domestic Violence in Ezekiel 16', *BibInt* 8 (2000), pp. 205–30.

100. Day, 'Rhetoric and Domestic Violence', pp. 214–15. One difference in the parallels exists. Day notes on page 216 of her article 'that the man's sense of contrition and vow to reform his behavior that is often seen during the final stage in real-life situations of domestic abuse is noticeably absent in this biblical version. YHWH is not sorry for what he has done'. As Exum warns, though, in these texts, 'God is a character in the biblical narrative (as much a male construct as the women in biblical literature) and thus not be confused with any one's notion of a "real" god'. Exum, 'Ethics of Biblical Violence', p. 264. Exum's comment was made in another context but it is particularly appropriate here.

101. Exum, 'Ethics of Biblical Violence', p. 267.

For our purposes, finding competing discourses means locating texts that contradict in some way the dominant/subordinate gender paradigm or offer an alternative to it.[102]

To begin, therefore, some consideration must be given to how masculinity is constructed in a text. For example, David Clines has analyzed the construction of masculinity in the David story (1 Sam. 16 to 1 Kgs 2) and compared it to the concept of masculinity in the modern West.[103] He found some similarities such as the fact that men are to be aggressive and successful in both cultural settings. More importantly, though, there were two major differences, both of which concern women. In the contemporary context, men are defined in opposition to women, so 'whatever women do is *ipso facto* what a real man must not do', and men 'are supposed to be sexually experienced and to be always interested in sex'.[104]

By comparison, Clines finds that masculinity is not defined in opposition to femininity in the David story. Instead, he found there that 'the spheres of men and women are so distinct, their cultural scripts so divergent, that neither defines self over against the other'.[105] Furthermore, Clines notes that, instead of the emphasis on sexual exploits that is part of contemporary masculinity, in the David story, women are 'marginal to the lives of the protagonists' and sex 'is perfunctory and usually politically motivated'.[106] Based on that comparison, Clines offers an intriguing insight:

> It is interesting to wonder how the evident lack of interest in sex in the David story, by contrast to our contemporary insistence on its near obligatoriness, fits in with the profile of masculinity in the text. Can it be that contemporary absorption in sex coheres with a masculinity that is not so sure of itself, that is troubled about self-definition and functionality?[107]

Just as the David story may offer an alternative to the oppositional gender paradigm (and provide a deeper awareness of our current gender constructions), so does the Song of Songs.[108] As Renita Weems writes, the Song of Songs offers 'an

102. It is usually assumed that cultures have a single monolithic gender ideology. However, anthropologists have found that one society may have multiple and even contradictory gender ideologies. See Anna Meigs, 'Multiple Gender Ideologies and Statuses', in Peggy Reeves Sanday and Ruth Gallagher Goodenough (eds.), *Beyond the Second Sex: New Directions in the Anthropology of Gender* (Philadelphia: University of Pennsylvania Press, 1990), pp. 99–112.

103. David J.A. Clines, 'David the Man: The Construction of Masculinity in the Hebrew Bible', in *Interested Parties: The Ideology of Writers and Readers of the Hebrew Bible* (JSOTSup, 205; Sheffield: Sheffield Academic Press, 1995), pp. 212–43.

104. Clines, 'David the Man', pp. 213–14.

105. Clines, 'David the Man', p. 231.

106. Clines, 'David the Man', pp. 225–26.

107. Clines, 'David the Man', p. 232. Clines is also aware of how contemporary constructions of masculinity influence our reading of the David story. Specifically, David's sexual exploits make him a 'real man' in our eyes whereas the possibility of homoeroticism in his relationship with Jonathan does not.

108. But see, for example, Clines, 'Why is there a Song of Songs, and What Does It Do to You If You Read It?', in *Interested Parties*, pp. 94–121. In this essay, Clines argues, among other things, that the Song of Songs is a male fantasy that, in the text's political matrix, 'implies the author's

account of love in which lovers love without domination'.[109] Most strikingly, the Song of Songs presents an unusual female character in the Hebrew Bible who is 'assertive, uninhibited, and unabashed about her sexual desires'.[110] Such a portrayal is unusual given that 'the Bible treats sexuality as a question of social control and behavior: who with whom and when'.[111] That control is justified on the basis of what Frymer-Kensky refers to as the 'problematic of sex'.

> This is the great problematic of sex. The ideal of the bonded, monogamous nuclear family conveys a positive place for sexuality within the social order. But at the same time, the same sexual attraction which serves to reinforce society if it is controlled and confined within the marital system can destroy social order if allowed free reign.[112]

The need for control over sexuality translates into procreation as the sole purpose for sexual expression and the notion that women must be controlled to ensure the legitimacy of the male heirs. These presumptions result in the very laws that, as argued here, constitute a form of violence against women. Ultimately, then, alternate gender ideologies must be based on a different concept of sexuality. Rather than being problematic, sexuality must be seen in more expansive and constructive terms. To that end, sexuality and the erotic have to be envisioned as expressions of spirituality.[113]

Exum, after discussing her threefold interpretive strategy, observed that these approaches to the prophetic literature do not 'constitute a solution to the ethical problem of biblical violence against women but an important rhetorical counter-strategy for dealing with it'.[114] Given the violent context today in which these violent texts are read, such a counter-strategy is desperately needed.

desire to repress the conflict of interests between the sexes by representing the female and male lovers as more or less equal, and their desire, capacities and satisfactions as more or less identical'. Clines, 'Song of Songs', p. 101. See also Clines, 'He Prophets: Masculinity as a Problem for Hebrew Prophets and Their Interpreters', in Alastair G. Hunter and Philip R. Davies (eds.), *Sense and Sensitivity: Essays on Reading the Bible in Memory of Robert Carroll* (JSOTSup 348; London: Sheffield Academic Press, 2002), pp. 311–28.

109. Renita J. Weems, 'Song of Songs', in *NIB* V (Nashville: Abingdon Press, 1997), p. 408.

110. Weems, 'Song of Songs', *NIB* V, p. 364.

111. Frymer-Kensky, *In the Wake of the Goddesses*, p. 197.

112. Frymer-Kensky, 'Law and Philosophy', p. 98.

113. See David M. Carr, *The Erotic Word: Sexuality, Spirituality, and the Bible* (New York: Oxford University Press, 2003). See also Jon Davies and Gerard Loughlin (eds.), *Sex These Days: Essays on Theology, Sexuality, and Society* (Sheffield: Sheffield Academic Press, 1997).

114. Exum, 'Ethics of Biblical Violence', pp. 268–69.

Appendix A

INCLUSIVE AND EXCLUSIVE LAWS OF THE BC AND DL[*]

1. *Inclusive Laws*

A. *Inclusive laws that explicitly refer to men and women*
1. *Inclusive laws: the treatment of male and female slaves*

a. *Striking a male or female slave*
Exod. 21.20-21.
When a slaveowner strikes a male or female slave with a rod and the slave dies immediately, the owner shall be punished. But if the slave survives a day or two, there is no punishment; for the slave is the owner's property.

Exod. 21.26-27
When a slaveowner strikes the eye of a male or female slave, destroying it, the owner shall let the slave go, a free person, to compensate for the eye. If the owner knocks out a tooth of a male or female slave, the slave shall be let go, a free person, to compensate for the tooth.

b. *Male or female slave gored by an ox*
Exod. 21.28-32
When an ox gores a man or a woman to death, the ox shall be stoned, and its flesh shall not be eaten; but the owner of the ox shall not be liable. If the ox has been accustomed to gore in the past, and its owner has been warned but has not restrained it, and it kills a man or a woman, the ox shall be stoned, and its owner also shall be put to death. If a ransom is imposed on the owner, then the owner shall pay whatever is imposed for the redemption of the victim's life. If it gores a boy or a girl, the owner shall be dealt with according to this same rule. If the ox gores a male or female slave, the owner shall pay to the slaveowner thirty shekels of silver, and the ox shall be stoned.

c. *Male or female debt slave*
Exod. 21.2-6
When you buy a male Hebrew slave, he shall serve six years, but in the seventh he shall go out a free person, without debt. If he comes in single, he shall go out sin-

* No significant textual issues are at stake in these verses. The quotations contained herein are from the New Revised Standard Version Bible, copyright © 1989 by the Division of Christian Education of the National Council of Churches of Christ in the USA. Used by permission. All rights reserved.

gle; if he comes in married, then his wife shall go out with him. If his master gives him a wife and she bears him sons or daughters, the wife and her children shall be her master's and he shall go out alone. But if the slave declares, 'I love my master, my wife, and my children; I will not go out a free person', then his master shall bring him before God. He shall be brought to the door or the doorpost; and his master shall pierce his ear with an awl; and he shall serve him for life.

Exod. 21.7-11

When a man sells his daughter as a slave, she shall not go out as the male slaves do. If she does not please her master, who designated her for himself, then he shall let her be redeemed; he shall have no right to sell her to a foreign people, since he has dealt unfairly with her. If he designates her for his son, he shall deal with her as with a daughter. If he takes another wife to himself, he shall not diminish the food, clothing, or marital rights of the first wife. And if he does not do these three things for her, she shall go out without debt, without payment of money.

Deut. 15.12-18

If a member of your community, whether a Hebrew man or a Hebrew woman, is sold to you and works for you six years, in the seventh year you shall set that person free. And when you send a male slave out from you a free person, you shall not send him out empty-handed. Provide liberally out of your flock, your threshing floor, and your wine press, thus giving to him some of the bounty with which the LORD your God has blessed you. Remember that you were a slave in the land of Egypt, and the LORD your God redeemed you; for this reason I lay this command upon you today. But if he says to you, 'I will not go out from you', because he loves you and your household, since he is well off with you, then you shall take an awl and thrust it through his earlobe into the door, and he shall be your slave forever. You shall do the same with regard to your female slave. Do not consider it a hardship when you send them out from you free persons, because for six years they have given you services worth the wages of hired laborers; and the LORD your God will bless you in all that you do.

2. *Inclusive laws: the treatment of men and women in family matters*

a. *Respect for mothers and fathers*

Exod. 21.15

Whoever strikes father or mother shall be put to death.

Exod. 21.17

Whoever curses father or mother shall be put to death.

Deut. 21.18-21

If someone has a stubborn and rebellious son who will not obey his father and mother, who does not heed them when they discipline him, then his father and his mother shall take hold of him and bring him out to the elders of his town at the gate of that place. They shall say to the elders of his town, 'This son of ours is stubborn and rebellious. He will not obey us. He is a glutton and a drunkard'. Then all the men of the town shall stone him to death. So you shall purge evil from your midst; and all Israel will hear, and be afraid.

b. *Widows*

Exod. 22.21-23 [22.22-24]

You shall not abuse any widow or orphan. If you do abuse them, when they cry out to me, I will surely heed their cry; my wrath will burn, and I will kill you with the sword, and your wives shall become widows and your children orphans.

Deut. 24.17-18

You shall not deprive a resident alien or an orphan of justice; you shall not take a widow's garment in pledge. Remember that you were a slave in Egypt and the LORD your God redeemed you from there; therefore I command you to do this.

Deut. 24.19-22

When you reap your harvest in your field and forget a sheaf in the field, you shall not go back to get it; it shall be left for the alien, the orphan, and the widow, so that the LORD your God may bless you in all your undertakings. When you beat your olive trees, do not strip what is left; it shall be for the alien, the orphan, and the widow. When you gather the grapes of your vineyard, do not glean what is left; it shall be for the alien, the orphan, and the widow. Remember that you were a slave in the land of Egypt; therefore, I am commanding you to do this.

3. *Inclusive laws: the treatment of men and women in the cult*

a. *Male and female cross-dressing*

Deut. 22.5

A woman shall not wear a man's apparel, nor shall a man put on a woman's garment; for whoever does such things is abhorrent to the LORD your God.

b. *Male and female prostitution*

Deut. 23.18-19 [23.17-18]

None of the daughters of Israel shall be a temple prostitute; none of the sons of Israel shall be a temple prostitute. You shall not bring the fee of a prostitute or the wages of a male prostitute into the house of the LORD your God in payment for any vow, for both of these are abhorrent to the LORD your God.

B. *Inclusive laws that implicitly refer to men and women*

1. *Female reference: sorcery*

Exod. 22.17 [22.18]

You shall not permit a female sorcerer to live.

2. *Male reference: sorcery*

Deut. 18.9-14

When you come into the land that the LORD your God is giving you, you must not learn to imitate the abhorrent practices of those nations. No one shall be found among you who makes a son or daughter pass through fire, or who practices divination, or is a soothsayer, or an augur, or a sorcerer, or one who casts spells, or who consults ghosts or spirits, or who seeks oracles from the dead. For whoever does these things is abhorrent to the LORD; it is because of such abhorrent practices that the LORD your God is driving them out before you. You must remain completely loyal to the LORD your God. Although these nations that you are about to dispossess do give heed to soothsayers and diviners, as for you, the LORD your God does not permit you to do so.

3. *Male reference: apostasy*

Exod. 22.19 [22.20]

Whoever sacrifices to any god, other than the LORD alone, shall be devoted to destruction.

Deut. 13.7-19 [13.6-18]

If anyone secretly entices you – even if it is your brother, your father's son or your mother's son, or your own son or daughter, or the wife you embrace, or your most intimate friend – saying, 'Let us go worship other gods', whom neither you nor your ancestors have known, any of the gods of the peoples that are around you, whether near you or far away from you, from one end of the earth to the other, you must not yield to or heed any such persons. Show them no pity or compassion and do not shield them. But you shall surely kill them; your own hand shall be first against them to execute them, and afterwards the hand of all the people. Stone them to death for trying to turn you away from the LORD your God, who brought you out of the land of Egypt, out of the house of slavery. Then all Israel shall hear and be afraid, and never again do any such wickedness.

If you hear it said about one of the towns that the LORD your God is giving you to live in, that scoundrels from among you have gone out and led the inhabitants of the town astray, saying 'Let us go and worship other gods', whom you have not known, then you shall inquire and make a thorough investigation. If the charge is established that such an abhorrent thing has been done among you, you shall put the inhabitants of that town to the sword, utterly destroying it and everything in it – even putting its livestock to the sword. All of its spoil you shall gather into its public square; then burn the town and all of its spoil with fire, as a whole burnt offering to the LORD your God. It shall remain a perpetual ruin, never to be rebuilt. Do not let anything devoted to destruction stick to your hand, so that the LORD may turn from his fierce anger and show you compassion, and in his compassion multiply you, as he swore to your ancestors, if you obey the voice of the LORD your God by keeping all his commandments that I am commanding you today, doing what is right in the sight of the LORD your God.

Deut. 17.2-7

If there is found among you, in one of your towns that the LORD your God is giving you, a man or woman who does what is evil in the sight of the LORD your God, and transgresses his covenant by going to serve other gods and worshiping them – whether the sun or the moon or any of the host of heaven, which I have forbidden – and if it is reported to you or you hear of it, and you make a thorough inquiry, and the charge is proved true that such an abhorrent thing has occurred in Israel, then you shall bring out to your gates that man or that woman who has committed this crime and you shall stone the man or woman to death. On the evidence of two or three witnesses the death sentence shall be executed; a person must not be put to death on the evidence of only one witness. The hands of the witnesses shall be the first raised against the person to execute the death penalty, and afterward the hands of all the people. So you shall purge evil from your midst.

2. *Exclusive Laws*

A. *Exclusive laws that apply only to women*

1. *Injury to a pregnant female*
   Exod. 21.22-25

When people who are fighting injure a pregnant woman so that there is a miscarriage, and yet no further harm follows, the one responsible shall be fined what the woman's husband demands, paying as much as the judges determine. If any harm follows, then you shall give life for life, eye for eye, tooth for tooth, hand for hand, foot for foot, burn for burn, wound for wound, stripe for stripe.

2. *Genital grabbing by a female*
   Deut. 25.11-12

If men get into a fight with one another, and the wife of one intervenes to rescue her husband from the grip of his opponent by reaching out and seizing his genitals, you shall cut off her hand; show no pity.

B. *Laws that exclude women by implication: cultic participation*
   Exod. 23.17

Three times in the year all your males shall appear before the LORD GOD.

   Deut. 16.16

Three times a year all your males shall appear before the LORD your God at the place that he will choose: at the festival of unleavened bread, at the festival of weeks, and at the festival of booths.

C. *Exclusive laws that treat women based on their relationship to men*

1. *Father and daughter: intercourse with an unbetrothed virgin*
   Exod. 22.15-16 [22.16-17]

When a man seduces a virgin who is not engaged to be married, and lies with her, he shall give the bride-price for her and make her his wife. But if her father refuses to give her to him, he shall pay an amount equal to the bride-price for virgins.

   Deut. 22.28-29

If a man meets a virgin who is not engaged, and seizes her and lies with her, and they are caught in the act, the man who lay with her shall give fifty shekels of silver to the young woman's father, and she shall become his wife. Because he violated her he shall not be permitted to divorce her as long as he lives.

2. *Engaged man and woman*

Deut. 22.23-24

If there is a young woman, a virgin already engaged to be married, and a man meets her in the town and lies with her, you shall bring both of them to the gate of that town and stone them to death, the young woman because she did not cry for help in the town and the man because he violated his neighbor's wife. So you shall purge the evil from your midst.

Deut. 22.25-27

But if the man meets the engaged woman in the open country, and the man seizes her and lies with her, then only the man who lay with her shall die. You shall do nothing to the young woman; the young woman has not committed an offense punishable by death, because this case is like that of someone who attacks and murders a neighbor. Since he found her in the open country, the engaged woman may have cried for help, but there was no one to rescue her.

3. *Husband and wife*

a. *Newlywed exemption*

Deut. 24.5

When a man is newly married, he shall not go out with the army or be charged with any related duty. He shall be free at home one year, to be happy with the wife whom he has married.

b. *Bride accused of sexual immorality*

Deut. 22.13-21

Suppose a man marries a woman, but after going in to her, he dislikes her and makes up charges against her, slandering her by saying, 'I married this woman; but when I lay with her, I did not find evidence of her virginity'. The father of the young woman and her mother shall then submit the evidence of the young woman's virginity to the elders of the city at the gate. The father of the young woman shall say to the elders: 'I gave my daughter in marriage to this man but he dislikes her; now he has made up charges against her, saying, 'I did not find evidence of your daughter's virginity'. But here is the evidence of my daughter's virginity'. Then they shall spread out the cloth before the elders of the town. The elders of the town shall take the man and punish him; they shall fine him one hundred shekels of silver (which they shall give to the young woman's father) because he has slandered a virgin of Israel. She shall remain his wife; he shall not be permitted to divorce her as long as he lives. If, however, this charge is true, that evidence of the young woman's virginity was not found, then they shall bring the young woman out to the entrance of her father's house and the men of her town shall stone her to death, because she committed a disgraceful act in Israel by prostituting herself in her father's house. So you shall purge the evil from your midst.

c. *Adultery*

Deut. 22.22

If a man is caught lying with the wife of another man, both of them shall die, the man who lay with the woman as well as the woman. So you shall purge the evil from Israel.

d. *Primogeniture*

Deut. 21.15-17

If a man has two wives, one of them loved and the other disliked, and if both the loved and the disliked have borne him sons, the firstborn being the son of the one who is disliked, then on the day when he wills his possessions to his sons, he is not permitted to treat the son of the loved as the firstborn in preference to the son of the disliked, who is the firstborn. He must acknowledge as firstborn the son of the one who is disliked, giving him a double portion of all that he has; since he is the first issue of his virility, the right of the firstborn is his.

e. *Incest*

Deut. 23.1 [22.30]

A man shall not marry his father's wife, thereby violating his father's rights.

f. *Restriction of remarriage*

Deut. 24.1-4

Suppose a man enters into marriage with a woman, but she does not please him because he finds something objectionable about her, and so he writes her a certificate of divorce, puts it in her hand, and sends her out of his house; she then leaves his house and goes off to become another man's wife. Then suppose the second man dislikes her, writes her a bill of divorce, puts it in her hand, and sends her out of his house (or the second man who married her dies); her first husband, who sent her away, is not permitted to take her again to be his wife after she has been defiled; for that would be abhorrent to the LORD, and you shall not bring guilt on the land that the LORD your God is giving you as a possession.

4. *Deceased husband and widow: levirate marriage*

Deut. 25.5-10

When brothers reside together, and one of them dies and has no son, the wife of the deceased shall not be married outside the family to a stranger. Her husband's brother shall go in to her, taking her in marriage, and performing the duty of a husband's brother to her, and the firstborn whom she bears shall succeed to the name of the deceased brother, so that his name may not be blotted out of Israel.

But if the man has no desire to marry his brother's widow, then his brother's widow shall go up to the elders at the gate and say, 'My husband's brother refuses to perpetuate his brother's name in Israel; he will not perform the duty of a husband's brother to me'. Then the elders of his town shall summon him and speak to him. If he persists, saying, 'I have no desire to marry her', then his brother's wife shall go up to him in the presence of the elders, pull his sandal off his foot, spit in his face, and declare, 'This is what is done to the man who does not build up his brother's house'. Throughout Israel his family shall be known as 'the house of him whose sandal was pulled off'.

5. *Female war captive*

Deut. 21.10-14

When you go out to war against your enemies, and the LORD your God hands them over to you and you take them captive, suppose you see among the captives a beautiful woman whom you desire and want to marry, and so you bring her home to your house: she shall shave her head, pare her nails, discard her captive's garb, and shall remain in your house a full month, mourning for her father and mother; after that you may go in to her and be her husband, and she shall be your wife. But if you are not satisfied with her, you shall let her go free and not sell her for money. You must not treat her as a slave, since you have dishonored her.

Appendix B

RELATIVE PRIVILEGES

	Privileged		*Non-Privileged*	
Male	A Male, Privileged, Israelite	B Male, Privileged, Non-Israelite	C Male, Non-privileged, Israelite	D Male, Non-privileged, Non-Israelite
Female	E Female, Privileged, Israelite	F Female, Privileged, Non-Israelite	G Female, Non-privileged, Israelite	H Female, Non-privileged, Non-Israelite

Notes:

1. Group A has privileges over groups B through H, but groups A through D (males) have privileges over groups E through H (females).
2. Being male or female is the 'master-status' trait.
3. Inclusive laws address groups A through H (Israelite males and Israelite females) but not groups B, D, F and H (non-Israelites). Inclusive laws present symmetrical gender roles.
4. Exclusive laws address groups E through H (females). Exclusive laws present asymmetrical gender roles.

Bibliography

Ackerman, Susan, '"And the Women Knead Dough": The Worship of the Queen of Heaven in Sixth-Century Judah', in Peggy L. Day (ed.), *Gender and Difference in Ancient Israel* (Minneapolis: Fortress Press, 1989), pp. 109–24.

Adam, A.K.M., *What Is Postmodern Biblical Criticism?*, Guides to Biblical Scholarship (Minneapolis: Fortress Press, 1995).

Adorno, Theodor, and Max Horkheimer, *Dialectic of Enlightenment* (trans. John Cumming; New York: Herder and Herder, 1972).

Adorno, Theodor, *Negative Dialectics* (trans. E.B. Ashton; New York: Seabury, 1973).

Aichele, George, and others, *The Postmodern Bible* (New Haven: Yale University Press, 1995).

Allwood, Gill, *French Feminisms: Gender and Violence in Contemporary Theory* (London: UCL Press, 1998).

Alt, Albrecht, 'The Origins of Israelite Law', in *Essays on Old Testament History and Religion* (trans. Robert A. Wilson; Garden City, NY: Doubleday, 1967), pp. 101–71.

Ashmore, James P., 'The Social Setting of the Law in Deuteronomy' (unpublished doctoral dissertation, Duke University, 1995).

Austin, J.L., *How to Do Things with Words* (Cambridge, MA: Harvard University Press, 2nd edn, 1975).

Bailey, Randall C., 'The Danger of Ignoring One's Cultural Bias in Reading Biblical Texts', in R.S. Sugirtharajah (ed.), *The Postcolonial Bible* (Sheffield: Sheffield Academic Press, 1998), pp. 66–90.

—'They're Nothing but Incestuous Bastards: The Polemical Use of Sex and Sexuality in Hebrew Canon Narratives', in Fernando F. Segovia and Mary Ann Tolbert (eds.), *Reading From This Place (Vol. 1): Social Location and Biblical Interpretation in the United States* (Minneapolis: Fortress Press, 1995), pp. 121–38.

Bal, Mieke, *Death & Dissymmetry: The Politics of Coherence in the Book of Judges* (Chicago: University of Chicago Press, 1988).

Barry, Peter, *Beginning Theory: An Introduction to Literary and Cultural Theory* (Manchester: Manchester University Press, 1995).

Barth, Fredrik (ed.), 'Introduction', in *Ethnic Groups and Boundaries: The Social Organization of Culture Difference* (Boston: Little Brown, 1969), pp. 9–38.

Bechtel, Lyn M., 'Shame as a Sanction of Social Control in Biblical Israel: Judicial, Political, and Social Shaming', *JSOT* 49 (1991), pp. 47–76.

—'What If Dinah Is Not Raped?', *JSOT* 62 (1994), pp. 19–36.

Bem, Sandra Lipsitz, *The Lenses of Gender: Transforming the Debate on Sexual Inequality* (New Haven: Yale University Press, 1993).

Benhabib, Seyla, *Critique, Norm, and Utopia: A Study of the Foundations of Critical Theory* (New York: Columbia University Press, 1986).

Benhabib, Seyla, and Drucilla Cornell, 'Introduction: Beyond the Politics of Gender', in Seyla Benhabib and Drucilla Cornell (eds.), *Feminism as Critique: On the Politics of Gender* (Minneapolis: University of Minnesota Press, 1987), pp. 1–15.

Benjamin, Walter, 'Theses on the Philosophy of History', in Hannah Arendt (ed.), *Illuminations: Essays and Reflections* (New York: Schocken Books, 1986), pp. 253–64.
Bennett, Harold V., *Injustice Made Legal: Deuteronomic Law and the Plight of Widows, Strangers and Orphans in Ancient Israel* (Grand Rapids: Eerdmans, 2002).
Berger, Peter L., *The Sacred Canopy: Elements of a Sociological Theory of Religion* (New York: Anchor Books/Doubleday, 1967).
Berger, Peter L., and Thomas Luckmann, *The Social Construction of Reality: A Treatise in the Sociology of Knowledge* (New York: Anchor Books/Doubleday, 1966).
Berquist, Jon L., *Controlling Corporeality: The Body and the Household in Ancient Israel* (New Brunswick, NJ: Rutgers University Press, 2002).
Birch, Bruce C., *Let Justice Roll Down: The Old Testament, Ethics, and Christian Life* (Louisville, KY: Westminster/John Knox Press, 1991).
Bird, Phyllis A., *Missing Persons and Mistaken Identities: Women and Gender in Ancient Israel* (Minneapolis: Fortress Press, 1997).
—'The End of the Male Cult Prostitute: A Literary-Historical and Sociological Analysis of Hebrew *Qādēš-Qĕdēšîm*', in J.A. Emerton (ed.), *VTSup 1995 Congress Volume* (Leiden: E.J. Brill, 1997), pp. 37–80.
Bloomquist, Karen L., 'Sexual Violence: Patriarchy's Offense and Defense', in Joanne Carlson Brown and Carole R. Bohn (eds.), *Christianity, Patriarchy, and Abuse: A Feminist Critique* (New York: Pilgrim Press, 1989), pp. 62–69.
Boecker, Hans Jochen, *Law and the Administration of Justice in the Old Testament & Ancient East* (trans. Jeremy Moiser; Minneapolis: Augsburg Publishing House, 1980).
Bordo, Susan, 'The Body and the Reproduction of Femininity: A Feminist Appropriation of Foucault', in Alison M. Jaggar and Susan Bordo (eds.), *Gender/Body/Knowledge: Feminist Reconstructions of Being and Knowing* (New Brunswick, NJ: Rutgers University Press, 1989), pp. 13–33.
—*Unbearable Weight: Feminism, Western Culture, and the Body* (Berkeley: University of California Press, 1993).
Botha, Pieter J.J., 'Submission and Violence: Exploring Gender Relations in the First-Century World', *Neotestamentica* 34 (2000), pp. 1–38.
Bottéro, Jean, *Mesopotamia: Writing, Reasoning and the Gods* (trans. Zainab Bahrani and Marc van de Mieroop; Chicago: Chicago University Press, 1992).
Bourque, Linda Brookover, *Defining Rape* (Durham: Duke University Press, 1989).
Bowen, Nancy R., 'The Daughters of Your People: Female Prophets in Ezekiel 13.17–23', *JBL* 118 (1999), pp. 417–33.
Bowker, Lee H. (ed.), *Masculinities and Violence* (Research on Men and Masculinities, 10; Thousand Oaks, CA: Sage Publications, 1998).
Boyd, Stephen Blake, W. Merle Longwood and Mark W. Muesse (eds.), *Redeeming Men: Religion and Masculinities* (Louisville, KY: Westminster/John Knox Press, 1996).
Brenner, Athalya (ed.), *A Feminist Companion to Exodus to Deuteronomy* (FCB, 6; Sheffield: Sheffield Academic Press, 1994).
—'On Incest', in Athalya Brenner (ed.), *A Feminist Companion to Exodus to Deuteronomy* (FCB, 6; Sheffield: Sheffield Academic Press, 1994), pp. 113–38.
—*The Intercourse of Knowledge: On Gendering Desire and 'Sexuality' in the Hebrew Bible* (Leiden: E.J. Brill, 1997).
—*The Israelite Woman: Social Role and Literary Type in Biblical Narrative* (Sheffield: JSOT Press, 1985).
Brett, Mark G., *Genesis: Procreation and the Politics of Identity* (Old Testament Readings; New York: Routledge, 2000).

Brett, Mark G. (ed.), *Ethnicity and the Bible* (Leiden: Brill Academic Publishers, 1996).

Brittan, Arthur, *Masculinity and Power* (Oxford: Basil Blackwell, 1989).

Brod, Harry, and Michael Kaufman (eds.), *Theorizing Masculinities* (Research on Men and Masculinities, 5; Thousand Oaks, CA: Sage Publications, 1994).

Brown, Joanne Carlson, and Carole R. Bohn (eds.), *Christianity, Patriarchy, and Abuse: A Feminist Critique* (New York: Pilgrim Press, 1989).

Brueggemann, Walter, 'Exodus' (*NIB* I; Nashville: Abingdon Press, 1994), pp. 675–982.

Buchwald, Emilie, Pamela R. Fletcher and Martha Roth (eds.), *Transforming a Rape Culture* (Minneapolis: Milkweed Editions, 1993).

Buck-Morss, Susan, *The Origin of Negative Dialectics: Theodor W. Adorno, Walter Benjamin, and the Frankfurt Institute* (New York: The Free Press, 1977).

Burnette-Bletsch, Rhonda J., 'My Bone and My Flesh: The Agrarian Family in Biblical Law' (unpublished doctoral dissertation, Duke University, 1998).

Butler, Judith, *Excitable Speech: A Politics of the Performative* (New York: Routledge, 1997).

—*Gender Trouble: Feminism and the Subversion of Identity* (New York: Routledge, 1990).

Calhoun, Craig. *Critical Social Theory: Culture, History, and the Challenge of Difference* (Oxford: Basil Blackwell, 1995).

Cameron, Averil, and Amélie Kuhrt (eds.), *Images of Women in Antiquity* (Detroit: Wayne State University Press, 1993).

Carmichael, Calum M., *Law and Narrative in the Bible: The Evidence of the Deuteronomic Laws and the Decalogue* (Ithaca, NY: Cornell University Press, 1985).

—*The Laws of Deuteronomy* (Ithaca, NY: Cornell University Press, 1974).

—*The Origins of Biblical Law: The Decalogue and the Book of the Covenant* (Ithaca, NY: Cornell University Press, 1992).

—*Women, Law, and the Genesis Traditions* (Edinburgh: Edinburgh University Press, 1979).

Carr, David M., 'Gender and the Shaping of Desire in the Song of Songs and Its Interpretations', *JBL* 119 (2000), pp. 233–48.

—*The Erotic Word: Sexuality, Spirituality, and the Bible* (New York: Oxford University Press, 2003).

Cassuto, Umberto, *A Commentary on the Book of Exodus* (trans. Israel Abrahams; Jerusalem: Magnes Press/The Hebrew University, 1967).

Clements, Ronald E., 'Deuteronomy', *NIB* II (Nashville: Abingdon Press, 1998), pp. 269–538.

—*Exodus* (Cambridge: Cambridge University Press, 1972), pp. 135–36.

Clines, David J.A., 'He-Prophets: Masculinity as a Problem for the Hebrew Prophets and Their Interpreters', in Robert P. Carroll, Alastair G. Hunter and Philip R. Davies (eds.), *Sense and Sensitivity: Essays on Reading the Bible in Memory of Robert Carroll* (London: Sheffield Academic Press, 2002), pp. 311–28.

—*Interested Parties: The Ideology of Writers and Readers of the Hebrew Bible* (JSOTSup, 205; Sheffield: Sheffield Academic Press, 1995).

Collins, John 'The Zeal of Phineas: The Bible and the Legitimation of Violence', *JBL* 122 (2003), pp. 3–21.

Collins, Patricia Hill, *Black Feminist Thought* (New York: Routledge, 1990).

—*Fighting Words: Black Women & the Search for Justice* (Minneapolis: University of Minnesota Press, 1998).

Connell, R.W., *Gender and Power: Society, the Person, and Sexual Politics* (Stanford: Stanford University Press, 1987).

—*Gender* (Cambridge: Polity Press, 2002).

—*Masculinities* (Cambridge: Polity Press, 1995).

Cooper-White, Pamela, *The Cry of Tamar: Violence against Women and the Church's Response* (Minneapolis: Fortress Press, 1995).

Cover, Robert, 'Nomos and Narrative', in Martha Minow, Michael Ryan and Austin Sarat (eds.), *Narrative, Violence, and the Law: The Essays of Robert Cover* (Ann Arbor: University of Michigan Press, 1992), pp. 95–172.

Crenshaw, Kimberlé, 'Demarginalizing the Intersection of Race and Sex: A Black Feminist Critique of Antidiscrimination Doctrine, Feminist Theory and Antiracist Politics', *University of Chicago Legal Forum* 129 (1989), pp. 139–67, reprinted in D. Kelly Weisberg (ed.), *Feminist Legal Theory: Foundations* (Philadelphia: Temple University Press, 1993), pp. 383–95.

Crüsemann, Frank, *The Torah: Theology and Social History of Old Testament Law* (trans. Allan W. Mahnke; Minneapolis: Fortress Press, 1996).

Daube, David, 'Biblical Landmarks in the Struggle for Women's Rights', *Juridical Review* 23 (1978), pp. 177–97.

Davies, Eryl W., 'Inheritance Rights and the Hebrew Levirate Marriage: Part 1'. *VT* 31 (1981), pp. 138–44.

—'Inheritance Rights and the Hebrew Levirate Marriage: Part 2', *VT* 31 (1981), pp. 257–68.

Davies, Jon, and Gerard Loughlin (eds.), *Sex These Days: Essays on Theology, Sexuality, and Society* (Sheffield: Sheffield Academic Press, 1997).

Davis, Angela Y., *Women, Race, and Class* (New York: Random House, 1981).

Day, Linda, 'Rhetoric and Domestic Violence in Ezekiel 16', *BibInt* 8 (2000), pp. 205–230.

Day, Peggy L. (ed.), *Gender and Difference in Ancient Israel* (Minneapolis: Fortress Press, 1989).

De Vaux, Roland, *Ancient Israel: Its Life and Institutions* (trans. John McHugh; New York: McGraw-Hill, 1961).

Derrida, Jacques, *Of Grammatology* (trans. Gayatri Chakravorty Spivak; Baltimore: The Johns Hopkins University Press, 1976).

Deutsch, Francine M., *Halving It All: How Equally Shared Parenting Works* (Cambridge: Harvard University Press, 1999).

Dews, Peter, *Logics of Disintegration: Post-Structuralist Thought and the Claims of Critical Theory* (London: Verso, 1987).

Dobash, R. Emerson, and Russell Dobash, *Violence against Wives: A Case against the Patriarchy* (New York: The Free Press, 1979).

Driver, G.R., and John C. Miles, *The Assyrian Laws* (Oxford: Clarendon Press, 1935).

—*The Babylonian Laws* (2 vols.; Oxford: Clarendon Press, 1956).

Edwards, Anne, 'Male Violence in Feminist Theory: An Analysis of the Changing Conceptions of Sex/Gender Violence and Male Dominance', in Jalna Hanmer and Mary Maynard (eds.), *Women, Violence, and Social Control* (Atlantic Highlands, NJ: Humanities Press International, 1987), pp. 13–29.

England, Paula (ed.), *Theory on Gender/Feminism on Theory* (New York: Aldine De Gruyter, 1993).

Epzstein, Léon, *Social Justice in the Ancient Near East and the People of the Bible* (trans. John Bowden; London: SCM Press, 1986).

Exum, J. Cheryl, 'Developing Strategies of Feminist Criticism/Developing Strategies for Commentating the Song of Songs', in David J.A. Clines and Stephen D. Moore (eds.), *Auguries: The Jubilee Volume of the Sheffield Department of Biblical Studies* (JSOTSup, 269; Sheffield: Sheffield Academic Press, 1998), pp. 206–49.

—*Fragmented Women: Feminist (Sub)Versions of Biblical Narratives* (Valley Forge: Trinity Press International, 1993).

—'The Ethics of Biblical Violence against Women', in John W. Rogerson, Margaret Davies and M. Daniel Carroll R. (eds.), *The Bible in Ethics: The Second Sheffield Colloquium* (JSOTSup, 207; Sheffield: Sheffield Academic Press, 1995), pp. 248–71.

Falk, Ze'ev W., *Hebrew Law in Biblical Times* (Provo, UT: Brigham Young University Press, 2001).

Fensham, Charles F., 'Widow, Orphan, and the Poor in Ancient near Eastern Legal and Wisdom Literature', *JNES* 21, (1962), pp. 129–39.

Fetterley, Judith, *The Resisting Reader: A Feminist Approach to American Fiction* (Bloomington: Indiana University Press, 1978).

Fewell, Dana Nolan, and David M. Gunn, *Gender, Power, & Promise: The Subject of the Bible's First Story* (Nashville: Abingdon Press, 1993).

Fineman, Martha Albertson, 'Preface', in Martha Albertson Fineman and Roxanne Mykitiuk (eds.), *The Public Nature of Private Violence: The Discovery of Domestic Abuse* (New York: Routledge, 1994), pp. xi–xviii.

—*The Neutered Mother, the Sexual Family, and Other Twentieth Century Tragedies* (New York: Routledge, 1995).

Finkelhor, David, 'Common Features of Family Abuse', in David Finkelhor, Richard J. Gelles, Gerald T. Hotaling and Murray A. Straus (eds.), *The Dark Side of Families: Current Family Violence Research* (Beverly Hills: Sage Publications, 1983), pp. 17–28.

Finkelstein, J.J., *The Ox That Gored* (Philadelphia: The American Philosophical Society, 1981).

Fitzpatrick-McKinley, Anne, *The Transformation of Torah from Scribal Advice to Law*, (JSOTSup, 287; Sheffield: Sheffield Academic Press, 1999).

Fletcher, Anthony, *Gender, Sex, and Subordination in England, 1500–1800* (New Haven: Yale University Press, 1995).

Foucault, Michel, *Discipline and Punish: The Birth of the Prison* (trans. Alan Sheridan; New York: Random House, 1977).

—*Power/Knowledge: Selected Interviews and Other Writings 1972–1977*, (ed. Colin Gordon; trans. Leo Marshall, Colin Gordon, John Mepham and Kate Soper; New York: Pantheon Books, 1980).

—*The History of Sexuality (Vol. 1): An Introduction* (trans. Robert Hurley; New York: Vantage Books, 1990).

—*The Order of Things: An Archaeology of the Human Sciences* (New York: Vantage Books, reprint edn, 1994).

Fowl, Stephen, 'The Ethics of Interpretation or What's Left Over After the Elimination of Meaning', in David J.A. Clines, Stephen E. Fowl and Stanley E. Porter (eds.), *The Bible in Three Dimensions: Essays in celebration of forty years of Biblical Studies in the University of Sheffield* (JSOTSup, 87; Sheffield: Sheffield Academic Press, 1990), pp. 379–98.

Francis, Leslie (ed.), *Date Rape* (University Park, PA: Pennsylvania State University Press, 1996).

Freeman, Jo, *Women: A Feminist Perspective* (Mountain View, CA: Mayfield Pub. Co., 5th edn, 1994).

Frug, Mary Jo, 'A Postmodern Feminist Legal Manifesto (an Unfinished Draft)', in Dan Danielsen and Karen Engle (eds.), *After Identity: A Reader in Law and Culture* (New York: Routledge, 1995), pp. 7–23.

Frymer-Kensky, Tikva, 'Deuteronomy', in Carol A. Newsom and Sharon H. Ringe (eds.), *Women's Bible Commentary* (Louisville, KY: Westminster/John Knox Press, 1998), pp. 57–68.

—*In the Wake of the Goddesses: Women, Culture and the Biblical Transformation of Pagan Myth* (New York: Faucett Columbine, 1992).
—'Law and Philosophy: The Case of Sex in the Bible', *Semeia* 45 (1989), pp. 89–102.
—*Reading the Women of the Bible: New Interpretations of Their Stories* (New York: Schocken Books, 2002).
—'Virginity in the Bible', in Bernard M. Levinson, Victor H. Matthews and Tikva Frymer-Kensky (eds.), *Gender and Law in the Hebrew Bible and the Ancient Near East* (Sheffield: Sheffield Academic Press, 1998), pp. 79–96.
Garbarino, James, *Lost Boys: Why Our Sons Turn Violent and How We Can Save Them* (New York: Free Press, 1999).
Gatens, Moira, 'A Critique of the Sex/Gender Distinction', in Sneja Gunew (ed.), *A Reader in Feminist Knowledge* (New York: Routledge, 1991), pp. 139–57.
Gemser, B., 'The Importance of the Motive Clause in Old Testament Law', *VTSup* 1 (1953), pp. 50–66.
Gerstenberger, Erhard S., 'Covenant and Commandment', *JBL* 84 (1965), pp. 38–51.
—Wesen und Herkunft des 'Apodiktishen Rechts', WMANT 20 (Neukirchen–Vluyn: Neukirchener Verlag, 1965).
Gilmore, David D., *Manhood in the Making: Cultural Concepts of Masculinity* (New Haven: Yale University Press, 1990).
Girard, René, *Violence and the Sacred* (trans. Patrick Gregory; Baltimore: The Johns Hopkins University Press, 1977).
Goody, J.R., 'Polygyny, Economy, and the Role of Women', in J.R. Goody (ed.), *The Character of Kinship* (Cambridge: Cambridge University Press, 1973), pp. 175–90.
—*The Logic of Writing and the Organization of Society* (Cambridge: Cambridge University Press, 1986).
Graetz, Naomi, *Silence is Deadly: Judaism Confronts Wifebeating* (Northvale, NJ: Jason Aronson Press, 1998).
Greenberg, Moshe, 'Some Postulates of Biblical Criminal Law', in M. Haran (ed.), *Y. Kaufmann Jubilee Volume* (Jerusalem: Detus Goldberg, 1960), pp. 5–28.
Griffin, Susan, 'Rape the All-American Crime', *Ramparts* 10 (September 1971), pp. 21–35.
Grosby, Steven, *Biblical Ideas of Nationality: Ancient and Modern* (Winona Lake, IN: Eisenbrauns, 2002).
Grosz, Katarzyna, 'Bridewealth and Dowry in Nuzi', in Averil Cameron and Amélie Kuhrt (eds.), *Images of Women in Antiquity* (Detroit: Wayne State University Press, rev. edn, 1993), pp. 193–206.
Groth, Bobbie, 'Lessons from the Spiritual Lives of Men Who Work in the Movement to End Violence Against Women and Children', *Journal of Religion and Abuse* 2 (2000), pp. 5–31 (italics in the original).
Gusfield, Joseph R., *Symbolic Crusade: Status Politics and the American Temperance Movement* (Urbana: University of Illinois Press, 2nd edn, 1986).
Haas, Peter, '"Die He Shall Surely Die": the Structure of Homicide in Biblical Law', *Semeia* 45 (1989), pp. 67–88.
Hamilton, Jeffries M., *Social Justice and Deuteronomy: The Case of Deuteronomy 15* (SBLDS, 136; Atlanta: Scholars Press, 1992).
—'*Hā'āreṣ* in the Shemitta Law', *VT* 42 (1992), pp. 214–22.
Hanmer, Jalna, and Mary Maynard, *Women, Violence, and Social Control* (Atlantic Highlands, NJ: Humanities Press International, 1987).
Hanson, Paul, 'The Theological Significance of Contradiction Within the Book of the Cove-

nant', in George W. Coats and Burke O. Long (eds.), *Canon and Authority: Essays in Old Testament Religion and Theology* (Philadelphia: Fortress Press, 1977), pp. 110–31.

Hanssen, Beatrice, *Critique of Violence: Between Poststructuralism and Critical Theory* (Warwick Studies in European Philosophy; New York: Routledge, 2000).

Hatty, Suzanne E., *Masculinities, Violence and Culture* (Sage Series on Violence against Women; Thousand Oaks, CA: Sage Publications, 2000).

Hauptman, Judith, 'Rabbinic Interpretation of Scripture', in Athalya Brenner and Carole Fontaine (eds.), *A Feminist Companion to Reading the Bible: Approaches, Strategies and Methods* (FCB; Sheffield: Sheffield Academic Press, 1997), pp. 472–86.

—*Rereading the Rabbis: A Woman's Voice* (Oxford: Westview Press, 1998).

Heard, R. Christopher, *Dynamics of Diselection: Ambiguity in Genesis 12–36 and Ethnic Boundaries in Post-Exilic Judah* (SBLSS, 39; Atlanta: Society of Biblical Literature, 2001).

Hegel, G.W.F., *The Phenomenology of Mind* (trans. J.B. Baillie; London: George Allen & Unwin, 2nd edn, 1964).

Hekman, Susan J., *Gender and Knowledge: Elements of a Postmodern Feminism* (Boston: Northeastern University Press, 1990).

Herman, Dianne, 'The Rape Culture', in Jo Freeman (ed.), *Women: A Feminist Perspective* (Palo Alto: Mayfield Publishing Company, 3rd edn, 1984), pp. 20–38.

Hester, Marianne, Liz Kelly, and Jill Radford (eds.), *Women, Violence and Male Power* (Buckingham: Open University Press, 1996).

Hewitt, Marsha Aileen, *Critical Theory of Religion: A Feminist Analysis* (Minneapolis: Fortress Press, 1995).

Hiebert, Paula S., '"Whence Shall Help Come to Me?": The Biblical Widow', in Peggy L. Day (ed.), *Gender and Difference in Ancient Israel* (Minneapolis: Fortress Press, 1989), pp. 125–41.

hooks, bell, 'Violence in Intimate Relationships: A Feminist Perspective', in *Talking Back: Thinking Feminist, Thinking Black* (Boston, MA: South End Press, 1989), pp. 84–91.

Hughes, Everett C., 'Dilemmas and Contradictions of Status', *The American Journal of Sociology* 50 (1945), pp. 353–59.

Jackson, Bernard S., 'Reflections on Biblical Criminal Law', in *Essays in Jewish and Comparative Legal History* (Studies in Judaism in Late Antiquity, 10; Leiden: E.J. Brill, 1975), pp. 108–52.

—'Modelling Biblical Law: The Covenant Code', *Chicago-Kent Law Review* 70 (1995), pp. 1745–1827.

—*Studies in the Semiotics of Biblical Law* (JSOTSup, 314; Sheffield: Sheffield Academic Press, 2000).

—'The Goring Ox', in *Essays in Jewish and Comparative Legal History* (Studies in Judaism and Late Antiquity, 10; Leiden: E.J. Brill, 1975), pp. 108–52 (115–16)

—'The Problem of Exodus XXI 22–5', *VT* 23 (1973), pp. 273–304.

Jaggar, Alison M., *Feminist Politics and Human Nature* (Totowa, NJ: Rowman & Allanheld, 1983).

Janzen, Waldemar, *Old Testament Ethics: A Paradigmatic Approach* (Louisville, KY: Westminster/John Knox Press, 1994).

Jay, Nancy, 'Sacrifice as Remedy for Having Been Born of Woman', in Clarissa W. Atkinson, Constance H. Buchanon and Margaret R. Miles (eds.), *Immaculate and Powerful: the Female in Sacred Image and Social Reality* (Boston: Beacon Press, 1985), pp. 283–309.

—*Throughout Your Generations Forever: Sacrifice, Religion and Paternity* (Chicago: University of Chicago Press, 1992).

Jehlen, Myra, 'Gender', in Frank Lentricchia and Thomas McLaughlin (eds.), *Critical Terms for Literary Study* (Chicago: University of Chicago Press, 2nd edn, 1995), pp. 263–73.

Johnston, Hank, Enrique Laraña and Joseph R. Gusfield, 'Identities, Grievances, and New Social Movements', in Hank Johnston, Enrique Laraña and Joseph R. Gusfield (eds.), *New Social Movements: From Ideology to Identity* (Philadelphia: Temple University Press, 1994), pp. 3–35.

Jonte-Pace, Diane E., *Speaking the Unspeakable: Religion, Misogyny, and the Uncanny Mother in Freud's Cultural Texts* (Berkeley: University of California Press, 2001).

Joy, Morny, Kathleen O'Grady and Judith L. Poxon (eds.), 'Editors' Introduction to "The Chosen People and the Choice of Foreignness"', *French Feminists on Religion: A Reader* (New York: Routledge, 2002), pp. 150–52.

—*Religion in French Feminist Thought, Critical Perspectives* (New York: Routledge, 2003).

Kamionkowski, S. Tamar, *Gender Reversal and Cosmic Chaos: A Study on the Book of Ezekiel* (JSOTSup, 368; London: Sheffield Academic Press, 2003).

Kim, Hyun Chul Paul, 'Gender Complementarity in the Hebrew Bible', in Wonil Kim, Deborah Ellens, Michael Floyd and Marvin A. Sweeney (eds.), *Reading the Hebrew Bible for a New Millennium: Form, Concept, and Theological Perspective* (Harrisburg, PA: Trinity Press International, 2000), pp. 263–91.

Kindlon, Dan, and Michael Thompson, with Teresa Barker, *Raising Cain: Protecting the Emotional Life of Boys* (New York: Ballantine, 1999).

Kirk-Duggan, Cheryl A., *Misbegotten Anguish: A Theology and Ethics of Violence* (St. Louis: Chalice Press, 2001).

Knight, Douglas A., 'Village Law and the Book of the Covenant', in Saul M. Olyan and Robert C. Culley (eds.), *A Wise and Discerning Mind: Essays in Honor of Burke O. Long* (BJS, 325; Providence, RI: Brown Judaic Studies, 2000), pp. 163–79.

—'Whose Agony? Whose Ecstacy?: The Politics of Deuteronomic Law', in David Penchansky and Paul L. Redditt (eds.), *Shall Not The Judge Of All the Earth Do What Is Right: Studies on the Nature of God in Tribute to James L. Crenshaw* (Winona Lake, IN: Eisenbrauns, 2000), pp. 97–112.

Kristeva, Julia, 'About Chinese Women', in Toril Moi (ed.), *The Kristeva Reader* (European Perspectives; trans. Leon S. Roudiez and Sean Hand; New York: Columbia University Press, 1986), pp. 138–59.

—*New Maladies of the Soul* (European Perspectives; New York: Columbia University Press, 1995).

—*Powers of Horror: An Essay on Abjection* (European Perspectives; New York: Columbia University Press, 1982).

—'Ruth the Moabite', in *Strangers to Ourselves* (trans. Leon S. Roudiez; New York: Columbia University Press, 1991), pp. 69–76.

—*The Kristeva Reader* (ed. Toril Moi; New York: Columbia University Press, 1986).

Kurzon, Dennis, *It Is Hereby Performed: Explorations in Legal Speech Acts* (Pragmatics and Beyond VII, 6; Amsterdam: John Benjamins, 1986).

Lafont, Sophie, *Femmes, Droit et Justice dans l'Antiquité orientale: Contribution à l'étude du droit pénal au Proche-Orient ancien* (OBO, 165; Editions Universitaires Fribourg Suisse/Gottingen: Vandenhoeck & Ruprecht, 1999).

—'Mesopotamia: Middle Assyrian Period', in Raymond Westbrook (ed.), *A History of Ancient Near Eastern Law* (HdO, 72/1; Leiden: E.J. Brill, 2003), pp. 521–63.

Laqueur, Thomas, *Making Sex: Body and Gender from the Greeks to Freud* (Cambridge, MA: Harvard University Press, 1990).

Law, Sylvia A., and Patricia Hennessey, 'Is the Law Male?: The Case of Family Law', *Chicago-Kent Law Review* 69 (1993), pp. 345–58.

Leiter, David A., 'The Unattainable Ideal: Impractical and/or Unenforceable Rules in the Ancient Israelite Legal Collections' (unpublished doctoral dissertation, Drew University, 1994).

Lemche, Niels Peter, 'Justice in Western Asia in Antiquity, Or: Why No Laws Were Needed!', *Chicago-Kent Law Review* 70 (1995), pp. 1695–1716.

Lenski, Gerhard E., *Power and Privilege: A Theory of Social Stratification* (Chapel Hill: The University of North Carolina Press, 1984).

Levenson, Jon D., 'Poverty and the State in Biblical Thought', *Judaism* 25 (1976), pp. 230–41.

Levenston, E.A., 'The Speech Acts of God', *Hebrew University Studies in Literature and the Arts* 12 (1984), pp. 129–45.

Levinson, Bernard M., 'Calum M. Carmichael's Approach to the Laws of Deuteronomy', *HTR* 83 (1990), pp. 227–57.

—*Deuteronomy and the Hermeneutics of Legal Innovation* (New York: Oxford University Press, 1997).

Levinson, Bernard M. (ed.), *Theory and Method in Biblical and Cuneiform Law: Revision, Interpolation, and Development* (JSOTSup, 181; Sheffield: Sheffield Academic Press, 1994).

Lipinski, E., 'The Wife's Right to Divorce in the Light of an Ancient Near Eastern Tradition', *The Jewish Law Annual* IV (1981), pp. 9–27.

Lloyd, Genevieve, *The Man of Reason: 'Male' and 'Female' in Western Philosophy* (Minneapolis: University of Minnesota Press, 2nd edn, 1993).

Lohfink, Norbert, 'Das Deuteronomische Gesetz in der Endgestalt-Entwurf einer Gesellschaft ohne marginale Gruppen', *BN* 51 (1990), pp. 25–40.

—'Poverty in the Laws of the Ancient Near East and of the Bible', *TS* 52 (1991), pp. 34–50.

Lorber, Judith, *Gender Inequality: Feminist Theories and Politics* (Los Angeles: Roxbury, 1998).

—*Paradoxes of Gender* (New Haven: Yale University Press, 1994).

Lorber, Judith, and Susan A. Farrell (eds.), 'Preface', *The Social Construction of Gender* (Newbury Park: SAGE Publications, 1991), pp. 1–5.

MacKinnon, Catharine A., *Feminism Unmodified: Discourses on Life and Law* (Cambridge: Harvard University Press, 1987).

—*Towards a Feminist Theory of the State* (Cambridge, MA: Harvard University Press, 1989).

Malul, Meir, *Knowledge, Control, and Sex: Studies in Biblical Thought, Culture, and Worldview* (Tel Aviv-Jaffa, Israel: Archaeological Center Publications, 2002).

Mananzan, Mary John, *et al.* (eds.), *Women Resisting Violence: Spirituality for Life* (Maryknoll, NY: Orbis Books, 1996).

Marcus, Sharon, 'Fighting Bodies, Fighting Words: A Theory and Politics of Rape Prevention', in Judith Butler and Joan Wallach Scott (eds.), *Feminists Theorize the Political* (New York: Routledge, 1992), pp. 385–403.

Marshall, Jay W., *Israel and the Book of the Covenant: An Anthropological Approach to Biblical Law* (SBLDS, 140; Atlanta: Scholars Press, 1993).

Martin, Bernice, 'The Pentecostal Gender Paradox: A Cautionary Tale for the Sociology of Religion', in Richard K. Fenn (ed.), *The Blackwell Companion to Sociology of Religion* (Blackwell Companions to Religion, 2; Oxford: Blackwell Publishers, 2001), pp. 52–66.

Matthews, Victor H., 'Honor and Shame in Gender-Related Legal Situations in the Hebrew Bible', in Victor H. Matthews, Bernard M. Levinson and Tikva Frymer-Kensky (eds.),

Gender and Law in the Hebrew Bible and the Ancient Near East (JSOTSup, 262; Sheffield: Sheffield Academic Press, 1998), pp. 97–112.
Matthews, Victor H., Bernard M. Levinson and Tikva Frymer-Kensky (eds.), *Gender and Law in the Hebrew Bible and the Ancient Near East* (JSOTSup, 262; Sheffield: Sheffield Academic Press, 1998).
McClenney-Sadler, Madeline Gay, 'Re-Covering the Daughter's Nakedness: A Formal Analysis of Israelite Kinship Terminology and the Internal Logic of Leviticus 18' (unpublished doctoral dissertation, Duke University, 2001).
Meek, Theophile James, *Hebrew Origins* (Toronto: University of Toronto Press, rev edn, 1950).
Meigs, Anna, 'Multiple Gender Ideologies and Statuses', in Peggy Reeves Sanday and Ruth Gallagher Goodenough (eds.), *Beyond the Second Sex: New Directions in the Anthropology of Gender* (Philadelphia: University of Pennsylvania Press, 1990), pp. 99–112.
Meintjes, Sheila, Anu Pillay and Meredeth Turshen (eds.), *The Aftermath: Women in Post-Conflict Transformation* (New York: Zed Books, 2001).
Melucci, Alberto, 'The Process of Collective Identity', in Hank Johnston and Bert Klandermans (eds.), *Social Movements and Culture* (Social Movements, Protests, and Contention, 4; Minneapolis: University of Minnesota Press, 1995), pp. 41–63.
Mendenhall, George E., 'Ancient Oriental and Biblical Law', *BA* 17 (1954), pp. 26–46.
Messner, Michael A., *Politics of Masculinities: Men in Movements* (Thousand Oaks, CA: Sage Publications, 1997).
Meyers, Carol, *Discovering Eve: Ancient Israelite Women in Context* (New York: Oxford University Press, 1988).
—'Everyday Life: Women in the Period of the Hebrew Bible', in Carol A. Newsom and Sharon H. Ringe (eds.), *Women's Bible Commentary* (Louisville, KY: Westminster/John Knox Press, revised and expanded, 1998), pp. 251–59.
—'Procreation, Production, and Protection: Male-Female Balance in Early Israel', *JAAR* 51 (1983), pp. 569–93.
—'The Family in Early Israel', in Joseph Blenkinsopp, Leo G. Perdue, John J. Collins and Carol Meyers (eds.), *Families in Ancient Israel* (Louisville, KY: Westminster/John Knox Press, 1997), pp. 1–47.
—'The Roots of Restriction: Women in Early Israel', *BA* 41 (1978), pp. 91–103.
—'To Her Mother's House: Considering a Counterpart to the Israelite *Bêt 'Āb*', in Peggy L. Day, David Jobling and Gerald T. Sheppard (eds.), *The Bible and the Politics of Exegesis* (Cleveland: The Pilgrim Press, 1991), pp. 39–51.
Miller, Patrick D., *Deuteronomy* (Interpretation; Louisville, KY: John Knox Press, 1990).
Minda, Gary, *Postmodern Legal Movements: Law and Jurisprudence at Century's End* (New York: New York University Press, 1995).
Mullen, E. Theodore, Jr, *Ethnic Myths and Pentateuchal Foundations: A New Approach to the Formation of the Pentateuch* (Atlanta: Scholars Press, 1997).
—*Narrative History and Ethnic Boundaries: The Deuteronomistic Historian and the Creation of Israelite National Identity* (SBLSS; Atlanta: Scholars Press, 1993).
Nakanose, Shigeyuki, *Josiah's Passover: Sociology & the Liberating Bible* (Maryknoll, NY: Orbis Books, 1993).
Nasuti, Harry P., 'Identity, Identification, and Imitation: The Narrative Hermeneutics of Biblical Law', *Journal of Law and Religion* 4 (1986), pp. 9–23.
Nelson, Richard D., *Deuteronomy: A Commentary* (OTL; Louisville, KY: Westminster/John Knox Press, 2002).

Neufeld, E., *Ancient Hebrew Marriage Laws* (London: Longmans, Green & Co., 1944).
Noth, Martin, *Exodus* (OTL; London: SCM Press, 1962).
—'The Laws in the Pentateuch: Their Assumptions and Meaning', *The Laws in the Pentateuch and Other Studies* (trans. D.R. Ap-Thomas; Edinburgh: Oliver & Boyd, 1966), pp. 1–107.
Oden, Robert A., Jr, 'Hermeneutics and Historiography: Germany and America', *SBLSP* 19 (Chico, CA: Scholars Press, 1980), pp. 135–57.
—*The Bible Without Theology: The Theological Tradition and Alternatives to It* (San Francico: Harper & Row, 1987).
Oliver, Kelly, *Reading Kristeva: Unraveling the double-bind* (Bloomington, IN: Indiana University Press, 1993).
Oliver, Kelly (ed.), *Ethics, Politics and Difference in Julia Kristeva's Writing* (New York: Routledge, 1993).
Olyan, Saul M., *Asherah and the Cult of Yahweh in Israel* (SBLMS, 34; Atlanta: Scholars Press, 1988).
Ortner, Sherry B., *Making Gender: The Politics and Erotics of Culture* (Boston: Beacon Press, 1996).
Otto, Eckart, 'False Weights in the Scales of Biblical Justice?: Different Views of Women from Patriarchal Hierarchy to Religious Equality in the Book of Deuteronomy', in Bernard M. Levinson, Victor H. Matthews and Tikva Frymer-Kensky (eds.), *Gender and Law in the Hebrew Bible and the Ancient Near East* (JSOTSup, 262; Sheffield: Sheffield Academic Press, 1998), pp. 128–46.
Patrick, Dale, *Old Testament Law* (Atlanta: John Knox Press, 1985).
Patrick, Dale (ed.), *Thinking Biblical Law*, Semeia 45 (1989).
Patte, Daniel, *Ethics of Biblical Interpretation: A Reevaluation* (Louisville, KY: Westminster/John Knox Press, 1995).
Paul, Shalom M., *Studies in the Book of the Covenant in the Light of Cuneiform and Biblical Law* (VTSup, 18 Leiden: E.J. Brill, 1970).
Perdue, Leo G., *et al.*, *Families in Ancient Israel* (Louisville, KY: Westminster/John Knox Press, 1997).
Pfau, Julie Ann, 'Dinah Is Still Silent: Trauma and the Unrealized Potential of Midrash' (unpublished Masters thesis, Emory University, 2002).
Phillips, Anthony, *Ancient Israel's Criminal Law: A New Approach to the Decalogue* (New York: Schocken Books, 1970).
—'Another Look at Adultery', *JSOT* 20 (1981), pp. 3–25.
—*Deuteronomy* (Cambridge: Cambridge University Press, 1973).
—*Essays on Biblical Law* (JSOTSup, 344; London: Sheffield Academic Press, 2002).
—'Some Aspects of Family Law in Pre-Exilic Israel', *VT* 23 (1973), pp. 349–61.
—'The Laws of Slavery: Exodus 21.2–11', *JSOT* 30 (1984), pp. 51–66.
—'Uncovering the Father's Skirt', *VT* 30 (1980), pp. 38–43.
Pinker, Steven, *How The Mind Works* (New York: W.W. Norton, 1997).
Plaskow, Judith, *Standing Again at Sinai: Judaism from a Feminist Perspective* (San Francisco: HarperSanFrancisco, 1990).
Pleins, J. David, *The Social Visions of the Hebrew Bible: A Theological Introduction* (Louisville, KY: Westminster/John Knox Press, 2001).
Poling, James N., *The Abuse of Power: A Theological Problem* (Nashville: Abingdon Press, 1991).
—*Understanding Male Violence: Pastoral Care Issues* (St. Louis: Chalice Press, 2003).

Pollack, William, *Real Boys: Rescuing Our Sons from the Myths of Boyhood* (New York: Harry Holt & Co., 1999).

Pressler, Carolyn, 'Sexual Violence and the Deuteronomic Law', in Athalya Brenner (ed.), *A Feminist Companion to Exodus to Deuteronomy* (FCB, 6; Sheffield: Sheffield Academic Press, 1994), pp. 102–12.

—*The View of Women Found in Deuteronomic Family Laws* (BZAW, 216; Berlin: W. de Gruyter, 1993).

—'Wives and Daughters, Bond and Free: Views of Women in the Slave Laws of Exodus 21.2–11', in Bernard M. Levinson, Victor Matthews and Tikva Frymer-Kensky (eds.), *Gender and Law in the Hebrew Bible and the Ancient Near East* (JSOTSup, 262; Sheffield: Sheffield Academic Press, 1998), pp. 141–72.

Radford, Jill, Liz Kelly, and Marianne Hester, 'Introduction', in Liz Kelly and Jill Radford Marianne Hester (eds.), *Women, Violence, and Male Power: Feminist Activism, Research and Practice* (Buckingham: Open University Press, 1996), pp. 1–16.

Ramazanoglu, Caroline, 'What Can You Do with a Man?: Feminism and the Critical Appraisal of Masculinity', *Women's Studies International Forum* 15 (1992), pp. 339–50.

Reineke, Martha J., *Sacrificed Lives: Kristeva on Women and Violence* (Bloomington: Indiana University Press, 1997).

Rendtorff, Rolf, 'The Gēr in the Priestly Laws of the Pentateuch', in Mark G. Brett (ed.), *Ethnicity and the Bible* (Leiden: E.J. Brill, 1996), pp. 77–88.

Roberts, Dorothy, 'Rape, Violence, and Women's Autonomy', *Chicago-Kent Law Review* 69 (1993), pp. 359–95.

Rofé, Alexander, 'Family and Sex Laws in Deuteronomy and the Book of Covenant', *Henoch* 9 (1987), pp. 131–60.

Rogerson, John W., Margaret Davies and M. Daniel Carroll R. (eds.), *The Bible in Ethics: The Second Sheffield Colloquium* (JSOTSup, 207; Sheffield: Sheffield Academic Press, 1995).

Rogerson, John W., and Philip Davies, *The Old Testament World* (Englewood Cliffs: Prentice-Hall, 1989).

Rosenberg, Warren, *Legacy of Rage: Jewish Masculinity, Violence, and Culture* (Amherst, MA: University of Massachusetts Press, 2001).

Roth, Martha T., *Law Collections from Mesopotamia and Asia Minor* (SBLWAW, 6; Atlanta: Scholars Press, 2nd edn, 1997).

Rubin, Gayle, 'The Traffic in Women: Notes on the "Political Economy" of Sex', in Rayna Reiter (ed.), *Toward an Anthropology of Women* (New York: Monthly Review Press, 1975), pp. 157–210.

Ruether, Rosemary Radford, *Gaia and God: An Ecofeminist Theology of Earth Healing* (San Francisco: HarperSanFrancisco, 1992).

—*Sexism and God-Talk: Toward a Feminist Theology* (Boston: Beacon Press, 1983).

—'The Western Tradition and Violence against Women', in Joanne Carlson Brown and Carole R. Bohn (eds.), *Christianity, Patriarchy, and Abuse: A Feminist Critique* (New York: Pilgrim Press, 1989), pp. 31–41.

Sanday, Peggy Reeves, *A Woman Scorned: Acquaintance Rape on Trial* (New York: Doubleday, 1996).

—*Female Power and Male Dominance: On the Origins of Sexual Inequality* (Cambridge: Cambridge University Press, 1981).

—*Fraternity Gang Rape: Sex, Brotherhood, and Privilege on Campus* (New York: New York University Press, 1990).

—'Rape and the Silencing of the Feminine', in Sylvana Tomaselli and Roy Porter (eds.), *Rape* (Oxford: Basil Blackwell, 1986), pp. 84–101.

—'The Socio-Cultural Context of Rape: A Cross-Cultural Study', *Journal of Social Issues* 37 (1981), pp. 5–27.

Sanday, Peggy Reeves, and Ruth Gallagher Goodenough, *Beyond the Second Sex: New Directions in the Anthropology of Gender* (Philadelphia: University of Pennsylvania Press, 1990).

Sbisà, Marina, and Paolo Fabbir, 'Models (?) for a Pragmatic Analysis', *Journal of Pragmatics* 4 (1980), pp. 301–19.

Schafran, Lynn Hecht, 'Is the Law Male?: Let Me Count the Ways', *Chicago-Kent Law Review* 69 (1993), pp. 397–411.

Scholz, Susanne, *Rape Plots: A Feminist Cultural Study of Genesis 34*, (Studies in Biblical Literature, 13; New York: Peter Lang Publishing, 2000).

Schüssler Fiorenza, Elizabeth, *But She Said: Feminist Practices of Biblical Interpretation* (Boston: Beacon Press, 1992).

—'Introduction', in Schüssler Fiorenza and M. Shawn Copeland (eds.), *Violence Against Women* (Concilium; London: SCM Press, 1994), pp. viii–xxiv.

—*Rhetoric and Ethic: The Politics of Biblical Studies* (Minneapolis: Fortress Press, 1999).

—'The Ethics of Interpretation: De-Centering Biblical Scholarship', *JBL* 107 (1988), pp. 3–17.

—'Ties That Bind: Domestic Violence Against Women', in Mary John Mananzan *et al.* (eds.), *Women Resisting Violence: Spirituality for Life* (Maryknoll, NY: Orbis Books, 1996), pp. 39–55.

Schwartz, Regina M., *The Curse of Cain: The Violent Legacy of Monotheism* (Chicago: University of Chicago Press, 1997).

Scott, Joan Wallach, *Gender and the Politics of History* (New York: Columbia University Press, rev. edn, 1999).

Scully, Diana, *Understanding Sexual Violence: A Study of Convicted Rapists* (Perspectives on Gender, 3; Boston: Unwin Hyman, 1990).

Searle, John R., *Expression and Meaning: Studies in the Theory of Speech Acts* (Cambridge: Cambridge University Press, 1979).

—*Intentionality, an essay in the philosophy of mind* (Cambridge: Cambridge University Press, 1983).

Searles, Patricia, and Ronald J. Berger, *Rape and Society: Readings on the Problem of Sexual Assault* (Boulder: Westview Press, 1995).

Segovia, Fernando F., ' "And They Began to Speak in Other Tongues": Competing Modes of Discourse in Contemporary Biblical Criticism', in Fernando F. Segovia and Mary Ann Tolbert (eds.), *Reading from This Place: Social Location and Biblical Interpretation in the United States* (Minneapolis: Fortress Press, 1995), pp. 1–32.

Sherwood, Yvonne, *The Prostitute and the Prophet: Hosea's Marriage in Literary-Theoretical Perspective* (JSOTSup, 212; Sheffield: Sheffield Academic Press, 1996).

Smart, Carol, *Feminism and the Power of Law* (New York: Routledge, 1989).

Smith, Anna, *Julia Kristeva: Readings of Exile and Estrangement* (Basingstoke: Macmillan, 1996).

Smith, Anne-Marie, *Julia Kristeva: Speaking the Unspeakable*, (Modern European Thinkers; Sterling, VA: Pluto Press, 1998).

Smith, Mark S., *The Early History of God: Yahweh and the Other Deities of Ancient Israel* (Grand Rapids: Eerdmans, 2nd edn, 2002).

Sonsino, Rifat, *Motive Clauses: Biblical Forms and Near Eastern Parallels* (SALDS, 45; Chico, CA: Scholars Press, 1980).

Stahl, Nanette, *Law and Liminality in the Bible* (JSOTSup, 202; Sheffield: Sheffield Academic Press, 1995).

Stark, Evan, and Anne Flitcraft, *Women at Risk: Domestic Violence and Women's Health* (Thousand Oaks: Sage Publications, 1996).

Steinberg, Naomi, 'Adam's and Eve's Daughters Are Many: Gender Roles in Ancient Israelite Society' (unpublished doctoral dissertation, Columbia University, 1984).

—'The Deuteronomic Law Code and the Politics of State Centralization', in Peggy L. Day, David Jobling and Gerald T. Sheppard (eds.), *The Bible and the Politics of Exegesis* (Cleveland: The Pilgrim Press, 1991), pp. 161–70.

Stol, M., 'Women in Mesopotamia', *JESHO* 38, (1995), pp. 123–44.

Stone, Ken, *Sex, Honor, and Power in the Deuteronomistic History* (JSOTSup, 234; Sheffield: Sheffield Academic Press, 1996).

Streete, Gail Corrington, *The Strange Woman: Power and Sex in the Bible* (Louisville, KY: Westminster/John Knox Press, 1997).

Swidler, Ann, 'Culture in Action: Symbols and Strategies', *American Sociological Review* 51 (1986), pp. 273–86.

Swirski, Barbara, 'Jews Don't Batter Their Wives: Another Myth Bites the Dust', in Barbara Swirski and Marilyn P. Safir (eds.), *Calling the Equality Bluff: Women in Israel* (Elmsford, NY: Pergamon Press, 1991), pp. 319–27.

Tarlin, Jan William, 'Utopia and Pornography in Ezekial: Violence, Hope and the Shattered Male Subject', in Timothy K. Beal and D.M. Gunn (eds.), *Reading Bibles, Writing Bodies: Identity and the Book* (New York: Routledge, 1997), pp. 175–83.

Thiselton, Anthony C., *New Horizons in Hermeneutics: The Theory and Practice of Transforming Biblical Reading* (Grand Rapids: Zondervan, 1992).

Thistlewaite, Susan Brooks, 'Every Two Minutes: Battered Women and Feminist Interpretation', in Letty M. Russell (ed.), *Feminist Interpretation of the Bible* (Philadelphia: Westminster Press, 1985), pp. 96–107.

Tigay, Jeffrey H., 'Excursus 22: The Alleged Practice of Cultic Prostitution in the Ancient Near East', in Jeffrey Tigay (ed.), *JPS Torah Commentary: Deuteronomy* (Philadelphia: Jewish Publication Society, 1996), pp. 480–81.

—'Excursus 24: Improper Intervention in a Fight', in Jeffrey Tigay (ed.), *JPS Torah Commentary* (Philadelphia: Jewish Publication Society, 1996), pp. 484–85.

Tomaselli, Sylvana, and Roy Porter, *Rape* (Oxford: Basil Blackwell, 1986).

Tong, Rosemarie, *Feminist Thought: A More Comprehensive Introduction* (Boulder, CO: Westview Press, 2nd edn, 1998).

Trible, Phyllis, *Texts of Terror: Literary-Feminist Readings of Biblical Narratives* (OBT; Philadelphia: Fortress Press, 1984).

Van der Toorn, Karel, *Family Religion in Babylonia, Syria and Israel: Continuity and Change in Forms of Religious Life* (Studies in the History and Culture of the Ancient Near East,VII; Leiden: E.J. Brill, 1996).

—'Female Prostitution in Payment of Vows in Ancient Israel' *JBL* 108 (1989), pp. 193–205.

—*From Her Cradle to Her Grave: The Role of Religion in the Life of the Israelite and Babylonian Woman* (trans. Sara J. Denning-Bolle; Sheffield: JSOT Press, 1994).

Van Leeuwen, Mary Stewart, *My Brother's Keeper: What the Social Sciences Do (And Don't) Tell Us About Masculinity* (Downers Grove, IL: InterVarsity Press, 2002).

Van Seters, John, *A Law Book for the Diaspora: Revision in the Study of the Covenant Code* (New York: Oxford University Press, 2003).

Von Waldow, H. Eberhard, 'Social Responsibility and Social Structure in Early Israel', *CBQ* 32 (1970), pp. 184–204.

Washington, Harold C., 'Violence and the Construction of Gender in the Hebrew Bible: A New Historicist Approach'. *BibInt* 5 (1997), pp. 324–63.

—' "Lest He Die in the Battle and Another Man Take Her": Violence and the Construction of Gender in the Laws of Deuteronomy 20–22', in Bernard M. Levinson, Victor H. Matthews and Tikva Frymer-Kensky (eds.), *Gender and Law in the Hebrew Bible and the Ancient Near East* (JSOTSup, 262; Sheffield: Sheffield Academic Press, 1998), pp. 185–213.

Waters, Mary C., *Black Identities: West Indian Immigrant Dreams and American Realities* (Cambridge, MA: Harvard University Press, 1999).

Weems, Renita J., *Battered Love: Marriage, Sex, and Violence in the Hebrew Prophets* (OBT; Minneapolis: Fortress Press, 1995).

—'Song of Songs', *NIB* V (Nashville: Abingdon Press, 1997), pp. 361–434.

Weinfeld, Moshe, *Deuteronomy and the Deuteronomic School* (Oxford: Clarendon Press, 1972).

Weisberg, D. Kelly (ed.), *Feminist Legal Theory: Foundations* (Philadelphia: Temple University Press, 1993).

Welch, D. Don, 'Introduction: The Moral Dimension of Law', in D. Don Welch (ed.), *Law and Morality* (Philadelphia: Fortress Press, 1987), pp. 1–27.

Wenham, Gordon, '*Bĕtûlāh:* "A Girl of Marriageable Age",' *VT* 22 (1972), pp. 326–45.

West, Candace and Don H. Zimmerman, 'Doing Gender', in Judith Lorber and Susan A. Farrell (eds.), *The Social Construction of Gender* (Newbury Park: SAGE Publications, Inc., 1991), pp. 13–37.

West, Candace and Sarah Fenstermaker, 'Ethnomethodology and "Idealist Determinism": A Reply to John Wilson', in Paula England (ed.), *Theory on Gender/Feminism on Theory* (New York: Aldine De Gruyter, 1993), pp. 357–61.

West, Robin, 'Jurisprudence and Gender', *University of Chicago Law Review* 55 (1988), pp. 1–72.

West, Traci C., *Wounds of the Spirit: Black Women, Violence, and Resistance Ethics* (New York: New York University Press, 1999).

Westbrook, Raymond, 'Adultery in Ancient Near Eastern Law', *RB* 92 (1990), pp. 542–80.

—'Cuneiform Law Codes and the Origins of Legislation', *ZA* 79 (1989), pp. 201–22.

—*Old Babylonian Marriage Law* (AfOB, 23; Horn F. Berger, 1988).

—*Property and the Family in Biblical Law* (JSOTSup, 113; Sheffield: Sheffield Academic Press, 1991).

—*Studies in Biblical and Cuneiform Law* (Cahiers de la *RB* 26; Paris: J. Gibalda, 1988).

—'The Female Slave', in Levinson, Matthews and Frymer-Kensky (eds.), *Gender and Law*, pp. 214–38.

—'The Prohibition of Marriage in Deuteronomy 24.1–4', in Sara Japhet (ed.), *Studies in Bible* (*Scripta Hierosolymitana*, 31; Jerusalem: Magnes Press, 1986), pp. 387–405.

—'What Is the Covenant Code?', in Bernard M. Levinson (ed.), *Theory and Method in Biblical and Cuneiform Law: Revision, Interpolation, and Development* (JSOTSup, 181; Sheffield: Sheffield Academic Press, 1994), pp. 15–36.

Westbrook, Raymond (ed.), *A History of Ancient Near Eastern Law* (2 vols., HdO, 72/1 & 2; Leiden: E.J. Brill, 2003).

White, Hugh C. (ed.), Speech Act Theory and Biblical Criticism: *Semeia* 41 (1988).

Wilson, Robert, 'The Role of Law in Early Israelite Society', in B. Halpern and D.W. Hobson (eds.), *Law, Politics and Society in the Ancient Mediterranean World* (Sheffield: Sheffield Academic Press, 1993), pp. 90–99.

Wing, Adrien Katherine (ed.), *Global Critical Race Feminism: An International Reader* (New York: New York University Press, 2000).

Yaron, Reuven, 'The Restoration of Marriage', *JSS* 17 (1966), pp. 1–11.

Yee, Gale, 'Ideological Criticism: Judges 17–21 and the Dismembered Body', in Gale Yee (ed.), *Judges & Method: New Approaches in Biblical Studies* (Minneapolis: Fortress Press, 1995), pp. 146–70.

Young, Iris Marion, 'Five Faces of Oppression', *The Philosophical Forum* XIX (1988), pp. 270–90.

Zakovitch, Yair, 'The Woman's Rights in the Bible of Divorce', *The Jewish Law Annual* IV (1981), pp. 28–46.

Zlotnick, Helena, *Dinah's Daughters: Gender and Judaism from the Hebrew Bible to Late Antiquity* (Philadelphia: University of Pennsylvania Press, 2002).

INDEX

INDEX OF REFERENCES

BIBLE

Index of Authors